MW00389690

...AND THE SONG
THAT I AM SINGING
IS A PRAYER TO
NON-BELIEVERS –
COME AND STAND
BESIDE US
WE CAN FIND A
BETTER WAY.

– JOHN DENVER – "RHYMES AND REASONS"

Borrowing Fire

Borrowing Fire

Rewriting the Eulogy for a Boy Named Wolf

First printing, December 2012

Published by
Abendmahl Press
P.O. Box 581083
Salt Lake City, Utah 84158-1083

ISBN: 978-0-9838025-2-5
Artwork by Ben Behunin, Eve Behunin, and Bert Compton
Designed by Ben Behunin and Bert Compton
Layout by Bert Compton - Compton Design Studio

Borrowing Fire

Rewriting the Eulogy for a Boy Named Wolf

by

Ben Behunin

To Nik Eaner -
Merry Christmas -

TO MY FRIENDS-
LIVING & DEAD,
WHO INSPIRE
ME TO LIVE
DELIBERATELY.
THANK
YOU!

Prelude

Pablo Picasso once said, "Art is the lie that reveals the truth." I first heard this quote in an art class almost twenty years ago. I am an artist, a potter to be precise. For the past sixteen years I have made my living as slinger of slime and a baker of mud pies, but I'm not sure I ever understood what Picasso was saying until I began writing.

As it turns out, truth is sometimes hard to swallow. It can be scary, intimidating and foreign. Unless we're ready to accept it at the exact moment it presents itself to us, we may not be able to hear it at all. If, however, truth presents itself to us in a more palpable package, if it looks and acts like a friend, and if we're prepared to receive it, we will usually invite it into our homes and hearts, giving it a portion of our time and interest. I hope that as you read this book, you will find within its pages, swaddled in the layers of story and art, truths that speak to your heart and mind.

A dear friend and mentor of mine, J. Terry Summerhays, passed away nearly a year ago. After a ten-month battle with cancer, Terry's body was tired, giving out on him far sooner than any of us were ready to let him go. He was an honorable man of faith and love. As I visited with him regularly over those last months, steadily watching his decline, I was often moved to tears by his wit and wisdom and the love he so freely expressed to me and his abundant family who gathered around him. The loved him, caring for him in his home, encouraging him and remaining hopeful until the very end. It was inspiring to watch; to witness the miracle of love that took place within the walls of his home. I visited with him the night before he died and was called back to his home shortly after his spirit departed this life. I was honored to be asked by his family to be an honorary pallbearer and to participate with his family in celebrating this giant of a man who lived life to its fullest, truly living everyday of his life. In his honor, his family planted a tree in their yard and asked me to make a ceramic sign, immortalizing the words he often shared with all of us before his passing, "It's all art."

Terry's was the forty-ninth funeral I attended as part of my research for this book, and it was one of the best. Not just because it was one of the rare funerals I attended where I actually knew the person who had died, but because Terry knew how to live. He'd figured it out. His was a love story—a love story that endures as his family continues to laugh and cry at the memories of the husband and father who loved them with all his heart.

In all, I have attended fifty-eight funerals as I have researched and written this book, most of which were for people I have never met. I suppose that would make me a funeral crasher. But over the course of this research, I have laughed and cried at the funerals of strangers. I have shared with their loved ones treasures from their stories and journeys. I was inspired and enlightened, but also depressed and disappointed. I went to funerals in churches and cathedrals, funeral parlors and cemeteries, funerals for rich people and poor people, married and single, parents and childless, old and young. It has forced me to consider the realities of my own mortality and has given me insights on the legacy I hope someday to leave behind. These experiences have perhaps influenced me most deeply in my roles as husband and father, making me think about how I am spending my time and how I hope my wife and children will think of me when I am gone.

It may sound egocentric and narcissistic to assume I'll be remembered at all, but the truth is, each of us leaves behind our mark on the world. Like a jet trail across the sky that remains long after the jet has passed, each of us will have some influence on our children and our children's children, possibly for generations to come. As I have listened to the stories shared by family and clergy of those who have passed, I have learned about hope and love, life and death, fear and pain, triumph and disappointment. But more than anything, the most meaningful lessons I have learned have all centered around one theme: Love.

As I have shared details, here and there about this project, many have asked me where in the world I came up with this idea. I don't know how other writers choose their themes and stories, but for me, I feel like the books I have written have chosen me rather than the other way around. On the day I finished my final edits for Becoming Isaac, the last book in the Niederbipp Trilogy, I went out to my studio, excited to get my hands back in the clay and rest my mind for a while. But it seems the universe had other plans for me.

Before that day I had outlined four other books, thinking that one day—sometime in the future—I would sit down and work on them. But on that day another idea entered my mind with such force that I had to sit down and take notes. I remember being frustrated that my hand could not keep up with the ideas that were put into my head. An hour and a half later, the whole book was outlined and seemed to scream for my attention, compelling me to begin and forget all my other plans.

In fairness, I will admit that this did not come out of nothing. I had just read the obituary of a high school classmate whom I had not seen or heard from since graduation nearly twenty years earlier. We were not close friends, but we had been amiable—two guys headed in the same basic direction, but on different paths. I was interested to read how, in the ensuing years, our paths and lives had become increasingly similar. We were both thirty-six years old. We were both fathers with young children. We were both Christians and were trying to raise our children in the light of the Lord. He studied politics. I studied art and business. After college, he'd moved far from our hometown. I had remained close to home. He was a successful lobbyist. I was a happy potter. His obituary noted that he was a classy dresser and was known for his collection of ties. I wear tie-dyed T-shirts and work pants that are generally covered with splatters of mud and glaze. Our lives were different; yet in many ways, they were very similar. But he was thirty-six years old—and dead—a victim of a heart failure. I was thirty-six years old and, as I would learn over the next two years, had a story to tell about life and death for those of us who remain among the living.

His funeral was to be held a few days later and I felt compelled to go. The services were held at a huge church, filled beyond capacity with people whose lives he had touched. There must have been close to six-hundred people in attendance. I learned that a crowd of similar size had attended a memorial service in his honor just days before in the town where he and his wife had lived for more than a decade. As I sat and listened to his eulogy and the stories from his life delivered by his siblings and friends, I realized how little I really knew about this man. Somehow, in the eighteen years since we had last seen each other, the boy had become a man—a man of compassion, love, patience, humility, honor and respect.

I left that day with a lot of thoughts in my head. I went home and hugged my kids a little tighter and kissed my wife a little longer. I looked over the notes I had taken about the book I knew I was supposed to write. I knew it would take time away from my work and family, but I knew somehow that this was what I needed to do.

I like bluegrass music, so several years ago I bought a mandolin, determined that I would teach myself to play. I haven't really failed, but I have yet to succeed. I became a beekeeper a few years ago because I love peanut butter and honey sandwiches. I have been much more successful with that venture. I mention these things only to suggest that I am not afraid of unusual hobbies, but becoming a funeral-crasher seemed especially odd—even for me. I wasn't at all sure how it would go.

I began trolling through the obituaries looking for interesting people who led interesting lives. Being a person of faith, I wanted to understand death through the eyes and hearts of people of all faiths, as well as those who claimed to have no faith at all. The outline for this book, which had come in a flash of either inspiration or insanity (I'll leave it to you to decide) would prove to open my heart and mind to dozens of new and beautiful situations as I became an observer of death and life in ways I might never have imagined.

The pages that follow are the result of more than two years worth of funeral crashing and the story that developed in my mind as I was influenced and inspired by common men and women who lived extraordinary lives.

And, oh, what lessons I have learned!

This experience has given me perspective and insight. It has taught me what it is to die. But more than that, it has taught me what it is to truly live. It has given me hope and strengthened my faith. It has left me desiring to live the best life I can—to make each day count for something good, and to love more abundantly.

I have never been obsessed with death or dying. I suppose I've been too busy living to ever think much about it. But I know I will die. Though my brain still believes I am twenty-one, my body quite often reminds me that I am indeed thirty-eight, and not getting any younger. These experiences have made me recognize the unfortunate truth that few of us will ever be able to choose how we will die. And maybe that's okay. For we can choose how to live. And I've discovered that how we live quite often profoundly effects how we die. I know there will come a time, hopefully in the distant future, when my body will be spent and death will come. I'm not ready for that day. I have too many pots to make, books to write and people to love. But I hope that on that day I will be ready to jump into the next adventure with the same enthusiasm that has inspired my life. I wrote this book for the same reason I wrote the Niederbipp Trilogy—I was compelled by the universe to do so. I hope it will bring you the same peace, hope and determination it has brought me to live purposefully and deliberately every day of your life.

Ben Behunin
December 2012

Acknowledgments

I have tried to give credit where credit is due for the quotes throughout this book. Where possible, I have listed the sources. The quotes written in the margins of this book were quotes I heard while attending two years worth of funerals. Many of these have been paraphrased from the original ideas I recorded and later pulled from the pages of my scattered notebooks. Many of them are my own thoughts that were inspired as I sat and listened to people talk about their dearly departed.

It is possible that you will find a story within these pages that sounds a lot like someone you know and love. You may even feel like I may have attended their funeral. If so, thank you for sharing your stories, your faith, and your experiences. They have enriched my life. I hope that as you experience these memories again, they will breathe new life into the stories, and inspire you to share your best stories with all who will listen.

Thanks for sharing.

Ben Behunin

Table of Contents

Prelude 7
Acknowledgments 12
The Package 15
Riding Shotgun 20
The She-Bear 32
Heart Stone 45
Second Chance 55
Lighting the Path 65
The Joy of Remembering 77
Unconditional 84
Questions 93
The Beginning of Wisdom 110
Eulogy For A Boy Named Wolf 122
A Six-Month Decade 133
The Armadillo and The Raven 146
Moving On 152
Searching For Dingledoodies 159
Trust 166
Seeds of Hope 177
Almost There 183
Max 194
Old Men Don't Ride Ponies 207
The Trade 212
The Legend of a Boy Named Wolf 221
Pumpkin Pie 230
The Request 237

Finding A Home 245
Surprises 249
Plans 259
Changes 268
The Gift of Nakedness 273
The Songs of Redeeming Love 283
Life is Beautiful 290
Raising Ebenezer 296
Of Light and Fire 314
Reflecting Light 323
Walking on Water 333
Finding the Something 345
Back To The Beginning 350
Postlude 358
Author's Note 362
The Eulogy of Ben Behunin 364

-Chapter 1-

The Package

WRITE IT ON YOUR HEART THAT EVERYDAY IS THE BEST DAY OF THE YEAR.
—RALPH WALDO EMERSON

"Are you ready?" Rachel asked from the doorway behind him.

"I think so," Paul responded. For at least twenty minutes he had been sitting on the front stoop, staring at the package, trying to decide if and when he would open it.

"Is that the package Katie sent?"

He nodded affirmatively, but didn't speak, still feeling overwhelmed by the revelations that had come with Katie's phone call. It had been more than a decade since he had last seen the old man, but never more than a week had passed in which he had not thought about him. There had been many times that Paul had wondered if was dead or alive—wondering what had become of the journal he'd entrusted to him. He had imagined many different scenarios over the years, but nothing like this. And the timing of it all made him wonder what games the universe was playing.

Mistaking his reflective mood as his reaction to the morning's heated discussion, Rachel sat down next to him, placing her hand on his forearm. "I'm sorry about earlier. I didn't really listen, did I?"

Paul forced a weak smile, but didn't answer.

"Someday I want to hear about this dream girl of yours. But if you don't mind, it would probably be better if it's not after I haven't seen you for four days."

Paul nodded, remembering how these rare, unusually long shifts at the fire station always created far more distance between them than either of them were ready accept. "Fair enough," he said softly, putting his arm around her shoulder. He knew it was pointless to remind her that the decision to take this extended shift had been her idea, enabling them to extend their vacation by four extra days. "Is Katie ready for this weekend?" he asked, pushing himself to let to go of his frustration by changing the subject.

"Yeah, I'm sorry the phone call interrupted our discussion. You know how she likes to talk."

"*How she likes to talk*?" he teased.

Rachel rolled her eyes, but smiled. "She had to tell me all about it. Think of it this way—I just saved you two hours worth of girl talk tomorrow night."

"What's tomorrow night?"

"Well, we decided that since we're getting there a day early, we should do dinner. She'll be busy with everyone else on Saturday, and we won't get to see each other much. They're planning on leaving for their honeymoon right after the wedding. You're okay with dinner, right?"

"Sure. It will be good to catch up with Mike—and Katie, of course. Are you ready to go?"

"I am. Did you get Eve packed?"

Paul pointed to their car, parked in the driveway, where Eve was already rigging up a tent in the back seat with her favorite blanket. "She packed one bag with nothing but art supplies."

Rachel smiled. "That sounds about right. Did you still want to stop in Chicago?"

"Oh, that's right—The Art Institute. Do you feel like looking at art for a couple of hours?"

"Is that a trick question?" She laughed softly.

Paul knew art wasn't her favorite thing, but she had always put up with her husband's interest in museums and galleries, especially after Eve began showing interest in art, too. "What do you think?" he asked.

"I think we better do it, especially if you're going to that funeral tomorrow. Eve really missed you this week without school to keep her occupied."

Paul nodded, looking down at the package in his hands. "What if you came with me?" he said after a moment.

"Where? You mean to the funeral?"

"Yeah."

"Really?" Rachel asked, pulling a funny face that made Paul smile. "I don't even know the guy. In fact, I've never even heard you mention his name. Wouldn't that be kind of weird to just show up and crash some stranger's funeral?"

His smile broadened. She knew him better than anyone ever had, but there was still so much about his past that she didn't know—so much that she seemed afraid to know. "I think you might like it," he said, trying hard to sound serious.

"Going to the funeral of a stranger? Really? But what would we do with Eve? I'm sure my mom will have to work tomorrow. I called and left a message, but she's wasn't expecting us until tomorrow night."

"What if we all went?"

"Are you serious?"

"Yeah, I am."

"Paul, I'm sorry, but that's not exactly my idea of a vacation. I've been to one funeral my whole life—my grandfather's. It was awful, seeing him in that casket, looking like a piece of plastic. I was traumatized for weeks. I really don't think it would be such a good idea to expose Eve to that."

"How old were you when you grandfather died?" Paul asked.

"Eight—maybe nine. Why?"

"I think I was about that age when my grandmother died. I remember freaking out when I saw her. My parents didn't prepare me to see her that way."

"And you want to expose Eve to that?"

Paul looked back down at the package. "You know how I always talk about raising our daughter not to be afraid of anything?"

"Yeah, but this is kind of different, don't you think?"

"Oh, I don't know. We're all going to die, sometime. I'd feel like a pretty lame parent if, after all we've tried to teach Eve, she was afraid of going to a funeral and looking into a casket."

"But don't you think we should wait until there's a funeral for someone we actually know?"

"Perhaps, but it seems like it might be easier to help her understand what that part of life is all about if she isn't emotionally tied to the person. Plus, it would give her a chance to get to know this guy by listening to the people who loved him."

She gave him a confused look before she spoke again. "I don't remember anyone saying anything at my grandpa's funeral—except the priest."

"That's because your grandfather was Catholic. You don't often hear much about a person at a Catholic funeral, especially if that person didn't regularly attend church. And after hearing the stories I've heard about your grandfather, I highly doubt his priest knew *anything* about him."

Paul turned to smile at Rachel before continuing. "This old man, Max, he's having his funeral at a Quaker church, which really surprises me considering what I know about Quakers, and what I remember about him. I guess I really didn't know him very well, but from what I do know, I'm sure this funeral ought to be very interesting."

She stared at him as if she were looking at a stranger.

"What?" he asked, trying not to laugh at the look on her face.

"Sometimes I feel like I don't even know you." She said it with a smile, but she looked at him a little bit closer, like she was checking him out for the first time. "You almost sound like you're the son of an undertaker and grew up in a funeral home. I'm trying to figure out why you would know so much about funerals?"

"I'm pretty sure you wouldn't believe me, even if I told you."

She turned her face and looked out at Eve playing in the car. "What does that mean?" she asked after a moment.

"It means the answer might take you somewhere you don't want to go."

She looked at him as if she were searching for clues written on his face. "Are you talking about the past?" she finally asked.

"What if I am?"

She put her hand on his arm again and leaned closer, resting her chin on his shoulder. "Does this have anything to do with that dream you keep having?"

He thought for a moment. "What if it does?"

She took a deep breath. "Is it a long story?"

"What if it is?"

"I'll take that as a yes. Is it a dark story?" she continued.

"Parts of it are, yes."

"Does it have a happy ending?"

"I suppose that all depends."

"On what?"

"On us."

She lifted her head from his shoulder. "On us?"

"Yeah."

"You and me?"

"And Eve, too." He looked thoughtful. "Come to think of it, I suppose there are actually a lot of people involved in this story who will decide if it has a happy ending or not."

"Sounds cryptic," she said with squinted eyes. "Am I going to like this story?"

"I think you will. But if you want to hear it, you're going to have to drive."

"Are you trying to trick me into driving all the way to Kenosha?"

He laughed. "There is only one way to find out."

CHAPTER 2
RIDING SHOTGUN

...WEEPING MAY ENDURE FOR A NIGHT,
BUT JOY COMETH IN THE MORNING.
—PSALMS 30:5

"How much longer till we get there?" Eve asked from the backseat as they pulled out of the gas station, ten minutes into their journey.

Rachel looked at her daughter through the rearview mirror before responding. "If a chicken-and-a-half laid an-egg-and-a-half in a day-and-a-half, how long would it take a grasshopper with a wooden leg to kick ..."

"... to kick all of the seeds out of a dill pickle?" Eve said, looking as if she might have heard that answer to her question more than a million times in her seven years of life. "I'm serious," she said. "I already started on some pictures for Grandma, but I need to know how many minutes I have to finish them."

Paul turned around from the passenger seat. "You have about five hundred minutes," he said after doing the math in his head while pulling a funny face that made Eve giggle.

"Is that a long time?" she asked.

"It's about ... sixteen cartoons long," he said, pulling another silly face. They had used the length of a typical cartoon program as a measure of a half hour since the time she was three and she had begun to understand the otherwise abstract reckoning of time. And even though she was now seven, that reckoning still made sense.

She nodded, doing her own math in her head. "I better hurry. Grandma has a really big gallery, and I promised her I was going to fill it up."

Paul smiled at his daughter again, wondering how many pictures it would take to fill up the walls of a two car garage.

"Can we listen to music?" Eve asked.

"Maybe in a little while," Rachel responded, stopping Paul's hand as he reached for the stereo. "Daddy promised Mommy that if she drove, he would tell us about the package he got in the mail."

"What kind of package?"

Paul looked at Rachel then back at Eve. He knew his chance of delaying the opening of the package was gone as soon as he saw the curiosity on Eve's face. "Oh, just a package from Aunt Katie. You might have seen it yesterday."

"What's in it?"

"Just an old book."

"Is it a storybook?"

"Uh, yeah, I suppose it is."

"Is it about a little girl?" Eve asked enthusiastically.

"No. Not this one," Paul responded.

"Is it about a boy then? Or a pony?"

Paul took a deep breath. "This one is about a boy," he said thoughtfully.

"What's his name?" She looked up from her drawing, expectantly.

Paul paused, thinking about the story he was about to begin. He knew there would be much of this story that he wouldn't be able to share with Eve—at least not now. But this story had been begging to be told for many years, waiting for the time and circumstances to be right. He knew that despite the many years he had had to think about sharing this with her, it would still not be easy to tell. He knew that many of the monsters which had haunted his younger years would be unleashed as their names and faces were recalled. But he had known since her birth that this was a story he wanted her to know—a story that could be amended over the coming years that might help her to avoid her own monsters. "His name was Wolf," he offered.

"That's a silly name for a boy," Eve said, crinkling up her nose as her smile consumed her face.

"Yes it is," Paul admitted. "He was named after his grandfather, Wolfgang."

"Was he a werewolf?" asked Eve.

"How do you know about werewolves?" he asked, one eyebrow raised.

"From mommy's books. She told me that werewolves are really people who change into wolves when there's a big moon."

Paul turned to look at Rachel. "What have you been reading?"

She smirked and shrugged her shoulders.

"No," he said, shaking his head and turning back to Eve. "This is not that kind of a story. There are no freakish hybrids or people with super powers in this story. It's just about a real boy named Wolf."

"Are there any vampires in this story?" Eve asked.

Rachel began laughing as Paul rolled his eyes. "No ... no vampires, no werewolves … just normal people."

"Cool," Eve said, turning her attention back to her drawing. "Does he have a dog?"

"No. His landlord wouldn't allow him to have a dog," Paul responded quickly.

"What's a landlord?"

"It's kind of like an ogre who owns old, run-down houses and rents them to desperate people who need to get out of the rain."

"You mean like Shrek?"

"No," Paul said, trying not to laugh. "No, Shrek is a funny ogre. Most landlords are the kind of ogres who put on their crankypants anytime you ask them to fix something, and then they keep charging you more rent so they can eat fancy, imported fish eggs and expensive cheeses that make their breath smell like pond scum."

Rachel laughed. "Honey, you better set her straight. She's going to have a landlord someday. You don't want to make her afraid of someone before she even meets them."

"Tell me I'm wrong."

She grinned after a moment's thought. "No, I guess you're right. Go on."

"I don't even know why we're talking about landlords. I can't say that landlords played a significant role in Wolf's life."

"He didn't let him have a dog. That would make me sad," Eve said, sounding melodramatic.

Paul shook his head, trying to keep a straight face. "Eve, we don't have a dog either. Does that make us ogres?"

She laughed. "Maybe. I don't really know. This is a silly story, Dad."

"Yes it is, and one I can already tell is going to take far longer than I anticipated."

"So why are you telling it?" asked Eve, looking suddenly serious.

"Well . . . because . . . it's important. I've actually been wanting to tell you this story since you were born."

"Does it have a happy ending?"

Paul looked at Rachel, who smiled, but kept her eyes on the road. "I think so—but it's not over yet. And the best part of that is—you get to help decide how the story will end. You get to decide if it's happy or not."

"How?"

"Well, you'll see as I get into the story."

"Okay, but …," Eve said, hesitating.

"But what?"

"It would be nice if that boy, Wolf, could have a dog or at least a pony."

Paul shook his head. "We'll see what we can do. But I should probably keep telling this story, or it's going to take me all the way to Grandma's and all the way back."

"Okay."

He took a deep breath before beginning again. "So this boy, Wolf, lived in a small, little village, far away from any cities. His grandfather, the one he's named after, was a man with big dreams. But he knew those dreams could never come true in his country, so he worked really hard, saved all his money, and came to America. On the boat that brought him here he fell in love with a pretty girl named Sybil. They both shared big dreams about having their own land and farm, and when they landed in New York, they got married and spent all their money on a farm in Wisconsin."

"Did they have a pony on their farm?" asked Eve.

"Of course. If you have a farm, it's pretty much a rule that you have to have at least one pony."

"What color was it?"

"Uh, what color do you think?"

"Hmmm, white?"

"That's a good guess, and because I'm not really sure, we'll say it was white. And just in case you wondered," he said, cutting Eve off before she could even open her mouth again, "they also had a dog and a cat and a cow and a farmhouse and probably some chickens and a pig or two. It took them a couple of years to get all that stuff, but they worked hard, and after a while they decided it was time to start a family."

"So the kids could help play with all those animals?" asked Eve.

"That was probably part of it. I'm not sure how it worked for them, but for most people, there comes a time in your life when you feel like you have enough love in your heart that you're ready to share it with someone else."

"Did they have a baby girl?"

"Nope. They had four boys— Hartmut, Karl, Wilhelm and Johann."

"Daddy, those are silly names."

"Yes, they are," he said with a snicker, "but they were German and sometimes Germans have funny names. Anyway, the boys grew up and became men. Each of them had dreams of raising their families on the same farm where they'd been raised. But the farm wasn't big enough for four families and four houses. So a few years before he died, their father decided to give the farm to the oldest and smartest son, Hartmut."

"That doesn't sound very fair."

"That's exactly what the other brothers said."

"Did the big brother make his little brothers leave the farm?" asked Eve, a look of concern on her face.

"Yes. As soon as each of the brothers married, they got kicked off the farm to find their own way in life. Wilhelm ended up becoming a diesel mechanic and moved to Oshkosh b'gosh, Wisconsin, and Johann, who changed his name to John as soon as his father died, moved to Minnesota and became a hockey coach."

"What happened to the other one?" asked Eve, holding up three fingers.

"Ahh, good you were paying attention. Karl married his high school sweetheart, and they moved into a stinky, little, single-wide trailer, just a stone's throw away from the railroad tracks in Adams-Friendship, Wisconsin."

"What did Karl become?"

"Karl became a … an ice fisherman."

"Why would anyone want to go fishing for ice?"

Rachel glanced at her husband with a curious smile.

"No, an ice fisherman is someone who spends the whole winter out on a frozen lake, drinking beer with his buddies while trying to catch fish."

"That sounds really boring … and cold," Eve responded.

Paul nodded. "It would be, but professional ice fishermen build special houses on the ice. Then they drill holes through the floor so they can fish all day long. Karl's house even had a bunk bed and a TV in it, so he could sleep there whenever his wife was angry at him. Did you know you can live in a house on the ice for four months a year?"

Eve shook her head.

"It's true. Four months a year, Karl spent his days and most nights out on the ice, only coming home to his stinky, little trailer once a week to take a shower and buy more beer.

"What did he do when there wasn't any ice?"

"Well, during the rest of the year he had lots of different jobs. Sometimes he chopped down trees to make firewood. Sometimes he worked at the gas station. Sometimes he was a janitor at the school. Sometimes he worked at a Christmas tree farm trimming trees. He had all sorts of crazy jobs. When summer was over, he quit whatever job he had, so he could get ready to become a professional deer hunter. By the time the hunt was over it was football season, and he would spend a couple of months watching football before the ice was thick enough for ice fishing to begin again."

"Did Karl have any kids."

"Yes. That's where Wolf comes in. Wolf was Karl's son. And Wolf had a younger sister named Jennie."

"Like your sister, Jennie?"

"Yep, that's right."

"Daddy, does Wolf grow up to become a prefreshional ice fisherman, too?"

Paul shook his head and took a deep breath. "No, baby, Wolf … uh, he had an accident on the ice when he was just a kid, and he never liked going on the ice after that. If you're afraid of ice, it's pretty much a rule that you aren't allowed to become a professional ice fisherman."

"What happened? Why was he afraid of the ice?"

"Well, that will have to be a story for another day. Let's just say he wanted to get a real job so he didn't have to live in a single-wide trailer for the rest of his life."

"Not that there's anything wrong with living in a trailer," Rachel added, looking at Eve in the rearview mirror.

"That's right," Paul said, nodding to his very politically correct wife. "It's just that Wolf wanted a better life for himself and figured since he was living in America where people could be whatever they wanted to be, he would dream a little bigger. He wanted to get a good job, and have a family, and live happily ever after."

"So, did he?" asked Eve.

"Well, so far. He's not dead yet, and there are still a lot of good years in his future. But there were some hard times in Wolf's life that made him wonder if he'd ever be happy again."

"Why?" Eve asked, looking concerned.

"This is a part of the story that's hard to tell, Eve. You see . . . sometimes people make choices that lead them to different places from where they really want to be."

"Why?" she asked, looking confused.

Paul looked thoughtful for a long moment, knowing his daughter would not accept an oversimplified answer. "Sometimes when you forget where you're going, and you decide not to ask for directions, you can make choices that can make you feel lost. Sometimes bad choices don't seem very bad in the beginning. And sometimes you don't recognize that you've made a bad choice until you're a long way down the road."

"Like when I didn't brush my teeth for a whole month because I left my pink toothbrush at Grandma's and didn't want to use the new green one Mommy gave me? And then I got a cavity?"

"Yeah, I guess it's kinda like that. But when you get bigger, the choices you make get bigger, too, and so do the consequences."

"So, did Wolf make some bad choices?" Eve asked.

"Yes. They didn't seem like bad choices, at least in the beginning. But when you make enough bad choices, sometimes it gets hard to fix things. Sometimes it can feel like you're out of control—like there's nothing you can do to make things better. Sometimes, when you don't have the all the tools you need, life can be pretty tough."

"What kind of tools?"

Paul paused, trying to make his story understandable for his daughter. "Remember last summer, when we built your treehouse in the backyard?"

Eve nodded.

"Remember all those trips we had to make to the hardware store to buy tools and wood and nails and stuff?"

Eve nodded again. "It was so boring, I thought I was going to die!"

Rachel laughed.

Paul ignored her. "And remember when Mr. Miller came over to help us? Do you remember what he brought with him?"

Eve looked thoughtful, then smiled. "You mean that long metal stick thing with yellow glass bubbles in it?"

"That's right. It's called a level. Before he came, I made a big mess of things. Nothing lined up with anything else. Do you remember?"

Eve smiled and nodded. "I was really worried about my treehouse, but not as much as Mommy. She told me I wasn't allowed to go inside until she had a prefreshional check to make sure it wouldn't fall down on me."

"Oh, really?" Paul said, trying to ignore Rachel's unsuccessful attempt to quell her own laughter. "What else did Mommy tell you?"

"She said that if it weren't for Mr. Miller, we would have had a whole bunch of firewood instead of a treehouse."

Paul laughed. "Your mother was right. I wanted to build you a cool treehouse, but no matter how hard I tried, I didn't have all the right tools to make it happen. When Mr. Miller brought us the right tools and showed me what I was doing wrong, it came together a lot better, right?"

Eve nodded vigorously.

"It was the same way with Wolf."

"He was trying to build a treehouse, too?"

"No, not exactly. Wolf was trying to figure out how to build a life."

"Is that harder than a treehouse?"

"Yes, yes it is," Paul said thoughtfully. "And it takes a lot more tools. It also helps if you have people around you like Mr. Miller who can show you how to use those tools. When you're building a life, it helps to have lots of people around you who love you and want to help you build the best life that you can."

"Like you and Mommy help me?"

"That's right."

Eve looked ponderous. "So, did Wolf have lots of people to help him?"

"Probably more than he thought he had. Sometimes it's hard, Eve, to admit you need help. It's like our treehouse. I knew it wasn't working out the way I pictured it in my mind, but I didn't want to admit I needed help, even when Mr. Miller came over with all his tools. I think there's a part of us all that believes we should be able to figure things out on our own—that we don't need anybody else. Maybe it's because we believe that if we can't figure life out by ourselves, that we're weak. And for those who discover that they really are weak and lost, there are usually only two choices: they can continue down that hopeless road, or they can stop and ask for directions."

Eve nodded, her eyes wide open. "So, which one did Wolf choose?"

"I guess he chose a little bit of both at different times in his life. He was fortunate enough when he was young to have some people to help him. When he was ten, he started working, mowing lawns to help his mom buy food for their family. By the time he was fifteen he was making more money than his father did, which wasn't much. But when you don't have any money at all, a little bit can seem like a whole bunch. When Wolf went to high school he had a teacher who became a good friend and helped Wolf to understand that if he wanted a better life than his parents had, he would have to work hard for it. He also helped Wolf apply for scholarships, so he wouldn't have to pay so much to go to college."

"Did Wolf get one?"

"As a matter of fact, he did. He got a scholarship that paid for half of his tuition."

"That's pretty good, right?"

"Yes, it was good for him, or at least it could have been good. But Wolf wasn't a very patient person. The college that gave him the scholarship was far away from the little village where he grew up. It was in a big town with lots of people, and Wolf didn't know anybody when he got there."

"Did he stay in a hotel?" asked Eve. "One with a pool and a big TV?"

"No," Paul said, laughing at Eve's animated expressions. "No, Wolf had worked very hard for his money, and he knew he didn't have enough to stay in a fancy hotel and still have enough to pay for his first month's rent. So he slept in the park for a few nights until he could find an apartment."

"Why didn't his parents help him?"

Paul shrugged his shoulders. "Wolf was a big boy by then. He was eighteen years old, and his mom was busy enough helping his sister who was only fifteen."

"But who cooked his dinner?" Eve asked, looking concerned.

"Wolf did."

"And who gave him his money?"

"Wolf had to get a job and earn his own money."

"Okay, but who did the laundry and the grocery shopping? Did he have a wife?"

"No, Wolf was too young to get married."

Eve shook her head and smiled. "Daddy, this is not a very good story."

"Why do you say that?"

"Because boys don't know how to do all of that stuff. Mom said that boys need to get married, so they can find a good woman who can help them grow up and remind them to brush their teeth and take a shower."

"Oh, did she?"

"Yes, she did. She said that you knew how to cook before you got married, but that was the only thing you knew how to do besides going to work. She said it has taken a long time to train you how to be a man. And she said that if she wasn't your wife, you would be a big fat mess."

Paul nodded. If what she said had not been so true, it might have been funny. "You're right," he said as Rachel started laughing. "You're right. It takes most guys a while to figure that out. What else did Mommy tell you about boys?"

"She told me to stay away from them for as long as I can, and when things change and I decide they're not all disgusting creepers, I should try to find a boy who loves me as much as you love Mommy."

"Even if that means you may have to cook and clean up after that boy?" asked Paul.

"I asked mommy about that, and she said that if you really love someone, it's worth taking care of them and doing things for them that they're not good at, even cleaning the bathroom," she said, pinching her nose closed with her fingers.

"I hope that's true," Paul said. He looked at Rachel and smiled. "I hope that's true."

-CHAPTER 3- THE SHE-BEAR

ETERNITY IS NOT SOMETHING THAT BEGINS AFTER YOU'RE DEAD. IT IS GOING ON ALL THE TIME. WE ARE IN IT NOW.
– CHARLOTTE PERKINS GILMAN

"Do you want me to continue with my story?" asked Paul

"Does it get better? So far it's been kinda boring," replied Eve.

Rachel laughed. "Don't all of Daddy's stories get better?"

"What does that mean?" he asked, surprised by the sudden hints of discontentment coming from his normally affable audience.

"It means most of your stories start in dark, lonely places and get happier as you get further into them," replied Rachel.

"They do?"

Rachel raised her eyebrows, focusing on the road.

"Yes, Daddy, most of them get better."

"Like what?" he asked, genuinely intrigued by this revelation.

"Like the story about the she-bear who became the queen of the forest. You know, the one you told me last week," answered Eve.

"What's so dark about that?"

Eve shook her head at her silly father. "Daddy, you told me that the she-bear was the runt of the litter and that her mother wouldn't feed her because she was going to die anyway and she didn't want to waste any food on her, and so the baby bear had to eat mud pies and tree bark until she taught herself how to fish."

"Is that a dark beginning?" Paul teased.

"Dad, she had to eat mud!" Eve said, much louder than needed.

"Okay, okay. But don't most people's stories start out darker than they are when they end?"

Eve looked thoughtful. "My life is pretty good," she said. "I've never had to eat mud."

Paul laughed. "Isn't your story better now than it was in the beginning?" he asked, turning to Rachel.

She nodded after a moment of thought. "Yeah, it's a lot better," she admitted.

"It's okay if your story starts in a dark place," Paul said, turning back to Eve, but addressing both of his girls. "When things are dark, you learn that you either have to be content with darkness or else learn to hold tight of every sunbeam that filters into your life. You learn to appreciate light for what it is; for the warmth it can give you and for the direction it offers to your feet and your mind. We seldom seek more light until we recognize that we've been sitting in the darkness, and realize there is more light to be had. Does that make sense?"

Eve nodded. "I think so."

"So, do you want me to keep telling my story?"

"Does it gets better from here?"

"Well, not quite yet. I could skip to the happy parts, but the happy parts are even happier if you hear the whole story."

"Does Wolf have to eat mud?"

"No," Paul said, trying not to laugh, "But he does have to eat some humbleberry pie."

"Okay, but maybe you could put in a pony or something to make it more exciting."

"I'll work on that. Will you remind me if I forget the pony?"

"Okay."

"Do you remember what I was talking about?"

"You were talking about Wolf being impatient with school," Rachel piped in.

"Oh, yeah, thanks. So, Wolf, didn't really like college. He got a job at Pizza Paradise and started working in the kitchen making pizzas. He was really good at it since he'd had so much practice making pizzas when he was a kid."

"Wait, you never said anything about pizza before," chimed Eve.

"Yeah, that's what Wolf did to earn money when he was in high school. His neighbor opened a pizza restaurant and gave Wolf a job because he'd done such a good job mowing his lawn."

"Lucky!"

"See, it's not such a bad story."

"Daddy, you make pizzas, too."

"That's right."

"Did you know Wolf?"

"You could say that, yes. He was an old friend of mine."

Eve nodded, looking significantly more interested since the mention of pizza.

"So, anyway, Wolf decided after a year of going to college that he really didn't like spending all of his time in school. He just wanted to make money. So he dropped out to make pizza."

"What does "dropped out" mean?"

"It means he stopped going to school."

"I didn't know you could do that," responded Eve. "Can I quit going to school, too, and stay home and make pizza?"

Rachel started laughing.

"You can do what ever you want to do," Paul responded.

"Really?"

"Yes, as soon as you're eighteen and move away. We'd prefer it if you went to college, but if pizza is your passion, we won't stand in your way."

Eve let out her breath in exasperation, making a sound like air coming quickly out of a balloon.

"Anyway," Paul continued, ignoring her response, "he gave up his dream of going to college to work at Pizza Paradise, full-time. His boss treated him well, and he never went home hungry. After a year, Wolf got promoted to manager and got a raise. That eliminated any desire to go back to school."

"Did his parents get mad that he dropped out?" asked Eve.

"They never found out."

"How come?"

"Well, before Wolf could tell his parents that his plans had changed, his mom died, and his dad went to jail."

"For what? How?" Eve asked with scrutinizing eyes, the same way she looked at Paul every time she was trying to figure out if he was serious or just pulling her leg as he so often did. But Paul didn't smile this time.

"His mother was walking home from her work at the grocery store one snowy night and was hit by a pickup truck as she was crossing the street … and she was killed." Paul watched as Eve stared into his eyes as if to make sure he was serious.

"She died in the road?"

"Yes," Paul said softly.

"All by herself? Was there anyone else with her?"

Paul pressed his lips together, then shook his head. "No. No one saw it happen. People in the village went to bed early, so they didn't find her until the next morning."

Eve looked very sad. "But what about the person who was driving the truck? Why didn't they stop? What happened to them?"

"The man went home, went to bed and tried to pretend it was all a bad dream."

"How do you know?"

"Ummm … Wolf told me. Eve, I've wanted to tell you this story for a long time, but I know it's sad. I … if I hadn't received this package from Aunt Katie, I probably would have waited a few more years to tell you. If you want me to stop, I can wait until you're older."

Eve had a very solemn look on her face, but she shook her head. "Keep going," she said softly.

Paul nodded, but before he could start again, Eve interrupted.

"Daddy, where is your package from Aunt Katie?"

"It's right here. Would you like to see it?" he asked, reaching for the package at his feet.

"Yes." She set aside her crayons as Paul handed her the package, filling her lap with the large, white envelope. With her finger, she traced the blue and orange letters at the top before running her hand over the return address. "This is from Auntie Katie?"

"That's right."

"This is the book about Wolf?"

"Yes."

"A man brought this to our house yesterday right before we went to the store."

"Is that right?"

"Yeah. Why did she send it to you if we were going to see her tomorrow?"

"I asked her the same thing when she called this morning. She said that a woman gave her some money and asked her to make sure it got to me as soon as possible."

Eve nodded, apparently satisfied with the answer. "Are there any cool pictures in it?"

"It's been a long time since I last saw it, but I seem to remember there being some pictures in it."

"Can we open it?"

Paul looked at his daughter. He loved that she was always curious. Despite his own curiosity, there remained a sense of uncertainty and hesitation which encompassed this package. His mind raced as he considered what this book would expose his daughter to. It seemed strange to him that he was even considering sharing this with her now. Since Eve's birth, he had tried with all his might to protect her from the person he once was and the mountains of baggage that came with the Schafer name. So far, the story about Wolf had enabled him to tell his own story without exposing the whole truth of who he was. But he knew that his bright, curious daughter would, without too many more details, be able to patch the full truth together. Was this safe? Would she be disappointed or ashamed of her father once she learned the whole truth?

"Daddy, can I open it?" Eve repeated.

Truth—the whole truth. Was that not what had changed his life forever? Was that not what had set him free from the monsters that plagued his soul?

"Daddy?"

"Yes, Baby, you can open it," Paul responded, lost in a parallel world of his own thoughts.

She smiled before reaching for the small, blue-handled, craft scissors in her open pencil box. She sliced the package open then picked it up to look inside. "It's a book," she said, looking surprised.

"Didn't I tell you it was a book?"

"Well, yeah, but you joke around a lot, Dad. I thought maybe you were kidding." She reached her hand inside the envelope and pulled the book out, laying it down on her lap. A bright, white prescription form was taped to the cover of the book with Katie's name on top.

"It's really from Katie! Can I read her note?" Eve asked.

"Sure, if you can," Paul said, smiling at the slightly smeared handwriting which authenticated it as Katie's own left-handed scrawls.

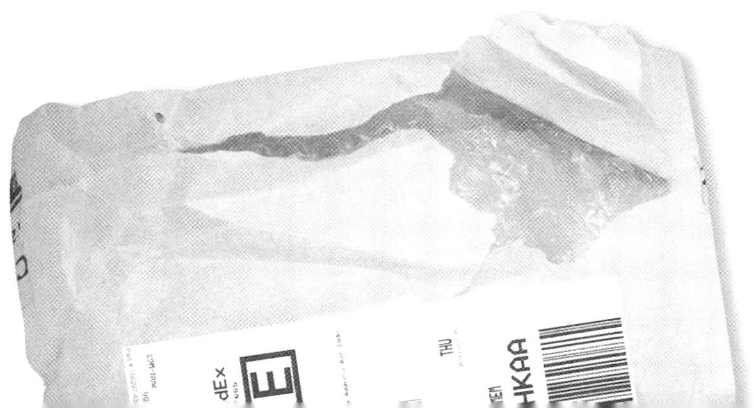

LIC.# 35.08

KATHRINE A. LEWIS, M.D.
KENOSHA HOSPITAL & MEDICAL CENTER
6308 8TH AVE
KENOSHA, WI 53143
TEL: (262) 656-2011 FAX: (262) 656-2012

NAME ______________________ DATE __________

ADDRESS ______________________

℞ PAUL, GET A CELL PHONE!!!
I HOPE I WILL HAVE SPOKEN TO YOU BY THE
TIME YOU GET THIS. IF I HAVEN'T, CALL ME! THE
OBITUARY FOR MR. GREEN IS INSIDE THE COVER.
I WASN'T SURE, BUT I THOUGHT YOU WOULD
PROBABLY LIKE TO ATTEND THE FUNERAL, IF YOU'RE
HERE. I CAN'T WAIT TO SEE YOU GUYS. GIVE THE
GIRLS A HUG FOR ME. SEE YOU SOON.

LOVE, KATIE

SIGNATURE

☐ LABEL
REFILL 0 1 2 3 4 5 PRN

Eve looked up, proud of herself for being able to read. "What's an o-b-i-t-u-a-r-y?"

Paul smiled, looking at Rachel. "It's kind of like an invitation."

"An invitation? To a party?"

"Well, sometimes. It's more like an invitation to get to know someone."

Eve looked confused.

Rachel shook her head. "Paul," she said with such an intonation that he didn't even have to look at her to know she was raising her eyebrow at him.

"Daddy, what is it really?" Eve asked playfully, catching on to her mother's hint that her father was not being entirely truthful.

"Okay, I guess most people don't really consider obituaries invitations, but I do. Everyday, in newspapers around the world, there is a section called obituaries." Paul opened the cover of the book and pulled out the long strip of newsprint. He looked closely at the photo at the top before smiling, then turned back to Eve. "This is an obituary for a very old friend of mine." He handed the strip of paper to her.

"John Maximilian Green," Eve read aloud. "Who is he?"

"A cranky old man I used to know, a long time ago."

"Was he your landlord?" asked Eve.

Paul laughed. "No, he wasn't that cranky. I think he was just lonely and forgot how to be nice."

Eve looked back at the picture. "He doesn't look cranky to me," she said, pointing to the pixilated photo. "He actually looks kinda happy."

"I guess he does," Paul said, craning his neck to take a closer look. He was surprised by the gentle smile the old man wore.

"Can I see?" asked Rachel, straining to see whatever she could through the rearview mirror.

Paul took the strip of paper back from Eve and showed it to Rachel.

"He looks like a nice, old man," she said after glancing at the photo. "What does it say about him?"

Paul moved the paper closer so he could better read the tiny writing.

John Maximilian Green
1918 - 2012

John Green, age 92, passed away Monday, June 16, 2012 of a brain tumor.

"Max", as he was known by his friends and family, was born in Berlin, Wisconsin, on July 10, 1918 to Joseph and Myrna Smithfield Green, and grew up on the family farm where he learned the value of hard work. After graduating from Berlin High in 1934, he borrowed twenty dollars from his father and set out for greener pastures. His aversion to cold weather and snow led him to California where he found work as a machinist.

In 1938, Max married his first wife, Jane Griffin in San Francisco. Their son, Clarence, was born two years later, followed by Joseph in '41 and Elizabeth in '42. Max was drafted into the Navy in May of 1942. Over the next three years, he survived three U-boat attacks, managing to stay alive despite horrific odds. A true member of the Greatest Generation, Max returned home from war, a decorated veteran.

When Jane passed away of pneumonia in 1947, Max was left with three young children to care for. Later that year, he married Margaret Manning, the widow of his best friend, Stanley Manning, becoming step-father to Stanley Jr. and Alice. Max took advantage of the G.I. Bill and received his education, graduating from Stanford in 1951 with a degree in accounting. Marie was born later that same year.

Max moved his family to Chicago in 1951 where he worked as an accountant for Encyclopedia Britannica, Inc., until he retired in 1980. Margaret died of cancer less than a year later. Shortly thereafter, Max was hired as a consultant by Snap-on Tools, Inc.,moving to Kenosha, Wisconsin in 1982. In his spare time, he took up bowling, where he met Millie Caldwell in 1984, marrying her later that year and becoming step-father to Jan, Peter and Stephanie. After Millie's death in 1989, Max went on a "sabbatical" for nearly ten years, turning his attention to fishing and philosophy.

Max spent the last decade of his life volunteering as a crossing guard at a local elementary school, rekindling relationships with his children, step-children, grandkids and great-grandkids, and becoming a devout Quaker and peace activist. Max will be sorely missed.

Funeral services will be held on Friday, June 21, at noon at the Quaker Church at 1730 Green Bay Road in Kenosha, Wisconsin. In lieu of flowers, please take someone you love to dinner or spend time with a child.

Paul looked up from the article with a smile on his face.

"What are you thinking?" Rachel asked.

"I was just thinking that I must have known Max during the period he called his "sabbatical."

"What does that mean, exactly?" Rachel continued to probe.

"I don't know for sure, but at the time I knew him, he often talked about his quest to make sense of life and our reasons for being here. I guess I understand now why he had so much trouble with that."

"What do you mean?"

Paul looked at the paper again. "I remember him talking about outliving a couple of wives. I'm sure it would be hard enough to lose one spouse, but to lose three … that just seems cruel, doesn't it?"

Rachel nodded, staring at the road ahead.

"Is that why he was cranky?" asked Eve.

Paul looked over his shoulder. "I think it must be. I … I don't think I really understood back then. I don't know if I could have—I had never been married before."

"Dad, why did Auntie Katie have this book? Does she know Wolf?" Eve asked, interrupting his memories.

"Uh, yes. She's known him ever since kindergarten. They grew up together."

"So, does she know that Wolf's mom got killed by a truck?"

Paul turned around, reminded of the story he'd been telling. "She didn't find out for several years after it happened, but yes, she knows. I'm sure Wolf must have told her."

"How did he find out?"

"Well, it took a few months, but the police finally found him at work in Kenosha and told him."

Eve wore a worried look on her face. "How did the police find out?"

"When her mom didn't come home that night, Jennie, got really worried. She stayed up waiting and finally called the police. The policeman didn't want to go out in the storm, so he said he would look for her in the morning. Jennie stayed up and waited, but her mom never came. The next morning, some people found Wolf's mother on the side of the road, half buried in the snow. The policeman went to the trailer by the tracks and told Jennie the sad news. Then the police went to the lake to tell Wolf's father. After they found him, passed out in his bunk in the ice fishing house, they discovered that the front end of his pickup truck was dented, and even all the snow that night couldn't hide the blood that was still on those dents. They took him and put him in jail."

"What does passed out mean?"

"He was drunk," Paul whispered somberly. "He'd spent the night before with his friends, drinking beer at the bar, and he decided not to go home because he was too drunk to even stand up."

Rachel touched Paul on the arm. He turned to look at her. Though she said nothing, her eyes were filled with tears.

"Dad, this story gets better, right?"

"It does, Baby, I promise, but not yet."

"How long will that man be in jail?"

Paul took a deep breath. "For the rest of his life. That man, Wolf's father, had had a drinking problem for many years. He'd gotten caught driving drunk before and had been in trouble with the police."

"Good," Eve said.

"What's good?"

"That he went to jail forever, so he can't hurt anyone else."

Her words stung Paul. He thought of all the pain and hurt his father's choice to drive drunk had brought into his life. There had been many other sorrows and disappointments that had come from his father's choices over the years, but this single act had become the monster that had nearly consumed him.

"Why did it take so long for the police to find Wolf?" Eve asked, pulling Paul back to the present.

"The police tried to contact him, but the phone number they had didn't work. They tried calling the college, but since he'd dropped out, they didn't have any information about him."

"Some people have cell phones," Eve said, innocently.

Paul shook his head. "Yes, but Wolf didn't know enough people he wanted to talk to in order to spend the money to get a cell phone. And besides that, cell phones weren't very common back then. By the time the police found him, it had been several months since Wolf had even called home."

"But what about Jennie? What happened to Jennie?" asked Eve.

"Jennie was only sixteen, and so she was sent to Osh Kosh to live with Wolf's uncle and aunt. After Wolf found out what happened, it took him a long time before he tried to find his sister, and by then she was in college and was busy with her own life."

"Why did he wait so long?"

"Because ... because Wolf didn't think about anybody else back then. He was hurting inside and angry at his father. He thought that he didn't need a family, that he could figure out life by himself. He knew he couldn't help Jennie, so he decided not to contact her until he could."

"But doesn't everybody need a family?" asked Eve.

Paul nodded. "Everybody needs someone to love. When people have a family, like we do, you don't have to look very far to find people to love. Wolf didn't have his family around him anymore, and so he went looking for friends who could take the place of his family. He made friends at work and some of those friends introduced him to their friends. That's when he began experimenting with drugs and alcohol, trying to get rid of the pain in his heart."

"Drugs are dumb," Eve said, resolutely.

"Yes, they are," admitted Paul, "but it took many years for Wolf to figure that out. During the day, he kept his mind busy by working, but sometimes at night, when he had time to think, he was haunted by … by monsters."

"Daddy, monsters aren't real."

"You're right, Eve. But sometimes, when life is dark, your mind can play tricks on you, and you can start to think that they are real."

Eve nodded.

"Sometimes it feels like they live inside your head and your chest, and they like to kick you in the heart or your stomach when you feel like you need love and there is no one there to love you. Sometimes, when people feel this way, they get tricked into believing that the only way they can feel better is if they take drugs or alcohol, so their brain and heart can rest from the hurt."

"Is that why Mr. Miller drinks beer?" Eve asked.

"Maybe sometimes," Paul responded. "Do you know Mr. Miller's story?"

"Kind of. Mom told me his wife died before I was born, and that he is lonely."

"That's right."

"Is that why we invite Mr. Miller to come to our house for dinner sometimes?"

Paul watched out of the corner of his eye as Rachel bit her lower lip. She had been reluctant at first when Paul had proposed inviting their neighbor to dinner from time to time. Over the subsequent years, Mr. Miller had become more than a neighbor. He was the closest thing they had to family in Ohio and he often looked in on Rachel and Eve when Paul was working at the fire station.

"That's right, Eve. Mommy and I both know how lonely it can be sometimes when you don't have people around you to love or when you don't feel like anybody loves you. Mr. Miller needs our love. He needs us to be his friends."

"Is that why Mr. Miller always likes to stay past my bedtime when he comes to visit?"

"Yes. Mr. Miller is still sad. He misses his wife every day. Did you know they were married for more than fifty years?"

"That's a long time."

"Yes it is."

"Why don't his kids come to visit more often?"

"They're busy with their own families, honey. He's a great-grandpa now, and he's getting older. He doesn't like to drive very far."

"And he's afraid his arms will get tired if he flies," Eve said, smiling just as she had when Mr. Miller had admitted his fear of flying at Thanksgiving dinner seven months earlier.

"That's right, Baby. I know he'd like to see his family more often, but since he can't, I'm glad that we can be his friends."

"Daddy, is Mr. Miller going to die, too?"

"Someday he will, yes."

"Will his family come to visit him then?"

Paul looked at Rachel. She looked at him briefly before turning her attention back to the road, leaving him to answer their daughter's question. "I hope so," he finally uttered after looking deep into his child's green eyes. "I hope they will come so they can learn who their father really was—so they can hear all his stories."

"Who will tell them his stories?" she asked.

"Maybe you can."

"Me?"

"Sure. You've heard a lot of his stories. You might have heard more of his stories than his own grandchildren have."

"I could tell them about the time when he was a little boy and he got chased by the bull and had to hide in the outhouse!" Eve said with great animation.

"I think they'd like that," replied Paul. "Sometimes we forget to tell our best stories to the people we love the most."

-Chapter 4- Heart Stone

God allows us to experience the low points of life in order to teach us lessons that we could learn in no other way. - C.S. Lewis

"So, what happened to Wolf?" asked Eve.

"Let's see … where was I?"

"You said that Wolf was being dumb with drugs," responded Eve, bluntly.

"That's right. He was trying to stop the pain he felt in his heart. There were lots of times that he felt out of control and hopeless, and the worst part was that he didn't feel like there was anything he could do to make things better. His life turned into a blur as he struggled to put on a happy face each day at work, and then he returned home to his empty apartment where he would often drink himself into a deep sleep.

"Things weren't always bad. Sometimes he would hang out with his friends, and things would be good for a while. After a couple of years, there were even whole weeks when he would feel like the sun was shining on him again. But that never lasted long."

"Why not?"

Paul took a deep breath. "Because he would see things that reminded him of his family, and the monsters would come back."

"Sometimes I think I see monsters after I watch a scary movie," replied Eve.

"It was kind of like that for Wolf, too, but lots of times it wasn't the scary things that made him sad. Lots of times it was seeing happy things, like families coming into the restaurant together, or a man and a woman holding hands. Lots of times, it was just that Wolf knew what he didn't have that made him feel sad."

"Why didn't he just get married, like you and mommy?"

Paul smiled, resting his hand on Rachel's knee. "Sometimes falling in love isn't so easy, especially if you really don't love yourself—if you don't really know who you are. Sometimes people have to figure out who they are first before anyone can fall in love with them. Wolf knew he was sad, but he didn't really know how to change his sadness—how to be happy."

"Sometimes the person you're supposed to marry isn't ready to fall in love yet," Rachel said softly.

Paul sat up and readjusted his position, twisting his neck back and forth to work out a kink. Rachel's words had been brief, but he knew they were meaningful, and as he settled back into the seat, he glanced at her. Though they had been married for more than a decade, there were still many things Paul knew she was uncomfortable talking about. He knew she had tamed many of her own monsters prior to meeting him, but she rarely spoke about any of them. From time to time, he caught glimpses of the remnants of those monsters in her words and in her writing. He often felt sad that she didn't trust him with these things. But he knew from his own experience and his own monsters that pushing her to talk about them was rarely helpful. And so he hadn't. Instead, he loved her in such a way that he hoped when the time was right, and she was ready, she would trust him enough to share those secrets and unload the burden he knew she carried.

"That's right," Paul said, resting his hand back on his wife's knee.

"Love is kind of a tricky thing, Eve, especially when it's love between a man and a woman. Sometimes it takes a long time to find the right person to love; the right person you want to marry and spend the rest of your life with. Mommy and I both had to date different kinds of people before we met each other and knew that we needed to get married."

"You went on dates with other people?" Eve asked with wide eyes.

"Sure. Lots of different people." Paul responded.

"Why?"

"It took me and mommy a long time to figure out what kind of person we wanted to commit to for the rest of our lives. We didn't have the best examples to look to in our parents, and we both knew we wanted something better in our own marriage. It's probably the most important decision you will make in your life."

"How will I know when I meet the right boy?" asked Eve.

Rachel turned to look at her husband, smiling. "You'll just know," she said. "Something in your heart will tell you that it's right, and you'll hold onto that good feeling for the rest of your life."

"Yeah, it's kinda like that," Paul said, winking at his wife.

"Daddy, you keep getting lost in your story."

"That's because you ask so many questions. How in the world am I supposed to remember where I am with all of your questions?"

Eve rolled her eyes, a skill she'd recently acquired from being around the girls at school, and one she had already used innumerable times to help her father remember that he was more than just a little bit goofy.

"Okay, so, Wolf fell in love with several different girls over the next few years, and while he was dating them, he was usually a little bit happier. But when they broke up, the old monsters came back again, and he would fall into the same darkness he'd known before. One time, he even got close to asking a girl to marry him. He had dated lots of different girls and he felt pretty sure that this was the one he wanted to spend the rest of his life with."

"What was her name?" asked Eve.

"Emily."

"Was she pretty?" asked Eve.

"Wolf thought she was very pretty," Paul said, catching his wife's sideward glance. "They dated for almost a whole year, and Wolf really wanted to marry her."

"Why didn't he?" asked Eve.

"Because … she didn't want to marry him."

"Why not?"

"Well, because he was a pizza boy. She wanted someone who made lots of money, not lots of pizzas. She stayed with Wolf until she met a handsome man from Chicago who had just finished law school. Then she dumped Wolf and ran away with the lawyer."

"Was Wolf sad?"

"Yes, he was very sad. He was sadder than he had ever been before."

"Even sadder than when his mommy died?" asked Eve.

"This was a different kind of sad, Eve. It made Wolf feel like everything he'd ever been sad about in his whole life came back at the same time and dropped onto his shoulders. He felt like he got pushed down into the cold dirt, down—like five hundred feet down until he couldn't see any light at all. He was so sad that he couldn't even think anything happy. When he tried to sleep, he had bad dreams that made him crazy. When he was awake, he felt so dark that he just wanted to die."

"How did he get happy again?"

"How do you know he did?" Paul queried.

"Because you told me this story gets better, and right now it's really sad."

Paul nodded. "Well, it does get better, but even though his life was already very dark, it had to get even darker before it got better."

"How did it get darker?"

Paul took a deep breath. "Christmastime came around."

"Christmas isn't sad," Eve responded, looking confused.

"It's not sad when you have people around who love you. But when there's no one to love, and you feel like nobody cares, Christmas can be a very sad time."

Eve nodded thoughtfully.

"On Christmas day, Wolf didn't have anyone around him to even wish him a Merry Christmas. His friends were all hanging out with their families, and no one invited him to come for dinner or to be with them."

"Why not? Didn't they care about him?"

"It's usually not very fun to be around sad people, and Wolf had been sad for a long time. I'm sure he tried hard to think of happy thoughts, but it was like all the monsters in his life were trying to eat every glimmer of light and every scrap of happiness he had ever known. All that day he sat in his quiet apartment feeling sorry for himself and becoming sadder and sadder until something inside him broke. When the night came, he couldn't handle it anymore and decided to go for a walk, even though it was snowing."

"Where did he go?" asked Eve.

"He went to a park at the lake, not very far from his apartment."

"Did he want to make a snowman?"

Paul shook his head. "No, but that would have been a better idea. No, Wolf had a big bottle of whiskey, and he decided he would try to drink it all and go to sleep in the snow, so he would never have to wake up again."

Eve stared at her father for a long moment. "He wanted to die?" she asked softly.

"Yes. He couldn't think of any good reasons to keep living."

"Is whiskey poisonous?" Eve thoughtfully asked.

"It is if you drink too much. Wolf wanted to make sure he didn't wake up again, so he took some pills, too."

"So … did he die?" Eve asked, holding her breath and looking very serious.

"No, but he probably would have. After he drank most of the bottle of whiskey and swallowed a handful of pills, he laid down in the snow and tried to go to sleep."

"Did he have any blankets, or a pillow?"

"No. By that time he was so drunk that he didn't

even know he was cold. He was just beginning to fall asleep when someone called his name."

"Who was it?"

Paul glanced at Rachel out of the corner of his eye. "It was a beautiful woman in a long white dress."

"Was she the Snow Princess?"

He smiled, charmed by his daughter's innocence. "I don't think so. She was much whiter than that, like the sun was shining on her—or through her—almost like her clothes and her hair were on fire."

"Was she an angel who came to take him to heaven?"

Paul shook his head. "I think she probably was an angel, but she didn't come to take him to heaven."

"Did she come to take him to the other place?" Eve asked, pointing downwards.

Paul smiled, but shook his head again. "No. She didn't come to take him anywhere. I think she came to make sure he didn't fall asleep—that he didn't die. I think she came to give Wolf a reason to live, to give him a piece of hope that he could hang onto even when his world was full of darkness."

"What does a piece of hope look like?" Eve asked.

Her question surprised him, and he stopped to think before responding. The woman had given him something that night, more than just the realization that there was something beyond the realms of mortality. She had reached into her robe and pulled out a white stone shaped like a rock that glowed brightly, placing it in the palm of his hand. Every time the dream had repeated itself over the years, he'd awakened with his hand clutched tightly in a fist, holding onto that stone with all the strength he could muster, afraid of letting go—afraid of it slipping through his fingers once again. And even though the stone was always gone when he awoke, the feeling it left in his heart always replaced the feeling of disappointment of an empty hand.

"Daddy, what does hope look like?" Eve repeated.

Paul took a deep breath. He knew the answer to her question was so much more than a mystical heart-shaped stone that radiated light. He looked at her, searching for words to explain. "What it looks like is probably much less important than what it feels like."

Eve stared at him, expectantly.

"Hope, at least the kind of hope that Wolf was given that night, gave him an expectation of better things. It made him aware that there was not only the possibility that there was something out there after death, but a certainty of the reality of a God and a creator who had a design for his life."

"The woman in the white dress told him all those things?"

"No, not exactly. What she gave him was only a view into eternity—a clue—maybe a handful of clues that led him to open his eyes and ears and heart to the hope of there being something more than the miserable life he'd experienced."

Eve nodded, but her face suggested his answer did not fully satisfy her question.

"What was it that he saw that made him believe those things—that gave him that hope?" Rachel asked.

Paul turned to look at her, surprised. She had always avoided this part of his history, never giving him a chance to explain, or even begin.

"I'm not sure exactly what it was that he saw, but it was beyond all the beauty he had ever seen in the world. It was a totally different place—a place where he wasn't cold anymore—where all the darkness was replaced with brilliant light. And in that light, all of the darkness in his heart was gone. And instead of loneliness, there were lots of people all around him who were happy to see him."

Paul shifted his position and turned again to look at Eve. "Wolf saw his mother there, but she was younger and happier than he had ever seen her before. He ran towards her, wanting to hug her, but as he reached out for her, all the people disappeared—everyone except the beautiful woman in the long, white dress. She told him that someone was coming to help him—that he needed to go and get better, and that people would be waiting to teach him and love him and help him learn the things he needed to learn before he could be ready to come back. She pointed her finger at his chest and told him that he wasn't ready to die because he hadn't learned how to live and to love. That wasn't what Wolf wanted to hear, so before she left, she gave him a very special gift. She handed him a bright, white stone, in the shape of a heart."

"Like a heart rock?" Eve asked excitedly. "Like the ones you help me find?"

"Yes, but this one was a little smaller, no bigger than a strawberry, and it was very special."

"Was it like the one we found at Lake Erie?"

"No, that was a good one, but this one glowed like it was a piece of the sun."

"Cool!"

"Yeah. Wolf had never seen anything so beautiful in his life. He couldn't help but stare at it in his hand, and when he looked up to thank her, the woman was gone, leaving him staring up into the falling snow."

"So, did someone come to help him?" asked Eve.

"Yes. Just like the woman told him. A man came and tried to pick him up out of the snow, but Wolf was too heavy, and he didn't want to go."

"Why not?" asked Eve, a puzzled look on her face.

"Because he thought if he could stay, he could find the woman in the white dress, and she could tell him more."

"But didn't you say he would die if he stayed?"

"Yes. I think the man who came to help him must have known that. When Wolf tried to resist, the man punched him in the stomach."

"Why did he punch him?"

"Because Wolf was being stubborn."

"But didn't that hurt Wolf?"

"Yes. In fact it cracked his ribs, but it probably saved his life."

"How?" asked Rachel.

"It made Wolf throw up most of the whiskey that was in his stomach. The man held Wolf's head by his hair as he threw up all over the snow.

When he was done, Wolf didn't have any fight left in him, and so the man dragged him all the way to hospital."

"The Kenosha Hospital?" asked Rachel, breaking her silence.

"Yes."

"Were they at Eichelman Park?" Rachel continued.

"Yes. Wolf was lucky they were. Eichelman Park is where we go sometimes when we visit Grandma," Paul explained. "It's only a quarter of a mile from the Kenosha Hospital."

"Isn't that where Auntie Katie works?" asked Eve.

"That's right."

"And I got my middle name from Aunt Katie, right?"

"Yes. Mommy and I both love Katie. She was a good friend to each of us when we needed her. Did you know that her real name is Kathryn?"

Eve nodded. "So, is Aunt Katie related to Mommy or you?"

Paul glanced at Rachel who was smiling, even though her eyes were wet with tears.

"She actually isn't related to either of us. She was my roommate and Daddy's friend from when he was your age. If it wasn't for Katie, Daddy and I might never have met and started dating."

Eve smiled and nodded. "So, what happened to Wolf? Did he see Katie when he was at the hospital?"

"Yes, he … um, it was Katie who helped save Wolf's life," Paul responded.

"How?"

"Katie was a new doctor back then. She had only been working at the hospital for about six months when the man brought Wolf to the emergency room on Christmas night. Katie helped Wolf get better. She helped him remember happy things and was his friend when he really needed a friend."

"So, did Wolf fall in love with Katie?" asked Eve.

Paul smiled. He had always admired Eve's ability to ask straightforward questions. "No. He never fell in love with her, but he loved her as a friend. She was almost like his sister in a lot of ways.

They actually knew each other from the time they were very young—remember, they grew up together."

Eve nodded and Paul was grateful she didn't ask any more questions that would cause him to reveal more to his daughter than he was ready to admit.

-Chapter 5-
Second Chance

There are moments when troubles
enter our lives
and we can do nothing to avoid them.
But they are there for a reason.
Only when we have overcome them
will we understand why they were there.
-Paulo Coelho

"So, what happened to Wolf at the hospital?" Rachel asked, speaking softly.

"I'm not exactly sure what happened, at least not for the first few days. Wolf remembers the man taking him into the emergency room and telling the doctors how he'd found him. He remembers them laying him down on a bed and covering him with warm blankets, but then … then he said it went dark for a long time, and he didn't wake up for a couple of days. Katie later told him that he was probably only minutes away from dying. And even though most of the poison had left his body, some of it got into his lungs when he threw up. His fingers and toes were also very cold, and he had hypothermia and three cracked ribs. He had to spend a few days in intensive care, hooked up to a machine that helped him breathe."

"He was only in the hospital for a few days?" asked Rachel, looking surprised.

"No, he was there for about two weeks all together. His pneumonia had to be treated, and he needed to rest so his body could heal."

"Did he get to eat popsicles and watch TV all day? That's what Mommy lets me do sometimes when I get sick."

Paul smiled at his daughter. "I don't think Wolf had any popsicles. I know he tried to watch TV, but people kept coming into his room."

"To bring him flowers and balloons?"

Paul laughed. "No, that would have been nice, but they actually came to visit Wolf's roommate—a really old man named Dr. Dinglebottom."

Eve started laughing. "Daddy, that's a silly name."

"I know it is. It was really just a nickname form his time in the war, but he'd been going by that for so many years that the name had stuck. Wolf tried to tell the doctor that his name was silly, but the old man said he liked the name because it always made children smile. He was a doctor for kids."

"You mean a pediatrician, like Dr. Bentley?" asked Eve.

"That's right! I forgot you know big words like that."

"Daddy, I've been going to my pediatrician at least a couple of times every year since I was born!" Eve replied.

"Right, sorry," he said, trying not to laugh at the face Eve was pulling. "Anyway, Dr. Dinglebottom was a very old man, but he liked his work so much that he just kept working—long after he was supposed to retire. He had worked at Kenosha Hospital for so long that he knew everyone who worked in the whole hospital. Even the janitors and the people who made the food wanted to visit him. He also had lots of friends and family members who came to see him. He had so many friends that it was hard to get any sleep. Just as someone was finishing their visit, someone else would show up, and they'd start talking about old times and telling stories."

"Was it kinda like bedtime stories at our house?" asked Eve.

"Uh, kinda. But Dr. Dinglebottom was really old, and like Wolf, he had pneumonia. Wolf didn't understand it at first. Most of the people who came were coming to say goodbye and remember all the fun times they'd had together and all the great things they'd learned from the old man. And as Wolf listened and watched, he did a lot of thinking. It was during those days that Wolf started hoping … hoping to make the kind of in impact in people's lives that Dr. Dinglebottom had made."

"Was Dr. Dinglebottom going on a trip? Is that why people came to say goodbye?"

Paul looked at Rachel, then back at his daughter, unsure of how he should answer her question. "Eve … Doctor Dinglebottom was dying. His body was old and worn out, and he was very sick. People came to see him because they knew they wouldn't see him again, and they wanted him to know that they were grateful for the love he'd given them."

"But he was at a hospital … and he was a doctor. Why didn't he just get better and go home?"

"Not everybody gets better, Eve, especially when they get old, or if their body becomes weak. Dr. Dinglebottom had lived a long life. He had raised his kids, and he even had great-grandchildren. I'm sure he had probably gotten sick lots of times before, and had usually gotten better, but his body was worn out."

"You mean like Rex?"

"That's right. Rex was over a hundred years old in dog years, and I think he had at least one spot for each of those years to prove it. Did you know that Rex worked at the fire station longer than any of the guys?"

Eve shook her head. "Even longer than you?"

"Sure. He was an old dog before I even met him."

"I was sad when he died. I liked it when he licked my face," she said, giggling.

"We were all sad, but none of us liked watching Rex limp around, not even able to get off of his bed some days."

Eve looked thoughtful, then nodded.

"It was kind of the same way with Dr. Dinglebottom. He had lived a long and happy life, but he knew his body was weak and tired. So he asked the doctors at the hospital not to hook him up to a breathing machine or make him live any longer than his body would let him."

"He wanted to die?"

"No, I wouldn't say he wanted to die, but he wasn't afraid of dying anymore."

"Because he wanted to go to heaven?"

Paul nodded. "He believed in heaven, and he was anxious to see if it would be everything he imagined. His wife had died several years before and one of his sons, too, and Wolf heard him talk about heaven with many of the people who came to visit him. Doctor Dinglebottom had more friends than anyone Wolf had ever met, and after a day or two, he decided it would be better to watch and listen than to be annoyed by all the visitors."

"Did people come and visit Wolf, too?"

"Only Katie. She came every day to check on him, even on the days she didn't work."

"Did she bring him balloons and flowers?"

Paul smiled. "No. She brought him something even better."

"A puppy?"

Rachel laughed.

"No. Puppies aren't allowed in the hospital. No, Katie brought Wolf a very special book."

"Was it a coloring book?"

"No, that would have been nice, too, but the book she brought Wolf didn't have any pictures. It didn't even have any words. She brought him a beautiful hand-made journal with a brown leather cover."

Paul watched as Eve looked down at the book on her lap. "Like this one?" she asked, looking up?

"Very much like that one. Actually, that is the book she brought him."

Eve lifted Katie's note off the cover of the book and set it aside. She ran her fingers over the rich brown surface, stopping at the edges that were scuffed and worn. She turned the book over, revealing a leather strap, the width and length of a shoelace, stitched to the back cover. On the spine, she discovered a half dozen sinewy threads, tightly stretched through hand drilled holes. Paul smiled to himself as he watched her examine every inch of the book's exterior. Then she lifted it to her nose and sniffed it.

"What does it smell like?" Rachel asked, having watched her daughter's interaction with the book through the rearview mirror.

"It smells like leather and … Mr. Miller's aftershave."

Paul look surprised. "Mr. Miller's aftershave?"

"Yeah, smell it—right here," she said, pointing to a darker area on the cover.

Paul took the book in his hands and held it close to his nose before inhaling deeply. Immediately, his mind was flooded with memories of a man he knew in a previous life—a man he knew by only one name—Max. "Old Spice," he whispered.

"So, why did Katie give Wolf that book?" Eve questioned.

"I think because she knew he needed it."

"How come?"

"Because she was his friend—and because when she visited him, she listened with her heart to what he told her. She knew he needed to remember what it felt like to have someone care about him. If I remember right, I think she even wrote him a note, just inside the cover."

Eve opened the book to the first page and looked up at her father with her bright green eyes, as if asking permission to proceed. He nodded his approval.

DECEMBER 30, 1998

TO WOLF, ONE OF MY OLDEST FRIENDS—

SOMETHING TOLD ME YEARS AGO, WHEN WE WERE JUST KIDS, THAT WE'D BE FRIENDS FOR A LONG, LONG TIME. I'VE MISSED SEEING YOU THESE PAST EIGHT YEARS, AND TODAY, I'M GRATEFUL TO STILL HAVE YOU IN MY LIFE.

MY AUNT GAVE ME THIS BOOK LAST CHRISTMAS. I WAS HAPPY TO RECEIVE SUCH A BEAUTIFUL GIFT AND HAVE THOUGHT MANY TIMES OVER THE PAST YEAR ABOUT THE THINGS I MIGHT WRITE IN IT. BUT SINCE CHRISTMAS NIGHT, I HAVE BEEN THINKING THAT SURELY YOUR STORY, WRITTEN ON THESE PAGES, WOULD BE FAR MORE INTERESTING THAN MINE.

I WANT YOU TO KNOW THAT I APPRECIATE YOUR FRIENDSHIP AND THAT I BELIEVE IN YOU. IN MY MIND, I CAN IMAGINE OUR PATHS CROSSING MANY TIMES OVER THE REST OF OUR LIVES, AND I HOPE THAT EACH TIME WE MEET, YOU WILL SHARE WITH ME SOME OF THE MAGIC YOU'VE GATHERED ALONG YOUR JOURNEY. REMEMBER, PAUL, THAT PAIN IS ALWAYS TEMPORARY, AND LIFE, WITH ALL ITS SURPRISES, IS ALWAYS WORTH FIGHTING FOR.

I LOVE YOU. YOUR FRIEND ALWAYS

KATIE LEWIS

Eve looked up from the book with a smile. "Katie was in love with Wolf!?"

Paul looked at his wife, resting his hand on her knee before he responded. "Katie was a friend to Wolf when he needed a friend more than anything else in this world—when he needed someone to love, but the love she had for Wolf was more like the love good friends have for each other. Kind of like a brother and a sister."

Eve looked confused.

"Love is kind of a funny thing. It's complicated, but having someone to love is one of the important ingredients in a happy life. That's one of the most valuable things that Wolf learned from Dr. Dinglebottom. He learned that if there is love in your heart, you can never be unhappy.

Sure, there will always be hard times and things that make you sad, but if you have someone to love, you will always be able to find something to be happy about. If you have someone to love, your life will always have meaning and purpose," Paul mused.

Eve nodded, but she still looked a little confused.

"Eve, remember how you surprised me with breakfast in bed on my birthday?"

She smiled and nodded.

"And remember how you made my favorite breakfast?" he continued.

"Toast with peanut butter and honey," she said confidently.

"That's right. And remember how it got all over your hands?" he asked.

Eve laughed. "Yeah, it got all over everything!"

"That's right. That was a big mess—a big, crazy, wonderful mess. Love is kind of like peanut butter and honey on hot toast; you can't spread it around without getting it all over yourself. When you love somebody, you treat them different—better than you would otherwise, and in the process, you become a better person. This is true of every kind of love, and the cool thing is you don't have to be in love with someone to have the same magic happen. Does that make sense?"

"Yeah," she replied. "I think I get it. Is that the kind of stuff Wolf wrote about in this book?"

"I'm sure there's a lot of that kind of stuff in there." Paul replied, knowingly.

Eve looked down at the book again, examining its size and weight. "He must know a whole lot about love."

"Well, he learned a lot about love, but in the beginning, back when this book was new, he hardly knew anything. In the beginning, when Katie gave him this book, he wasn't even sure he wanted to write anything in it at all."

"Why not?" Eve asked.

"Oh, probably for the same reason Katie hadn't written anything in the book during the year she owned it. She didn't know if she had anything good enough to write in such a cool book. Wolf didn't think he knew anything either and he didn't want to ruin it."

Eve flipped through the corner of the book revealing writing on every page. "I guess he changed his mind."

"Yes, he did. It didn't take long for him to realize there was interesting stuff going on all around him, and he figured he better write it down before he'd forgot. And as he began opening his eyes, and ears, and heart, and began listening to all the things happening on the other side of the curtain that separated his space from Dr. Dinglebottom's, Wolf realized more and more that the lady from his dream was right. He wasn't ready to die because he really hadn't learned how to live. But there was something else that the doctor had that intrigued Wolf. He had faith in a God Wolf had never known and a curiously bright hope for a man whose life seemed to be coming to an end."

Paul shifted in his seat, trying to get comfortable before he continued. "As he watched Dr. Dinglebottom over the next few days, Wolf saw how the doctor's faith caused him to reach out to others, and to embrace them in a way that seemed much deeper than just physically. He even reached out to Wolf, and treated him like a friend even though they'd only just met. But Wolf was reluctant at first to accept or return the warmth the doctor extended to him because he didn't feel worthy of it."

"What does worthy mean?" Eve asked.

Paul took a deep breath, considering his response. "I guess it means that he didn't believe he deserved the love and concern that the doctor was giving him."

"Because he didn't know him very well?" Eve asked.

"I'm sure that was probably part of it. But it had been a long time since Wolf had even loved himself. If he had ever known he was lovable, he had forgotten a long time before. I suppose there were lots of things he'd forgotten during the time he'd been doing drugs. A part of him turned off and became dark in the years since he learned of his mother's death, and there were lots of things that didn't matter after that. He'd been lost for so long—in such a deep, dark place, that being exposed to Dr. Dinglebottom, and all the happiness that oozed out of him, was almost like stepping out of a cave and walking out into the brightest day in summer without any sunglasses."

Eve squinted her eyes as her imagination digested her father's words.

"At first, Wolf didn't know what to do with so much light and happiness. I think he was probably a little bit afraid of it in the beginning. It seemed so different compared to the place he'd been, but there was also something very familiar about it that intrigued him. He watched the doctor carefully, trying to figure out what he was seeing—what he was feeling.

"A couple of nights after he'd begun paying attention to the doctor, Wolf had a dream that was so real, it woke him up. It was actually the same dream he'd had the night he was brought to the hospital. But this time, as he woke up and looked around, feeling warm and dry, he was grateful to be alive. But the dream also left him with questions—questions he'd never thought of before—questions he wasn't even sure had answers."

"What kind of questions?" Eve asked.

"Oh, all sorts of questions, I suppose, about life and death—and heaven and hell. Having experienced what felt like hell the night he'd almost died, and experiencing it again in his dream, he knew he didn't want that. He knew how dark and cold that felt. But in his dream, he also saw something that felt very different.

"As he thought about the things he'd felt and seen, he was also confused by something. Wolf had never been a religious person. He had wondered about spiritual things from time to time, but had never given them much thought. Many times, throughout his life, he'd heard people talk about right and wrong, and heaven and hell, and about good people and bad people. He'd never felt like he was a bad person—if there was such a thing, but in his heart, he also knew that many of the choices he'd made were not good. As he thought about his dream, he knew there was something more—something better—something brighter, warmer, and more incredible than anything he'd ever imagined. There was something there, just beyond his reach— some missing piece of life—an existence that no words could describe.

"As he lay there that night, looking up at the ceiling of his hospital room, he started thinking about his life, trying to figure out where he was and what he was doing. Having experienced the intensity of light, he recognized the reality of darkness. He recognized that the difference between the two was much more than just color. The darkness, besides being void of light, was also cold and heavy, and like a sopping wet blanket, completely incapable of offering comfort or warmth."

Eve's eyes were wide as she listened to her father speak.

"But on the other end of the spectrum, light also had properties that were far more profound than just the absence of darkness. Wolf began thinking about all the things he felt when he finally looked at the woman who was calling his name. There was warmth, but in a way that was much more that just the feel of the sun on your face. It was something that seemed to swallow him up completely, but not in a scary way that kept him from moving. More like … an avalanche of everything good and positive sliding down on top of him, but instead of suffocating under the load of it all, it filled his mind and heart—his whole body—with hope and happiness—a feeling like he could do anything and everything at the same time. Thinking about it, he was filled with the greatest feeling of peace he'd ever known. But it was a strange kind of peace. Instead of making him feel calm and relaxed, he felt a surge of energy that made him want to do and be something amazing, while giving him all the confidence that he could be something better than he was. After feeling all those things, he decided he'd better start writing them down while he could remember the discoveries he'd made that night."

" So that's what he wrote in the book?" Eve asked.

"That was part of it, but that was really only the beginning."

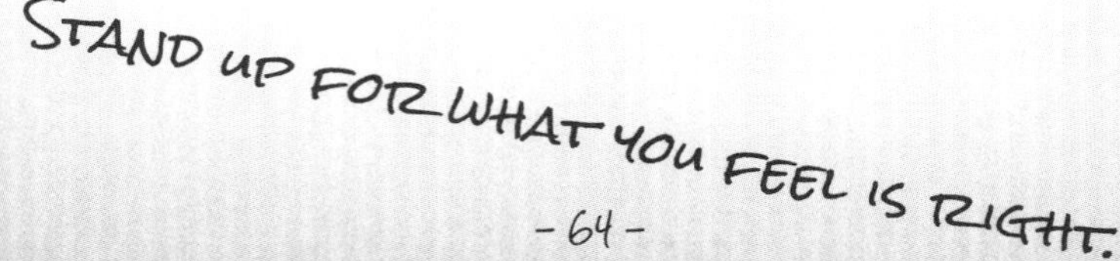

-Chapter 6-
Lighting the Path

THE PURE AND SIMPLE TRUTH IS RARELY
PURE AND NEVER SIMPLE.
—OSCAR WILDE

"What other things did he write down?" Eve asked, turning one page then another and another, as if she were looking for something. On the fifth page, she stopped at a yellowed piece of newsprint that had been taped to the page—a pixilated photograph of a man with a big smile. Paul watched as Eve ran her finger over the masking tape that held the photo to the page.

"Who is this?"

"That's Dr. Dinglebottom." Paul replied

"He has a nice smile."

Paul took a closer look, and nodded. "He practiced that smile a lot."

"Why is his picture here?" Eve wanted to know.

"Because Wolf wanted to remember what he looked like. That picture came from his obituary."

"You mean … from when he died?"

"Yes."

"Where did he die?"

"At the hospital, in the room he shared with Wolf."

Eve looked up slowly from the picture, her eyes filled with concern. "Was Wolf scared?"

"No. I'm sure he probably wondered why he wasn't, but as it turned out, there was nothing to be afraid of. I think that was a big turning point for Wolf. When you're young and healthy you don't usually think about death and dying because you're too busy living."

Eve nodded. "I don't ever think about it."

Paul nodded. "The experience Wolf had the night he almost died left him with a lot of questions about what he'd seen and felt. And in the middle of trying to sort through all those things, something amazing was happening. Just a few feet away, Dr. Dinglebottom was struggling to find his way out of this world. For Wolf, that was the most beautiful thing he had ever experienced."

"What's so beautiful about watching an old man die?" asked Rachel.

"That's the very question Wolf has spent the last twelve years trying to figure out. There was something in that room during the last day of the doctor's life—an intense warmth and peace. Wolf felt some of that the night he almost died, but this was different. Instead of the warmth being there for just a few moments, it came and stayed, almost like the ceiling and walls of their room disappeared and the sun moved a million miles closer.

"It was such a wonderful feeling that Wolf didn't want to sleep because he was afraid he would miss whatever was happening. So instead, he listened closely as the doctor's family and friends shared stories about him and all the cool things he'd done for them and so many others.

And when the end finally came, Wolf was surprised by how peaceful it was as they all watched and listened to the doctor take his final breaths and slip away."

"Was Wolf sad when Dr. Dinglebottom died?"

"Sure. He was the best roommate Wolf had ever had, but sadness was only a small part of what he felt. The doctor's kids were there when he died. And they stayed for a while, talking about the love he'd shared

"NEVER FIGHT ABOUT ANYTHING MORE THAN TWO WEEKS OLD."

with them and the hope of heaven he'd given to each of them. Wolf listened carefully to everything they had to say, trying to make sense of the things he was feeling. Their vision of heaven seemed so real that he could imagine the doctor was already there. It wasn't until after the doctor's family left, and the men from the mortuary had come to take his body that Wolf began missing him.

"Wolf had known for a few days that this was going to happen, and he'd tried to prepare himself for it. But he couldn't have known how the doctor's death would make him feel. He was surprised by many of his emotions, but most of all, the feeling of envy—envy for the happiness and peace that surrounded the old man, and envy at the number and quality of friends the doctor had accumulated over his life.

"It was just a couple of days later that Katie brought Wolf the newspaper with the doctor's obituary and that picture," he said, pointing to the journal. "The funeral was to be held the day after Wolf was scheduled to be released from the hospital. And even though he was still feeling overwhelmed with all that he'd experienced, he decided he wanted to go and see what else he might learn."

"Where was it?" asked Rachel

"At the Methodist Church in Kenosha."

Rachel nodded. "Why did Wolf decide to go?"

"Because … he was thirsty."

Rachel and Eve both gave him a funny look.

Paul smiled. "I guess that probably sounds strange, but the day after the doctor died, Wolf recognized a major change in the feeling in his room—like he'd been drinking from some sort of magic fountain, and suddenly the fountain was gone, leaving behind a huge void. Wolf went to the funeral because he knew, after living a lifetime starved of that magic—whatever it was—he knew he wanted more." Paul paused for a moment, looking thoughtful. "He went because he knew the doctor had something that he needed, and he hoped he might discover what that magic was before it was too late."

"THERE IS A PURPOSE TO OUR EXISTENCE. WE WILL DISCOVER THAT PURPOSE AS WE SEEK GOD'S LIGHT."

"Was Dr. Dinglebottom a magician?" Eve asked, looking quite excited.

"Yes, but not the way you're thinking. His magic was limited to just a couple of tricks, but he knew how to do them very well."

"Could he make things disappear?"

"No, his tricks were much better than stuff like that. He knew how to love people. It was almost like he could look into their hearts and see the way they needed to be loved. Then he would give them just the right kind of love to help them feel better."

"Is that really magic?"

"I think that must be the rarest kind of magic there is. And for most people, it's a very difficult magic to learn."

"So …, " Rachel said, trailing off before she even got going.

"So …?" Paul responded after she didn't continue.

"I guess I'm just trying to figure this out. Wolf just showed up at this Doctor's funeral after knowing him for, what—a week? What was he expecting?"

"I'm certain he had no idea what to expect. That was the first time he'd ever been in a church."

"And he didn't feel weird walking into an unfamiliar church, so he could go to a funeral for someone he barely knew?" Rachel continued.

"I think he probably would have, if he'd spent much time thinking about it. But sometimes, when you don't know what you're getting into, and you have no preconceived notions, it's easy to do something different and new. That's the way it was for Wolf anyway. As he sat in the pews, waiting for the service to begin, he was surprised to recognize in the faces of many of the other people who had come, a searching and a longing to know the same things he had come for. It was almost like they were hoping to catch a peek backstage, hoping that the secrets behind the magic would be revealed in a way that could be easily understood and duplicated."

"Did he find what he was looking for?"

"No."

TELL GOOD STORIES

Rachel looked at him incredulously. "Really?"

"Then what's in this book?" Eve asked, flipping through the pages filled with writing as if to make certain her eyes had not deceived her.

"I didn't say he didn't learn anything. I only said he didn't learn what he was hoping for, at least not all of it. Wolf went to that funeral, looking for answers to all of his questions, but as it turned out, he came away with more questions than answers."

"How many questions did he have?" asked Eve.

"Hundreds, I suppose."

"Were they good questions?"

Paul nodded, remembering the many times he'd taught his daughter the importance of asking good questions. "Most of them, yes. You see, even though Wolf was twenty-six years old, he really hadn't figured out what life was all about. I think Wolf was probably looking for an easy answer to all of his questions, but instead, he got something even better. It was like he went to the funeral with an empty cup, hoping to scoop up enough water to satisfy his new thirst for understanding. Instead he got a few precious drops of truth. And though that wasn't enough to satisfy him, it was enough to make him realize that the water he wanted required more than just dipping his cup into a deep well. He learned that day that if he really wanted the kind of truth that made Dr. Dinglebottom so happy, he would have to work for it. He had to be willing to make changes in his life."

"Is that the kind of stuff they talk about at funerals?" asked Eve.

"Sometimes, yes. But not always. I think Wolf hoped that all funerals would be like the Doctor's funeral. But only the people who truly learn how to live can have a funeral like that."

"So, what made his funeral different than others?" asked Rachel.

"There was hope. I think if all funerals could have that kind of hope, people would line up to go to them."

"What kind of hope is that?"

Paul took a deep breath. "Remember how I was talking about how Wolf had experienced both darkness and light in his dream?"

Rachel and Eve both nodded.

"Maybe people have to experience a piece of the darkness, like Wolf did, before they can fully appreciate the hope light brings. Wolf recognized that kind of hope in the doctor while they were roommates, and he recognized it that day in the faces of the doctor's children as they walked into the chapel for his funeral."

"What does hope like that look like?" asked Rachel.

"It looks like humble confidence," Paul nodded his head and smiled. "I suppose that sounds like a contradiction. But when Wolf watched the Doctor's kids that day, he was surprised that there didn't seem to be any sadness in their faces. He saw lots of tears on the faces of many of the grandchildren—tears that expressed the sadness they surely felt at losing someone they loved. But their parents wore completely different expressions. Many of them even smiled at all the people who had come, and tthey told funny stories. Even though it was a cold winter day, it felt like they brought the sunshine in with them.

"Why were they happy?" asked Eve.

"That's exactly what Wolf wondered."

"Did he ask them?"

"He didn't have to. Each of the doctor's kids got to give a speech about their dad."

Rachel looked sideways. "Each of his kids gave a speech?"

"Yes. That's what the doctor wanted. The minister explained that Dr. Dinglebottom requested that each of his kids have a chance to talk about their dad and share the reasons for the hope they had."

"I've never heard of a funeral like that. I thought that it was just the minister who usually speaks."

"I think in most cases, that's true. But it often depends on the religion of the person who died and the desires of the family. I guess Dr. Dinglebottom's minister was open to the request."

Rachel's brow was furrowed, as if she was trying to grasp the idea of someone other than a minister speaking. "I don't know if I could give a speech at my dad's funeral, or if he'd even want me to."

"But things would probably be different if he was a … a different kind of dad and grandfather."

Rachel nodded.

"Is grandpa going to die?" Eve asked.

"No, honey. Probably not for lots of years," Rachel responded, looking through the rearview mirror.

"Good. Why don't we ever see him and Grandma Judy?"

Rachel glanced at Paul, then turned her attention back to the road. "Would you like to see them?"

"I don't know. I was just wondering why we never do."

"I'm not sure either," Rachel lied. It had been at least two years since they had last seen her father, and their short visit had been cold and disheartening. Her father had been less than welcoming, showing little interest in Rachel or her family. Disappointed that nothing had changed in the four years since their previous visit, or in the twenty years before that, she turned her back on that relationship, unwilling to continue to be disappointed and hurt. "So, what did the doctor's kids have to say?" she asked, anxious for the subject to change.

"Oh, lots of great stuff," Paul said, reaching for the journal. "Each one of them talked about a different aspect of their father." He flipped the page and silently read several lines before continuing. "His oldest son talked about how his father grew up on the family farm during the depression and learned that hard work was the only way to get anything good out of life. Even though Wolf had only known the doctor for about a week, he figured he knew a lot about him from listening to all the stories. But as he sat in that funeral, he realized he barely knew anything at all."

"What do you mean?" asked Eve.

"I think you can probably learn more about a person at their funeral than you can in any other way."

"How so?" asked Rachel.

"Well, think about this doctor for example. Many of the doctors and nurses who came had worked with him for years, but I'm sure they

"Dad always answered all of my questions."

learned a lot about him that day from his kids who had known him a lot longer. There were probably stories told that day that many people had never heard. When you go to a person's funeral, if it's a good funeral, you might get to learn all sorts of great stuff about that person."

"Like what?"

"You name it. Stuff about fantastic family vacations, or the story of their first kiss, or the things that made them happy. Everybody has their own story, and most of them are interesting."

"What was interesting about Dr. Dinglebottom?" asked Eve.

Paul looked back to the journal. "He almost drowned when he was ten because the fish he caught was so big it pulled him into the creek. He wouldn't let go of the fishing pole because he'd borrowed it from his brother without asking and didn't want to get caught."

Eve smiled. "What else?"

Paul turned again to the journal. "He took his family on fun family vacations and fishing outings, and he often came home from work early so his family could have game night, and they'd stay up late playing fun games and eating cookie dough."

"Hey, that sounds like our game nights." Eve replied. "I love game night."

"So do I," he said, reaching around his seat to pat his daughter's hand.

"What else did they do?"

He turned a page in the book. "They made jam together every summer—hundreds of bottles of strawberry, raspberry and gooseberry jam from the berries they picked in their own backyard."

"Hey, we make jam, too." Her eyes grew wider.

"That's because it's a good time to make family memories. There's just something about smashing fruit between your fingers that brings a family closer together."

"And it tastes good, too. Did you know that Monika, my friend at school, has to buy jam because her parents don't even know how to make it? I told her she could come to our house, so you can teach her."

LEARN HOW TO MAKE JAM!

"That sounds like fun."

"Did you know that was one of the things that made Mommy fall in love with Daddy?" Rachel asked, looking through the rearview mirror.

"Jam?"

Rachel smiled and nodded. "Your Daddy asked me to help him make jam when we were just friends."

"So, you're the one who taught Daddy how to make jam?"

"No, I had never made jam before—and I'm pretty sure he hadn't either. I think he was just trying to figure out a way to spend more time with me."

Eve looked at her parents like they'd suddenly become more interesting.

"And your father has been tricking me into helping him make jam ever since."

"You make it sound like it's a form of torture," Paul responded, feigning injury.

Rachel laughed. "No, I'm glad we do it. It's a fun thing to do."

"What other things did Wolf learn about Dr. Dinglebottom?" asked Eve.

"He was drafted into the army when he was twenty-one and spent three years in France working as a medic."

"What's a medic?"

"It's someone who takes care of soldiers who get hurt during the war."

"Like a doctor?"

"Kind of, but they usually don't have the same training or a hospital to work in. Their job is mostly to stop the bleeding when someone gets hurt."

"Yuck! Blood! Why would anyone want to do that?"

"He wanted to be a medic because he didn't want to have to shoot anyone."

Eve looked suddenly somber. "Were there any other choices?"

Paul shook his head. "War is an awful thing. Dr. Dinglebottom's kids said he almost never talked about his time in France, but it influenced the rest of his life."

"Is that's why he became a doctor?"

"Yes. When he came home from the war, the government gave him some money to go to school. He decided to become a doctor so he could help people. He met his wife at a university dance. She was on a date with his best friend and he was on a date with a different girl, but he knew he was going to marry her the first time he saw her. They were married for almost fifty years before she died."

"How did she die?"

"Cancer."

CANCER SUCKS!

"That's sad."

"Yes, it is. She was his best friend in the whole world and the one who helped him develop the faith and hope that helped him to become the man he was."

"He didn't have faith and hope before?" Rachel asked, looking a little surprised.

Paul shook his head. "No, not according to his daughter. She said he always felt like he wasted a lot of time in his younger years by being cynical."

"What does cynical mean?"

"It means unbelieving and negative."

"That doesn't sound like the Dr. Dinglebottom you've been talking about," Rachel said.

"That's exactly what Wolf thought. He couldn't believe that such a kind, optimistic man could ever have had a negative thought. But his youngest daughter told the story of a younger Dr. Dinglebottom—before all the game nights and the raspberry jam; before he even became Dr. Dinglebottom."

"What was he before he became a doctor?"

"He was a sleep-deprived, overworked medical school student and war veteran who was trying to figure out how to be a doctor and a husband and a father all at the same time. And through all of that, he was dealing with the emotional pain of his war years. On top of that, there were lots of days that made him wonder if he'd made a huge mistake by choosing to become a doctor."

"What did he want to be instead?"

"He wasn't sure. He only knew that he felt lost. There were days that he wondered if he got married too early and had kids too soon. What made things even worse was that between crying babies and his nightmares about the war, he rarely got a good night's sleep. He felt like he was failing at everything he tried to do."

"What did his wife do?" asked Eve.

"She loved him, even when he was cranky. And she prayed for him, even though he told her it was useless. And she took the kids to church every Sunday so he could have some time to rest."

"He didn't like prayers or church?"

"Not back then."

"How come?"

"Because he didn't believe in God."

Rachel turned to him and studied his face as if she was wondering where he might be going with this. "That doesn't sound like the man you've been describing."

"I know. A lot of things had changed in his life by the time he met Wolf."

"But why didn't he believe in God?" asked Eve, looking concerned.

"Well, he'd grown up believing in God, but by the time he came home from the war, he found it was easier to believe there was no God than to try to believe in a God who allowed the injustice and pain of war to happen."

"So, he stopped believing in God?" asked Eve, looking surprised. "Did he forget the secret?"

The question surprised Paul. Since the time they began praying with her before tucking her into bed each night, Paul had shared something with his daughter that he hoped she would always remember. It had

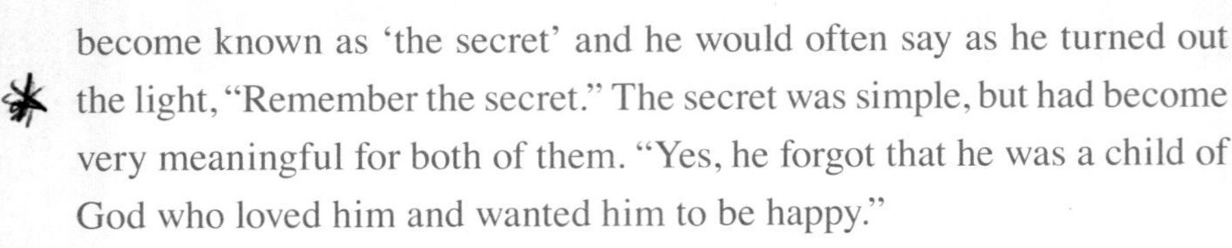

become known as 'the secret' and he would often say as he turned out the light, "Remember the secret." The secret was simple, but had become very meaningful for both of them. "Yes, he forgot that he was a child of God who loved him and wanted him to be happy."

"How did he forget? Did his parents forget to help him to remember like you and Mommy help me?"

Paul glanced at Rachel and saw her eyes, brimming with tears. "Yes," he said, turning back to Eve, feeling a little distracted. "He forgot."

LIVE IN THE PRESENT

GO TO HEAVEN FOR THE CLIMATE AND HELL FOR THE COMPANY.

- MARK TWAIN

"WE ARE MORE CAPABLE WHEN WE COME TOGETHER THAN WHEN WE STAND ALONE."

"I KNOW GOD LOVES ME AND EVERY MEMBER OF THIS CRAZY, MESSED UP, HUMAN RACE."

LET NOT YOUR HEART BE TROUBLED John 14:27

-CHAPTER 7-
THE JOY OF REMEMBERING

HOW WONDERFUL IT IS THAT NOBODY NEED WAIT A SINGLE MOMENT BEFORE STARTING TO IMPROVE THE WORLD.
—ANNE FRANK

"So, how did he remember, Daddy?"

"Who said that he did?" Paul replied

"Daddy! You can't tell a story about a really nice man, and then talk about his problems without telling us how he fixed them."

"How do you know he did?"

"Daddy! You can't become a nice man like Dr. Dinglebottom without fixing your problems."

Paul smiled, acknowledging the profound but simple truth his daughter had just spoken. "You're right, Eve."

"So, how did he do it?"

"He didn't do it alone. He had a lot of help."

"Who helped him?"

"His wife, and his children."

"How?"

MAKE EVERY HOUSE YOU LIVE IN YOUR HOME.

"They loved him, even when he didn't remember that he deserved to be loved, even when he didn't love himself. I think his wife must have known who he really was, deep down inside. Instead of focusing on the things that were broken, she focused on the things that were good. But all of his kids said the thing that made the biggest difference was their little brother, Joe. Joe was born with Down Syndrome."

"Hey, that's like Carter, at my school."

Paul nodded. "Carter is a pretty special kid, isn't he?"

"I think everyone is his buddy."

"Joe must have been the same way, but things were different back then with kids who were born with Down Syndrome. People didn't have the same understanding that they do now. Most kids with Downs never went home from the hospital. Instead, they were sent to institutions where they usually died before they turned twelve."

"So … they didn't get to be with their mommy and daddy?"

Paul shook his head.

"That doesn't seem fair."

"That's exactly what Dr. Dinglebottom's wife said. When their doctor suggested that they should worry about the five kids they already had at home and leave Joe at the hospital, she freaked out. Instead, she took him home and made sure he was raised with the same amount of love that her other children received.

"Dr. Dinglebottom's daughter talked about how Joe became the glue that held their family together, teaching them love and acceptance. And in that environment, her father began to soften. She talked about a conversation she'd had with her dad when she was struggling with her own faith. She wanted to know specifically what it was that had brought him back to a belief in God after being away from the faith for so many years.

"She said that her father couldn't talk about it without choking up. It was Joe, and the innocence of the unconditional love that oozed out of him that melted and tenderized his heart. His scientific mind couldn't offer any reasonable explanation for the love his son shared

OH, 'TIS LOVE, 'TIS LOVE THAT MAKES THE WORLD GO ROUND. —LEWIS CARROLL with everyone he met. It made him wonder if children, like Joe, were gifts from heaven to help us to remember what love is.

"But the thing that meant the most to Wolf was something that she said her father had told her. Somewhere, in the deep recesses of his mind, there was a nearly forgotten memory of a pure and enduring love that he remembered had been given to him without conditions. It was Joe who had triggered that memory. And that memory gave the doctor's life new purpose and understanding. He hoped that by sharing that kind of love with others, they too would open their hearts and minds and remember that God is love. That was an important thing for Wolf to hear. He knew that what she was saying was true."

"How?" asked Eve.

"Because of the way it made him feel." He turned a couple of pages, scanning the words until he found what he hoped he might find. "I could tell you about it," he said, turning back to his daughter, "or I could read you what Wolf wrote, if you want."

"Can you read it?"

Paul nodded, turning back to the journal.

SOMETHING HAPPENED TODAY DURING THE DOCTOR'S FUNERAL. AS I LISTENED TO HIS CHILDREN TALK ABOUT THEIR FATHER AND THE INFLUENCE HE HAD ON THEIR LIVES, I FELT A STRANGE WARMTH IN MY CHEST.

READING WHAT I JUST WROTE—IT SOUNDS SO WEIRD—BUT I DON'T KNOW HOW ELSE TO DESCRIBE IT. AS I HAVE CONSIDERED THAT FEELING, I REMEMBERED THAT I HAVE HAD THAT FEELING BEFORE. THAT NIGHT AT THE LAKE—THE NIGHT I ALMOST DIED—THE WOMAN IN THE LONG WHITE DRESS—I HAD A SIMILAR FEELING WHEN I SPOKE TO HER. I REMEMBER FREEZING IN THE DARKNESS, LYING THERE

NEXT TO THE BENCH IN THE SNOW. BUT SOMETHING HAPPENED WHEN SHE SPOKE TO ME. THERE WAS A WARMTH THAT FILLED ALL THE AIR AROUND ME. THAT FEELING CAME BACK WHEN I HAD THE DREAM AGAIN IN THE HOSPITAL. I FEEL IT AGAIN NOW, AS I WRITE THESE THINGS DOWN.

MAYBE THIS FEELING—THIS WARMTH—MAYBE IT ISN'T SO STRANGE AFTER ALL. I REALIZE NOW THAT IT WAS THERE WHEN I WATCHED THE DOCTOR'S CHILDREN GATHER AROUND HIM DURING HIS FINAL HOURS. THERE WAS SOMETHING HIS DAUGHTER SAID TODAY THAT HAS MADE ME WONDER. SHE SAID THAT JOE'S LOVE HELPED HER DAD REMEMBER A PURE AND UNCONDITIONAL LOVE THAT HE KNEW HE HAD FELT BEFORE. AS I HAVE THOUGHT ABOUT THAT, I REMEMBER FEELING SOMETHING LIKE WHAT SHE DESCRIBED. BUT THIS MEMORY SEEMS SO DISTANT; IT'S ALMOST AS IF IT HAPPENED IN ANOTHER LIFE. IS THIS WHAT THE DOCTOR'S DAUGHTER WAS TALKING ABOUT? IS THIS THAT SAME FEELING OF LOVE? SHE SAID THAT HE BELIEVED GOD IS LOVE. IS THAT WHAT I'M FEELING? AM I FEELING GOD?

FOR THE LAST FIVE MINUTES, I HAVE BEEN SITTING HERE TRYING TO FIGURE OUT WHAT THIS IS—THIS ALMOST TANGIBLE FEELING. I RECOGNIZE THAT WHATEVER IT IS, IT SEEMS TO BE SOMEHOW CONNECTED TO TRUTH. I DON'T THINK I'VE EVER CONSIDERED THAT TRUTH MIGHT HAVE A "FEELING." BUT EVEN NOW, AS I WRITE DOWN THESE THOUGHTS, I AM FEELING THAT SAME WARMTH. AND IN THIS WARMTH, I FEEL HOPE—MORE HOPE THAN I CAN EVER REMEMBER FEELING. IS THAT WHAT LOVE IS? IT SEEMS SO DIFFERENT THAN ANY LOVE I HAVE KNOWN BEFORE. MAYBE I'VE NEVER KNOWN WHAT love is. Or maybe what I thought was love is something else entirely. Or maybe this kind of love is only associated with truth.

I recognize that I have never known much of that in my life—either love or truth. But having experienced it, it seems I can't possibly be happy without it. I feel like I crave it more than I have ever craved anything. How do I get more of it?

And still there remains a big ~~qesti~~ question in my mind. Where is this warmth, this love coming from? I have never believed in God before. But today, after all the things that have happened to me since that terrible night—after all the things I have felt and learned, it almost seems like it would be easier for me to deny that I have a right hand than to deny the reality of this feeling. My skeptical, cynical mind would have me believe it's just a reaction to all the trauma my body has been through. But in light of this warmth and the feelings of love, I recognize that my cynicism and skepticism have never produced anything like this. They have never brought me peace. They have only brought me questions that seem completely devoid of answers.

I wonder if this is what the doctor learned from his son. I wonder if he ever felt the same way I do tonight. Something tells me he did. And there is hope in that. I feel it. I have some big regrets about what I did, but I don't know if I could have heard this, or felt this any other way. Somehow, in my efforts to stop the insanity and end my sadness and pain,

IT SEEMS I HAVE BEEN SHOWN A WAY TO END THE MISERY WITHOUT LOSING MY LIFE IN THE PROCESS. FOR THE FIRST TIME IN MY LIFE I WANT TO BELIEVE THERE IS A GOD. I WANT TO BELIEVE THERE IS HOPE FOR ME. I WANT TO BELIEVE THERE IS SOMEONE WHO IS LOOKING OUT FOR ME, WHO CARES WHETHER I LIVE OR DIE. TONIGHT, I WONDER IF THE OPPORTUNITY WAS ALWAYS THERE, WAITING FOR ME TO OPEN MY EYES AND SEE. I WONDER WHAT ELSE I'VE MISSED, BLINDED BY MY CHOICES AND THE PATH I HAVE FOLLOWED. TONIGHT, I WANT TO LIVE. I NEED TO FIND OUT WHAT THIS IS. IF THIS IS GOD, I NEED TO KNOW. I NEED TO KNOW THE SOURCE OF THIS FEELING OF WARMTH, AND LOVE, AND HOPE.

Paul looked up from the journal and turned his head so he could see into Eve's big, green eyes.

"That was a good thing for Wolf to learn, huh?" she asked.

"Which part?"

"That true things have good feelings. That's what you and Mommy taught me."

Paul nodded, unable to speak without losing his composure. He glanced at Rachel. Her cheeks were wet with tears. He wondered what she was feeling but knew that now was not the time to ask. Though there was much of sadness in the history of this boy named Wolf, it was his story—a story that had been waiting to be told for more than a decade. This journal, his journal, now for the second time in his life, had become a vehicle to understanding. And as he considered these things and the timing of it all, his daughter's words echoed through his mind. "True things have good feelings." He was certain she had no idea of the magnitude of the truth she had just spoken, nor the pain that one truth might help her avoid if she could remember it. He reached out and took her small hand in his, and in that moment, he knew that all the anguish and trouble he'd experienced in his younger years was worth it.

His daughter's life would be much different—much better than his own in so many ways because of that truth.

"Yes," he finally said, squeezing her small hand. "True things have good feelings. I hope you will always remember that."

IT IS IN GIVING THAT WE RECEIVE, IT IS IN DYING THAT WE ARE BORN INTO ETERNAL LIFE.
-ST. FRANCIS OF ASSISI-

THOSE WHO DON'T BELIEVE IN MAGIC WILL NEVER FIND IT.
-ROALD DAHL

OH, THE EXPERIENCE OF THIS SWEET LIFE. -DANTE

› CHAPTER 8 ‹ UNCONDITIONAL

NOT ALL OF US CAN DO GREAT THINGS. BUT WE CAN DO SMALL THINGS WITH GREAT LOVE. –MOTHER TERESA

"What does unconditional mean?" asked Eve.

"Why do you ask?"

"You said it in that part you just read."

"I did?" He scanned over the pages until he found it, reading it again.

SHE SAID THAT JOE'S LOVE HELPED HER DAD REMEMBER A PURE AND UNCONDITIONAL LOVE THAT HE KNEW HE HAD FELT BEFORE.

"Yeah, that's it. What is unconditional love?"

Paul looked thoughtful for a long moment before responding. The question was a difficult one to answer. For him, it had come to mean many things at different times over the past decade, and he knew that any words he could use to describe or define it would, without question, limit the word's scope and breadth. Still, he knew he had to try to offer his daughter the best answer he could. He took a deep breath before squeezing her small hand again. "It is the love God has for all of us. It … it is a love that … that never ends, that goes on forever, regardless of who we are or the choices we make. It is a love filled with mercy … and hope … and understanding … and grace."

Eve nodded slowly. "So, I guess it probably feels good, like true things?"

Paul nodded. "Like the truest thing you have ever heard. And when you feel it, it's like it starts a fire in your chest and you know it's real, and good, and true."

Eve leaned forward and looked at the open journal. "When did Dr. Dinglebottom feel that unconditional love?"

"What do you mean?"

"You said he remembered feeling it before."

Paul swallowed, then nodded.

"Before what?" Eve continued.

"I'm not entirely sure."

"But Wolf remembered having that feeling, too?"

"Yes."

"When?"

Paul considered his answer carefully. He wanted her to know, but he knew the answer would likely spawn only more questions. He knew the answers he had were both limited and deeply personal, and yet this was his daughter—his only living child. If he couldn't tell her, who could he tell? He knew this knowledge—this distant memory—had helped him, giving him answers and hope when he needed it most. In many ways, this memory had formed who he had become. Like a tiny seed, it seemed to have been planted deep in his mind, waiting for the time when the soil of circumstance would offer it a fertile place to grow. It could be said that this memory was his earliest, and yet he knew that it came from a time when time itself had no meaning.

Paul glanced at Rachel, but she did not turn to face him, keeping her eyes instead on the road before them. "What if I answer you with a story?" he finally responded.

"What kind of story?"

"A story about you."

"A true story?"

"Yeah. It's a story from when you were just a little girl, maybe only two or three years old. One day, when we were driving in the car, you asked us where your brother was."

"I did?"

"Yeah."

"How come?"

"I don't know. Your mom and I … we were both very surprised by your question because we had never talked to you about Andrew, your brother who died before you were born. And we had never told you that we couldn't have any more babies. I remember pulling the car over to the side of the road, so we could listen to what you were saying. When we asked how you knew about your brother, you told us that you knew him when you used to live with God."

Eve smiled. "I remember that," she said, staring off to the faraway memory.

"Not long after that, I came home from work one day and mommy shared with me that you had told her that you couldn't remember what God looked like anymore."

Eve nodded. "I don't remember ..."

"But there was once a time that you did remember?"

Rachel glanced in the rearview mirror, waiting for her daughter's answer.

Eve nodded again. "I was just a little kid back then."

"I don't know how it works, or how to explain it, Eve, but I think Wolf must have had a similar memory. Maybe we all do—somewhere, buried deep in our minds. It was only when Wolf felt the warmth of that love again that he remembered he'd felt it before. Most of the details were gone, but there were still fragments of that beautiful feeling."

Eve nodded. "I remember that feeling, too. Do you think people can learn how to love that way?"

"You mean unconditionally?"

Eve nodded.

"The song is over, but the melody will always linger..."

"Yes. But I don't think it's very easy. Some people, like Carter, at your school, seem to be born with the ability to love without judging or being afraid of loving someone too much. But for the rest of us, it seems like it takes a lot of practice."

"What kind of practice?"

"Well, loving someone unconditionally means … to love with your whole heart, without stopping to think about it. It means closing your eyes so your heart can see and feel. It means understanding without judgement. It means loving someone despite the disappointing choices they might be making. Those are hard things for most of us to learn."

"So if it's so hard, how can people learn?"

"I don't know if anyone can learn how to love unconditionally without recognizing the mercy and love God has for each of us, in spite of our weaknesses. When we see that God looks past our flaws, and loves us anyway, it becomes easier to love other people without judging them. And when we do that, it becomes easier to see answers instead of only problems. Without that understanding, we tend to avoid questions that we know have answers we won't like."

EVERY SAINT HAS A PAST. EVERY SINNER HAS A FUTURE.
—SIGN OUTSIDE CHURCH

Eve looked a little confused. "Why?"

"Oh, lots of reasons, I suppose. Sometimes we're not ready for the answers because it would require a change in the way we think or act. Sometimes, when you've been thinking or believing one way for a long time, it's hard to stop or even open your eyes and recognize that another way might be better. Does that make sense?"

Eve nodded, but the look on her face was not convincing.

"Sometimes people can't see the answers because their own questions get in the way," Rachel offered.

"But you told me that questions are good," Eve responded.

Rachel looked through the rearview mirror, staring at her daughter for a long moment before she answered. "They are good, but only if you are willing to listen for the answer." She glanced at Paul before continuing. "When your brother died, I was really sad for a long time. I couldn't figure out why God would let an accident like that happen; why Andrew had to die before he could breathe his first breath. And I guess I needed to be angry for a while before I could hear the answer He gave me."

"What was the answer?"

She turned to Paul again before looking back into the mirror. "It was love," she said softly.

"Love? Love was the reason Andrew died?"

Rachel shook her head. "No, I don't think so. I still don't know the answer for that. I wish you had a big brother sitting in the back seat next to you. I wish things were different … but … I hope that one day, I'll understand why these things happen. I couldn't hear, or feel it at first, because all I could think about were the questions … and the anger. But love made me feel that everything would be okay."

"How did you finally hear it?" asked Paul.

Rachel took a deep breath. "Aunt Katie gave me a book."

"A book about love?" asked Eve.

Rachel shook her head. "No, it was kind of like that one. It was a journal."

"What did it say?"

"It didn't say anything at all. It was just filled with blank lined paper."

"How could a blank book help you?" Eve asked, looking even more confused.

"I didn't think it would at first, but it made me slow down and think about my life and everything that had happened. It made me remember the good things. And it gave me a place to get rid of all my anger."

"Like going to time out?"

Rachel smiled. "Yes. Sometimes grown-ups need a time out, too, where we have to slow down and think about the things we've done. "

Paul turned back to Eve. "Asking questions is a very important part of growing up. But you could ask a million awesome questions and never get an answer if you don't stop to listen. Like Mommy said, sometimes listening with your ears isn't enough. In order to hear the most important answers, you have to listen with your heart."

Eve nodded, but still looked confused and Paul found himself wondering if she was ready to hear and comprehend this kind of heavy talk. "What's bothering you?" he asked, hoping she might give words to the look of confusion on her face.

"How old would my brother be—if he was alive?"

Paul glanced quickly at Rachel. Though it had been many years since that terrible tragedy, they had rarely spoken about it, and never this openly, especially with Eve.

"Well, let's see," he said, stalling. "How old are you?"

She looked at her father and shook her head. "Daddy, I'm seven and a half!" she replied, loudly.

"Really? Already?" he responded, trying to pretend he was completely shocked. "It seems like you were only five just a few days ago. Are you sure?"

"Daddy, you know how old I am. Stop kidding me."

Paul nodded. "If you're seven and a half, that means your brother … would be almost nine."

He watched Eve's face light up.

"Hey, that's how old Carter is."

"Is that right?"

"Yeah. Did you know that he asked me to marry him?"

"He did?"

"Yep. On the last day of school."

"What did you tell him?"

"I told him I'd have to ask my parents."

"I'd say that's a reasonable answer, considering that you're seven."

"And a half!"

"Right. Sorry."

"After summer vacation, I think I'll tell him I'm too little to be married, but that we can be friends forever and always."

STAND UP FOR WHAT YOU FEEL IS RIGHT.

"It sounds like you've been thinking about this."

"I have. He's really nice. Do you think it would be okay if I asked him if he would be my substitute brother, since my brother died?"

Her question caught Paul completely off-guard. He looked at Rachel, hoping she might help.

"Why do you ask, honey?" Rachel asked, looking through the rearview mirror.

"It would be fun to have a brother. You would really like him. He makes everybody feel happy."

"I … umm … we …"

"Tell us why you're thinking this," Paul responded.

"Because of your story."

"Which part?"

"The part about Dr. Dinglebottom's son, Joe."

Paul nodded, encouraging her to continue.

"You said that Joe helped Dr. Dinglebottom remember important things. I … I thought that maybe it would be nice to have Carter come over sometimes to help us remember important things, too."

"Do you think we need help?" Paul asked.

"I don't know. Sometimes, maybe. I just don't want to forget. He's really nice. I feel good when I play with him at recess."

Paul smiled, stretching his arm out to pat her knee. "That's an important thing to remember … that being nice helps you to feel good."

Eve beamed back at her father. "Do you think that's what helped Dr. Dinglebottom change?"

"What do you mean?"

"Being nice to his son? Do you think that made him be a better person?"

Paul smiled again. "I'm sure it helped a lot. It's a lot easier to learn how to love unconditionally when you have a good teacher, like Joe. Joe taught the doctor many things. But if it hadn't been for the love of his wife, things would probably have been a lot different. One change I'm sure he had to make in order to learn about love is that he had to recognize how amazing and patient his wife was. I think it might be easier for women to love unconditionally."

"Why do you say that?" asked Rachel.

"Because you have to practice so much patience with the men around you."

"And that's easy?" she mused, raising one eyebrow.

"I'm not saying it is. You just get a lot more practice, that's all."

Eve watched the interaction between her parents with intrigue. She knew her father was right. He had given her mother plenty of practice in the patience department. But she knew her mother loved her father, and that knowledge had been a great source of security in her life. She smiled as she watched her father set his hand gently on her mother's knee.

"So, what happened to Dr. Dinglebottom when his wife died?"

Paul turned back to face his daughter. "He decided to go back to work."

"How come?"

"He wanted to keep himself busy so he wouldn't be sad."

"Did it work?"

"Yes." Paul turned the page and pointed to words scrawled in the top corner.

"Dr. Dinglebottom believed that all happy people had three things in common—they had someone to love, something to do, and something to look forward to. After his wife died, he forgot those three things for a little while, and life wasn't very much fun."

"So, what made him remember?"

"I think his family must have helped him remember. After having someone around to love, when they die, it leaves a gigantic hole in your heart."

"Did he find another wife?"

"No, and even though his family helped him feel loved, most of them didn't live very close. That's why he went back to work—so he

DR. DINGLEBOTTOM'S RECIPE FOR HAPPINESS
1. SOMEONE TO LOVE
2. SOMETHING TO DO
3. SOMETHING TO LOOK FORWARD TO

could look forward to getting up every morning and being surrounded by lots of kids who needed his love."

"And he got happy again?"

"Yes. His kids said that the last eight years of his life were the happiest years he'd ever had. Even though he missed his wife everyday, helping people gave him lots of reasons to be happy. But he didn't stop there. He decided he needed something to look forward to, so he started doing the things that scared him when he was younger."

"Like what?"

"Like parachuting twice a month with a group of World War II veterans; and he went back to Europe for the first time since the war, visiting some of the same places that he'd had nightmares about. He even learned how to dance, so just in case there is dancing in heaven, he'd be able to show his wife a good time without stepping on her toes like he had most of his life. On his days off he made trips to visit his kids and grandkids. And in the evenings, he took several college classes, learning how to write poetry and use a computer, so he could email his family."

"He sounds like a cool dude," Eve said.

Paul nodded. "He was. There were lots of reasons to be inspired by him, but after all the things that Wolf had seen and learned about the doctor, I think it might have been his youngest daughter's speech that was the most important thing for him to hear."

"How come?"

"Because it gave Wolf hope that someone—even as messed up as he was—could make something better of himself. It made him want to live long enough to figure out how to be as happy as Dr. Dinglebottom."

"WHEREVER A BEAUTIFUL SOUL HAS BEEN, THERE IS A TRAIL OF BEAUTIFUL MEMORIES."

LEARN HOW TO FISH.

(CHAPTER 9) QUESTIONS

ALWAYS GO TO OTHER PEOPLE'S FUNERALS, OTHERWISE THEY WON'T COME TO YOURS.
-YOGI BERRA

"I need to go potty," Eve said, looking suddenly uncomfortable.

Rachel looked at her daughter through the rearview mirror, then at the clock on the dashboard, then at her husband. "I think there's a rest stop coming up in just a few miles."

"Good. How much further until we get to grandma's?"

"Still about five hours, honey. Are you hungry yet?"

"Yeah.

"Hey, I brought our fun money," Paul said, reaching for the duffle bag at his feet.

Rachel rolled her eyes. "I hope you have it counted out this time."

"Are you kidding? And take all the fun out of it?"

"I don't think it's that fun to look like a family of panhandlers when you're paying for cheeseburgers."

Paul lifted the quart size plastic bag and set it on Eve's lap. "We're rich," he exclaimed, ignoring his wife's killjoy attitude.

Eve smiled broadly and hefted the bag of change in her hands. "I bet there's probably enough in here for almost a thousand cheeseburgers," she exclaimed.

"I hope so. I'm starving," Paul responded.

"Can we get shakes, too?"

"Of course. We're on vacation. That's what fun money's for."

Eve nodded, her smile filling her face.

Rachel couldn't help but smile back at her daughter's oversized front teeth that had finally grown in within the last six months. "Couldn't we at least put the coins in rolls? Doesn't it embarrass you guys to pay for your stuff in change?"

"Hey, it took us a long time to collect all that change; and besides, it's still money isn't it?" Paul countered.

"And it's fun to count." Eve added.

Rachel shook her head, but smiled amiably as she veered right off the turnpike, down the exit ramp to the rest stop.

"How long have we been saving our fun money?" Eve asked.

"Do you mean this time, or ever?"

"Ever."

Rachel looked at her husband. "Since your dad and I got married."

"Why did you start?"

"Because we were poor and on a tight budget, but we still wanted to have fun. Mommy brought home her change from the grocery store, and I saved my change from the gas station. It all went into the jar for us to use on things we wouldn't normally buy."

"Like saltwater taffy and snow cones," Eve said, knowingly.

"That's right. And cheeseburgers and onion rings and Krispy Kremes."

Since the time Eve was a baby, they had begun saving their fun money for vacation time when they would use it to pretend they were millionaires. It had become something they all looked forward to, though only two of them admitted it.

The beautiful morning had morphed and melted into a muggy early afternoon, so after parking, they quickly made their way into the air-conditioned rest stop. While they waited in line for burgers, Paul helped Eve count change to give themselves a head start.

BE KINDER THAN NECESSARY - MOTHER TERESA

The pimple-faced burger boy was less than amused by the coins, even though Eve had stacked them on a tray in neat rows. As they ate, Paul revealed his surprise to Eve about their plans to spend a couple of hours at the Chicago Art Institute. Her enthusiasm about the detour, as well as Rachel's desire to avoid Chicago's rush hour traffic, propelled their consumption. After filling up the gas tank, they motored on.

"Daddy, can you tell me more stories about Wolf?" Eve asked, shortly after they pulled back onto the turnpike.

"You're not bored?"

"No, not yet." She picked up the book and flipped quickly through the pages, stopping at another pixelated photo. "Who is this?" she asked, pointing to the photo.

Paul craned his neck around the seat to get a closer look. "I can't remember her name. What does it say there?"

Eve's eyes scanned the page. "Edna Thomas Maller," she said slowly. "Is this one of Wolf's friends?"

"Yes."

"How did he know her?"

"Well, he … a … he met her at her funeral."

Eve gave her father a confused look.

Paul laughed. "After Wolf went to Dr. Dinglebottom's funeral, he thought he might see if … well, if maybe he could learn something else about life by going to other people's funerals."

"Going to other people's funerals?" Rachel asked, casting him a sideways glance.

"Yeah. Ya, know," he said, turning back to Eve, "people die everyday, even in Kenosha, Wisconsin. Wolf met a whole bunch of people at their funerals."

"So he just showed up at people's funerals, even though he didn't know them?" Rachel asked.

"Well, I wouldn't go that far. These people weren't entirely strangers. He usually knew at least a little bit about them."

"How?"

"He, uh … he read about them in the newspaper. In the obituaries." Paul replied.

Rachel shook her head in disbelief. "So … you weren't kidding before? He just invited himself to strangers' funerals?"

"I guess you could look at it that way. But Wolf figured if it was printed in the paper, it was basically an invitation for anyone who wanted to come."

Rachel laughed. "Doesn't that seem kinda crazy?"

"Mmmaybe … a little bit … now. But at the time, Wolf was hungry to learn everything he could. He'd messed up his own life pretty good, but he'd been given a second chance to make things right. And though he'd learned lots of good things at Dr. Dinglebottom's funeral, it was only enough to make him want more."

"More what?" Rachel asked, dubiously.

Paul ignored the tone of his wife's question and answered without a hint of self-doubt. "He wanted more understanding. More answers. More magic. It was like the clouds that had been blocking the sun from shining on him were finally beginning to part, and a big sunbeam landed on his head and woke him up from a long, cold winter."

"So he went to people's funerals?" Rachel persisted.

"Yeah. What's so crazy about that?"

"It just seems like a really depressing thing to do. Especially if Wolf had already been depressed, and tried to end his own life. That just doesn't seem that healthy … or *normal*."

"Maybe Wolf wasn't really a normal guy, whatever *normal* means. He had a lot of things he needed to figure out, and going to funerals helped him work through those things."

"How?" asked Eve.

"By giving him answers, and helping him figure out what really matters in life."

"Like what?"

"Well, when you start where Wolf was, having been in a gloomy place for a long, long time, you tend to get excited about anything that even resembles light. He was desperate to learn everything he could. He was looking for teachers."

"At funerals? Really?" Rachel continued.

"Okay, so maybe it is a little strange," he said, turning to face Rachel, knowing if he couldn't help her understand this it would be pointless to continue.

"Listen," he said, resting his hand on her knee until she turned to face him, "I know this sounds like just another one of my crazy stories, but I promise you it's not. Dr. Dinglebottom's funeral, as well as the last days of his life—those things changed the way Wolf thought about life. He figured that maybe he might learn other good stuff from other people. It was kind of like the doctor gave Wolf a treasure map."

"A treasure map?" Eve asked, looking excited.

Paul nodded, turning back to Eve. "Yes. After all he'd seen and experienced, Wolf believed there was a treasure, maybe not one made of silver or gold, but something even better."

"Like rubies?" Eve asked, pointing her finger to a word on the open page of the journal.

He looked closer, trying to read upside down. "What does it say?"

THERE IS GOLD, AND A MULTITUDE OF RUBIES:
BUT THE LIPS OF KNOWLEDGE ARE A
PRECIOUS JEWEL
-PROVERBS 20:15.

"That's from Proverbs," he said, pointing to the reference written just below what Eve had read.

"What does it mean?" asked Eve.

"It means that … well, that wisdom and true understanding are even more rare and precious than the riches of the world."

Eve studied her father's face for a long moment before nodding. "And that's what Wolf wanted?"

"Yes." He looked down at the journal thoughtfully. "Wolf had seen enough of life, both good and bad, to know that he wanted the treasure that Dr. Dinglebottom had. Wolf knew that happiness wasn't about money or fame, it was about making choices that lead to real happiness. That's where the treasure map comes in."

"So, there really was a map then?" asked Eve.

Paul smiled at his daughter kindly, but shook his head. "It was a little more complicated than that, and maybe that's the way it needed to be. If someone had just given him a map that told him exactly where the treasure was hidden, he would have missed out on a lot of really important things and people and experiences along the way."

"So … did he ever find the treasure," Eve asked, sounding quite uncertain.

"Yes," he said, winking at his daughter. "At least part of it. But remember, the story isn't over yet."

"He found it, even without a map?"

Paul nodded, looking down at the journal. "That book there, that kinda became Wolf's treasure map."

"How?" she asked, flipping through the journal once again as if she were looking for a map folded neatly between the pages.

Paul watched Eve for a moment before responding. "That book," he said, pausing until she looked up into his eyes, "contains a lot of secrets."

"What kind of secrets?" she wondered.

"Secrets about happiness. Those secrets taught Wolf to slow down, so he could listen to the truth that whispers on the gentlest of breezes. And those breezes and the whispers that came to him gave his life new direction, like clues that gently nudged and encouraged him along the path to the treasure he so desperately wanted."

"So the map to the treasure is in here?" Eve asked, looking quite confused.

Paul nodded.

"Where?"

"On nearly every page."

"Can you show me?"

"Sure," he said, reaching for the book. He turned a page, then another before stopping and turning back to Eve. "Do you want to read it, or should I?"

"You can. But Daddy, can you read it in a silly voice?"

Rachel smiled, but kept her eyes on the road.

Paul cleared his throat before sliding into a thick southern drawl. "You mean like this, Little Miss?"

She erupted in laughter, nodding her head affirmatively.

"Very well," he said, continuing the drawl as he turned to the book.

I'VE BEEN THINKING A LOT ABOUT THE FUNERAL I WENT TO TODAY FOR POLLY ROSE PETERS ROBINSON JACOBS GARRETT GIBSON. I WENT BECAUSE HER OBITUARY WAS FASCINATING. SHE OUTLIVED FOUR HUSBANDS AND WAS NINETY-EIGHT YEARS OLD! HER OBIT SAID HER POSTERITY, BETWEEN HER OWN KIDS AND HER STEP KIDS, GRANDKIDS, GREAT-GRANDKIDS AND EVEN GREAT-GREAT-GRANDKIDS NUMBERED MORE THAN 200. I WAS ALSO INTERESTED IN THIS ONE BECAUSE IT WAS AT THE MORMON CHURCH OUT ON RACINE STREET. I'VE NEVER BEEN IN A MORMON CHURCH BEFORE, AND IT WAS DIFFERENT FROM ANY CHURCH I'VE BEEN IN SO FAR. THERE WAS NO BACK WALL TO THE CHAPEL. INSTEAD IT OPENED UP INTO A BASKETBALL GYM, COMPLETE WITH HOOPS AND GLASS BACKBOARDS. AND THERE WAS NO CROSS OR ALTAR AT THE FRONT OF THE CHURCH, WHICH MADE ME WONDER AT FIRST IF MORMONS are Christians. There must have been five hundred people there, and most of those had to sit on folding chairs that were set up on the gym floor. That's where I sat. I thought it was safe sitting near the back, but people just kept coming. All the chairs were filled, and there were lots of people who had to stand. ———

Another thing I noticed that was very different than other funerals is that the people who came weren't wearing black and most of them actually looked happy. And for a school day, I was surprised by how many kids were there. They were all dressed up, wearing their Sunday best. Before the service even started, about fifty kids walked up to the front of the church and sang a song. I don't remember ever hearing it before, and the words of the song have made me think all day. They sang about being children of God. I guess that makes sense; I mean if God is our Heavenly Father, then we would have to be his children. But the way they sang it made it seem somehow real, like they really believed it.

One little boy, probably about nine years old, was so loud that you could totally hear him singing above the rest of the kids. I'm not sure he knew all the words because he seemed to get mixed up on the second verse, so he just sang the first verse again, even louder than the first time. I was a little embarrassed for the

KID, BUT AS I LOOKED AROUND I SAW THAT EVERYBODY WAS SMILING, NOT TO MAKE FUN, BUT ALMOST LIKE THEY WERE HAPPY DESPITE HOW BAD HE WAS.

I HAVE BEEN TO TWELVE FUNERALS NOW, AND THIS ONE WAS THE MOST SIMILAR TO DR. DINGLEBOTTOM'S. THERE WAS NO PRIEST WHO WAS IN CHARGE, JUST A MIDDLE-AGED MAN IN A BLUE SUIT WHO CALLED HIMSELF A BISHOP. HE CALLED EVERYONE HE INTRODUCED BROTHER OR SISTER SO-AND-SO. BESIDES THE KIDS, THERE WAS A GROUP OF WOMEN WHO SANG A SONG, BUT THEY WERE MUCH BETTER. THE SONG WAS CALLED "COME THOU FOUNT OF EVERY BLESSING" ACCORDING TO THE PROGRAM. IT WAS AMAZING—DEFINITELY THE MOST BEAUTIFUL SONG I HAVE EVER HEARD, AND I HAVEN'T BEEN ABLE TO GET THE MELODY OUT OF MY HEAD ALL DAY. THERE WAS SOMETHING THAT HAPPENED TO ME WHEN I HEARD IT. IT WAS THAT SAME FEELING FROM DR. DINGLEBOTTOM'S FUNERAL, BUT IT HIT ME WITH SUCH FORCE THAT I FOUND MYSELF CRYING. I FELT STUPID UNTIL I LOOKED AROUND AND NOTICED THAT OTHER PEOPLE WERE CRYING, TOO. I'VE HAD A HARD TIME IMAGINING WHAT HEAVEN IS LIKE, BUT THAT SONG MADE ME HOPE THAT HEAVEN IS FILLED WITH MUSIC AS BEAUTIFUL AS THAT.

Paul paused for a moment as memories of that day filled his mind and heart. When he began again, the silly southern drawl he'd been using was gone, replaced with a much more reverent tone.

... streams of mercy, never ceasing,
call for songs of loudest praise.

These words from the song have left me thinking about the change of course my life has taken. For several weeks now, I have been thinking about God in a way I never have before. For most of my life, if I thought about Him at all, I usually pictured Him as a mean and vengeful person who allowed unfortunate things to happen to my life. So I tried not to think much about Him, subconsciously hoping that He would go away and leave me alone. But the night I almost died and the dreams and experiences I have had going to funerals since then have given me some different ideas. As I think about the words of that song and all the things I have felt today—it all makes me think that maybe God is less concerned about judging me and more concerned about mercy and love.

This woman, Polly, as her family referred to her, was really someone special. As her family and the bishop spoke about her, I found myself crying about the stories they told. She went through hell with the death of each of her husbands. But instead of being angry and bitter, they said she put her trust in God, always resigning herself to the belief that God must need her husbands more than she did. It made me realize that I know nothing about trusting God. I never have. But there was a feeling of peace in the words her family spoke of her, a feeling that what they were saying was true and important.

This was the first time since Dr. Dinglebottom's funeral that I found myself crying as I sat and listened to funeral speeches. But this one was different. I never knew this woman in life, but I left her funeral feeling like I did, like somehow I was part of her ginormous family. I cried today at the funeral of a total stranger! What is happening to me?

But I laughed, too. She had a wonderful sense of humor. One of her step-daughters spoke about how Polly came into the family and brought her own children. She said that it was uncomfortable at first as they were all still missing their own mother. They hated the idea of having strangers in their home. After several months things were still strained between a couple of the girls. So in the middle of one particularly noisy fight, Polly stepped in between them and asked who was right. Both the children claimed to be right. She asked who was wrong, and they both pointed fingers at the other. So she handed them each a spoon and told them it was time to settle things once and for

All by fighting it out to the death. She closed the door behind them and left them staring at each other, holding their weapons of murder until they both began to laugh at the absurdity of it all. The step-sisters became best friends, and have remained close for decades.

From all that I heard about this woman today, it seems like she really knew how to live. She never had much money, and she worked hard every day of her life. But she was happy. Her last husband passed away six years ago, leaving her alone to care for their small farm—mowing the lawn, caring for the fruit trees in the summer, even chopping her own wood to heat her home in the winter. Each fall she bottled bushels of fruit to share with her family and still always managed to have cookies in the cookie jar for anyone who stopped by.

This was the kind of funeral I hoped for when I started this journal. If I could find a funeral like Polly's everyday, I'd probably quit my job so I could just go to funerals and soak up all those happy feelings. It has left me feeling that, like that song said, "... God's mercy never ends." Just when I was wondering after last week's funeral if I was wasting my time, I feel compelled to continue my quest to find the meaning of life. Today, I think I found a big piece of it: to seek joy,

DESPITE THE CHALLENGES AND TRIALS THAT LIFE BRINGS YOU. I WONDER IF POLLY EVER KNEW DR. DINGLEBOTTOM. IF SHE DIDN'T IN THIS LIFE, I HOPE SHE DOES NOW. IN SO MANY WAYS, THEIR ATTITUDES ABOUT LIFE ARE THE SAME. AND MAYBE THAT'S WHY I CONNECTED WITH THIS WOMAN AS I READ HER OBIT– SHE FOUND JOY. IS THAT WHAT I AM LOOKING FOR? IS THAT WHAT COMPELS ME TO GO TO FUNERALS? AM I LOOKING FOR JOY?

LATELY I FIND MYSELF STOPPING TO LISTEN TO MY OWN HEART BEAT IN MY EARS OR FEEL THE PULSE IN MY NECK OR WRIST. I AM CONSTANTLY SURPRISED BY THE FEELINGS OF GRATEFULNESS THAT I AM STILL ALIVE. AND TODAY I AM GRATEFUL FOR ANSWERS. I AM GRATEFUL FOR POLLY, MY NEW FRIEND, WHO HAS GIVEN NEW HOPE TO THIS CRAZY QUEST OF MINE. AFTER A DOZEN FUNERALS, I THINK I FINALLY REALIZE WHAT I AM LOOKING FOR. I AM LOOKING FOR JOY. I AM LOOKING FOR TEACHERS TO POINT ME IN THE RIGHT DIRECTION SO I CAN FIND MY OWN.

Paul looked up from the page to find Eve smiling.

"Can I see her picture?" she asked.

Paul flipped back a couple of pages where the yellowed picture was taped to the top corner.

"She looks like an angel."

"I think she must have been an angel—even before she died," Paul said, running his finger over the tape that held the picture to the page.

"What do you mean, even before she died?" Eve queried.

Paul set the book down on his lap then turned back to Eve. "I think there must be people who figure out the secrets of life before the rest of us do. It's almost as if God opened a window into heaven long enough for them to learn all the important things—the things that really matter the most— so they can teach the rest of us." He lifted the book from his lap, setting it down on Eve's lap. "This picture became an important clue for Wolf."

Eve took a closer look, running her finger over the newsprint as if she hoped it would offer up the clue to her, too. "How?" she finally asked.

"Look at her eyes and her smile."

She looked down at the photo. "She looks very happy?"

Paul nodded. "You don't get a smile like that without working on it for a long, long time. Very few of us smile without having a good reason to be happy. After Wolf went to that funeral, he spent a lot of time looking at that photo, wondering what it was that made her smile the way she did.

"Did he find out?"

"I'm not completely sure, but I think he must have gotten a pretty good idea from the clues he had. He imagined this picture was taken at a birthday party for one of her great-grandkids. Maybe she had just given away the beautiful sweater that she had spent most of January knitting as she sat next to her wood stove trying to keep her sore, crooked fingers from getting stiff. Or maybe she had just gotten first place in the Kenosha County Annual Bake Off for the apple pie she had been perfecting for the past forty years by trying it out on her family and her neighbors until it was so good it knocked the judges socks off."

"Or maybe this picture was taken at one of her weddings," Eve suggested.

"We'll probably never know for sure," Paul shrugged as he beamed at his daughter, "but we do know that her smile had been practiced for years. Despite losing four husbands and the countless challenges that followed, as well as all the other challenges that life gives each of us, she was happy, and her well-practiced smile and the lines on her face seem to suggest this wasn't the first time she had something to smile about.

I'm sure that smile was part of the reason Wolf went to her funeral. And it was that smile," Paul said, smiling with his own toothy grin, "that helped Wolf discover a very important clue—that happy people look happy. And knowing Polly had somehow found the happiness he wanted made him push forward in his own search for happiness. Despite the discouragement he'd had the week before, he knew he was on the right track again. That the treasure was still out there, waiting for him to find it."

-LIFE IS A GAME OF SCRABBLE—WE DON'T GET TO CHOOSE OUR LETTERS, BUT WE HAVE TO USE WHAT WE ARE GIVEN."

-IT'S ALL ABOUT LOVE, KINDNESS, RELATIONSHIPS, AND WHAT WE CAN DO TO MAKE THE WORLD A BETTER PLACE.

-IT IS WELL KNOWN THAT AMONG THE BLIND THE ONE EYED MAN IS KING. -GERARD ERASMUS

-TRUTH CAN NEVER BE TOLD AS TO BE UNDERSTOOD, AND NOT BE BELIEVED.—WILLIAM BLAKE

- ONE CATCHES MORE FLIES WITH A SPOONFUL OF HONEY THAN WITH TWENTY CASKS OF VINEGAR. -KING HENRY IV

-"IF HE COULD HAVE FOUND A WOMAN HE COULD TOLERATE, HE WOULD HAVE HAD A HUNDRED KIDS."

"LET US CHEERFULLY DO ALL THAT IS WITHIN OUR POWER."

Notes and Quotes:

I expect to pass through this life but once. If therefore there be any kindness I can show or any good deed I can do to any fellow being, let me do it now and not defer or neglect it, as I shall not pass this way again. –Quaker Proverb

---

We were not sent into this world to do anything into which we cannot put our hearts. –John Ruskin

---

No matter how many communes anybody invents, the family always creeps back. –Margaret Mead

---

When one tugs at a single thing in nature, he finds it attached to the rest of the world. –John Muir

---

No man is free who is not the master of himself. –Epictetus

Could a greater miracle take place than for us to look through each other's eyes for an instant? –Thoreau

Those who dream by day are cognizant of many things which escape those who dream only at night. —Edgar Allan Poe

---

I need thy presence every passing hour. What but thy grace can foil the tempter's power? Who, like thyself, my guide and stay can be? Through cloud and sunshine, Lord, abide with me. "Abide With Me" —Henry Francis Lyte

---

No one is rich enough to avoid mortal experiences. —Julie Beck

---

Your happiness will be in proportion to your charity. —George Smith

---

It is never too late to be what you might have been. —George Eliot

---

Ask, and it shall be given you; seek, and ye shall find; knock, and it will be opened unto you. —Matthew 7: 7

What is Hell? I maintain that it is the suffering of being unable to love. —Dostoyevsky

-CHAPTER 10- THE BEGINNING OF WISDOM

BY THREE METHODS WE MAY LEARN WISDOM: FIRST, BY REFLECTION, WHICH IS NOBLEST; SECOND, BY IMITATION, WHICH IS EASIEST; AND THIRD, BY EXPERIENCE, WHICH IS BITTEREST. – CONFUCIOUS

"So, he kept going to funerals?" asked Eve.

Paul nodded "He figured he had two choices. He could continue on the path he was on, filling in the treasure map as he went along, or he could just be happy with what he had already learned."

"Which one did he choose?"

Paul stretched his arm across to reach the journal, flipping a couple of pages until he came to a small strip of once-white paper, yellowed under the Scotch tape which fastened it to the page.

"He might have stopped if it hadn't been for that," he said, pointing.

> There are only two mistakes one can make along the road to truth; not going all the way and not starting. -Buddha

Eve read the words aloud, slowly. "He had to keep going, didn't he?" she asked after a moments pause.

Paul nodded. "Wolf considered stopping many times, but he always came back to that truth he found one day in his fortune cookie. He knew he couldn't be content, no matter how hard he tried, until he learned everything he could. He'd already tried the other mistake—not starting. There's something funny about truth and wisdom—the more you learn, the more you want to learn, and the more humble you become as you begin to recognize all the stuff you don't know."

"So, how do you know when you have enough?" asked Rachel

"I'm not sure there is such a thing as enough. Truth and wisdom bring understanding, light and happiness. And I'm convinced that the more of that stuff you can gather up and hold onto, the better your life will be.

"From the good funerals he went to, he'd learned that the people who embraced as much truth and wisdom as they could find seemed to live happier, more meaningful lives. I don't know if their lives were any easier, but it seemed like they had an ability to make sense of their trials and find joy along the way. It's almost as if they had a flashlight to illuminate their path that could keep them from stumbling over the rocks and briars that life brings us."

Eve turned several more pages filled with writing and doodles and black and white photographs. "How many funerals did he go to?"

"I'm not sure, but he went to at least one every week for almost a year."

"That's a lot of funerals," Eve replied.

"Yes, it is. He had a lot to learn."

"Couldn't he think of any better ways to learn about those things?" asked Rachel.

"He eventually figured out lots of different ways to get the answers he needed, but in the beginning, he wasn't entirely sure what he was looking for, or even what questions to ask. It was kind of like I said before, he was thirsty, and he figured if he wanted a drink, he needed to go to the fountain."

"So, were most of the funerals like Polly's and Dr. Dinglebottom's?" asked Eve.

Paul laughed. "Unfortunately, no. He suffered through many funerals that weren't very helpful."

"Why not?"

"Some of them were depressing. Some people never figured out what life is all about. Paul stretched out his arm and turned back several pages in the journal. "This was a really hard one for him to go to, and it almost made him throw in the towel."

RAYMOND COREY

Eve read the name aloud before looking up. She rubbed her fingers over the masking tape that might once have secured a photograph to the page like the others, but in this case, the photograph was gone. "How did he die?"

"He drowned. He was ice fishing with his buddies, drank too much beer, fell through some thin ice and by the time his drunk friends got the help he needed, it was too late. He was only thirty-two years old."

"Did he have a family?" asked Rachel.

"Kind of. He had a girlfriend and at least two children with different women, but he was never married."

"I'm guessing his funeral wasn't held at a church."

"No." Paul craned his neck again to look at the writing in the journal. "It was at the Kingman Funeral Parlor." He shook his head. "And that was probably only because of his parents. If it had been up to Raymond and his buddies, I think they might have thought it would have been better if it was held at a bar. Most of his friends showed up drunk anyway. After the funeral director said a few words, they had an open mic and several of his friends stood up and sang AC/DC's 'Highway to Hell.'"

"SOME PEOPLE JUST HAVE DUMB KIDS!"

Rachel shook her head and tried not to smile.

"Yeah, Wolf went away from that funeral feeling pretty depressed. But I guess he learned something from even the really painful funerals."

"Like what not to be?"

"Exactly. Sometimes we can learn our best lessons from bad examples."

"What kind of lessons?" asked Eve.

Paul looked contemplative. "I'm pretty sure it was during that funeral that Wolf decided he never needed to drink again. There were too many parallels between Wolf's family history and the circumstance of Raymond's life and death. And there is something very powerful about looking down into a casket and seeing someone whose life parallels your own in too many ways. It makes you stop and think and wake up. Wolf decided drinking didn't fit into any long-term model of a happy life he could imagine. In reality, he knew it had only brought him and his family trouble, and he knew he wanted to leave those traditions behind."

Rachel looked at him sideways as if she was seeing something new in the man she'd been married to for the past decade. "Was it hard for him to stop drinking?" she asked when he turned to face her.

Paul nodded. "In the beginning, yes. Most of the people he worked with drank, and they couldn't understand why he stopped. But Wolf knew he couldn't have it both ways. The more he learned, the more he became convinced that staying sober was a big part of finding the happiness he was looking for."

Eve reached for the journal and turned the page. "Who's that?"

"Uh, his name is Robert Jacobson."

"Why did Wolf go to his funeral?" she asked.

"I'm not sure," Paul said, scanning the page for something interesting. "I think Wolf must have gone to this one because it was at St. Peter's."

"What does that have to do with anything?" asked Rachel.

"Wolf had never been to St. Peter's, or any Catholic

church for that matter. He wanted to know what a Catholic funeral was like."

"What did he find out?"

"Well, you definitely can't judge all Catholic funerals by that one, but it was pretty cold."

"Cold?"

"I'm sure it probably would have been different if the priest had actually known Bob, but since he didn't, he just talked about a lot of other stuff that didn't seem to offer any comfort."

"Like what?"

"Well," he turned to the journal. "Bob was born in 1931, so the priest talked about being born during the depression and growing up poor, which was probably a pretty good guess, considering the timing and circumstances. He talked about World War II ending when he was in high school. He talked about the Cold War and the Korean War and the Vietnam War and the Hippie Era and named all the presidents of the United States along the way. Then he read a few things from the Bible, you know, "ashes to ashes and dust to dust sort of thing." There were a couple of hymns, and then he asked the pallbearers to come forward and take Bob to his final resting place."

"What did Wolf get out of a funeral like that?" asked Rachel

"More than you might expect. It was a good historical overview of the previous seventy years."

"Were there any stories?" asked Eve.

"No. I don't think the priest knew any of Bob's stories. Bob really wasn't a church-going sort of man. It wasn't a great funeral, but it could have been worse."

"How?" asked Rachel with a smirk on her face.

Paul flipped through the book, stopping about halfway through. "This was a really painful funeral for Wolf."

"Painful?"

"Yeah, just really embarrassing."

"YOU'LL REMEMBER THE QUALITY LONG AFTER YOU FORGET WHAT YOU PAID FOR IT."

"Did he get caught? Did they find out that he had no idea who the dead person was?" asked Rachel.

"No, though that did happen a few times. This one was painful for another reason. The pastor kept forgetting the dead lady's name."

"Ughhh, that must have been really embarrassing."

"Yeah, and he was even reading his whole sermon from his notes. I think he must have been using the notes from the last funeral he conducted. The lady's family was pretty upset that they were paying him a bunch of money, and he couldn't even get her name right."

"How much does a funeral cost?"

"It really depends. Somewhere between five and ten thousand dollars, by the time you figure in all the fees like caskets and embalming and digging the grave. They probably paid that pastor at least two hundred dollars, and he didn't even have to write it—he just copied most of it out of a book. He probably would have had more to say if he'd actually known the woman. I think the only reason she had her funeral at that church was because she was baptized there, but she had never really attended."

"Why did Wolf go to that one?" asked Eve.

"He had never been to a Baptist funeral before, and she seemed interesting enough, at least from her obituary."

"What about that one?" Eve asked, pointing to the picture on the opposite page.

Nancy Gasperini

He scanned the page before looking up. "This was a good one."

"Why?"

"Because she had a great story. She must have figured out what life was all about early on because even though she was young when she died, she filled up her years with a lot of great stories."

"Like what?" asked Eve.

Paul turned back to the book. "Do you want me to read what Wolf wrote?"

"Sure," responded Eve.

This was a hard funeral to go to, but I'm trying to figure out why. This lady lived a great life, but she died too young, which is kind of weird to say considering I have been to several other funerals for people who were younger than she was. Maybe I feel this way because after meeting her at her funeral, I feel bad that I didn't know her before she died. She must have really been amazing. Nancy died from a blood clot that went to her lungs just a couple of weeks after she had her knee replaced. The reason she had to have knee surgery is because she wore it out having fun with her kids. Her motto in life was that it is better to wear out than rust out. I think of all the people I've met going to funerals so far, she had the most fun.

Both of her daughters gave speeches about their mom and told some amazing stories about her. She was the queen of garage sales and used to drag the girls with her every Saturday morning. They would pack a lunch and sometimes be gone all day, stopping to have picnics at the lake. She taught them how to catch tadpoles, so they could watch them turn into frogs. She worked at the county library and always brought home the newest children's books to share with her girls, even long after they had grown out of children's books. They said she wasn't much of a cook, but she always had fun with food, serving her specialty of macaroni and tomato sauce on her finest china by candlelight.

Her husband died in a car accident when the girls were young, and money was always tight. But she never let that get in the way of them having fun. One thing she did that I thought was really cool was that she always kept a bowl of spare change on the kitchen counter. On Friday nights they would count out their change and then walk to the Dairy Freeze to buy ice cream cones. They called it their fun money.

"Hey, that's just like our fun money!" Eve said, excitedly.

Paul nodded and smiled. "It must have been a good idea." He continued to read before she could ask any questions.

It sounds like such a simple thing, but it was cool to see how a small thing like eating an ice cream cone on a park bench meant so much to them—even now when they are both in their thirties and have young kids of their own. One of the girls said something that was really cool. She said that they never went to the beach or to Disneyland or on exotic vacations like their friends did with their families. But they knew their mother loved them because of all the time she spent with them. She said she wouldn't trade her memories of skipping rocks and nature walks and ice cream cones for a million trips to Disneyland. And she hoped she would be able to raise her children to have an appreciation for the small things in life.

That made me think a lot about my own life. I don't remember ever going on a family vacation—there was never any money for anything like that. I don't think I even left the county until I was ten or eleven. And even though my dad was never around much—and when he was he had no idea how to be a dad—I

HAD A GREAT MOM. SHE WORKED HARD, AND SHE LOVED US. I DON'T THINK I EVER APPRECIATED THE LITTLE THINGS SHE DID. SHE USED TO GO WITHOUT LUNCH, SO SHE COULD SAVE HER MONEY TO GO TO THE LAUNDROMAT AND MAKE SURE JENNIE AND I HAD CLEAN CLOTHES TO WEAR TO SCHOOL.

Paul's voice cracked, but he swallowed hard and kept reading.

IT HAS BEEN A LONG TIME SINCE I HAVE EVEN THOUGHT ABOUT MOM. IT SEEMS STUPID THAT I HAVE TO GO TO A FUNERAL TO REMEMBER HER. SHE'S BEEN GONE FOR SIX YEARS, OR IS IT SEVEN? I WAS JUST TRYING TO REMEMBER THE LAST TIME I TOLD HER THAT I LOVED HER. I THINK IT MUST HAVE BEEN WHEN I LEFT FOR COLLEGE. I NEVER FIGURED THAT WOULD BE THE LAST TIME I'D SEE HER. I WISH I WOULD HAVE CARED MORE. I HOPE SHE KNEW I DID. I WONDER IF SHE KNOWS I'M THINKING ABOUT HER. I'VE NEVER THOUGHT MUCH ABOUT HEAVEN, OR EVEN IF THERE IS ONE. BUT IF THERE IS, I HOPE THAT ONE DAY I CAN SEE HER AGAIN AND THANK HER FOR LOVING ME.

Paul turned away from the book and looked out the side window, trying to control his emotions. More than twelve years had past since the day he wrote this, but the sorrow and ache lingered fresh in his mind. His mother had died too early—before he could make things right; before he could tell her that he loved her at least one more time. She'd had a rough life, one he was certain was full of disappointments. But she was his mother. She'd done all she could to try to make his life better than her own. What had he done with her memory?

"What's wrong, Daddy?" Eve asked, resting her hand on his shoulder.

He turned slowly towards her. "I was just thinking about Wolf and his mother."

"How come?"

IT IS POSSIBLE TO PARTAKE OF THE BITTER CUP WITHOUT BECOMING BITTER. —NEAL MAXWELL

"Because this funeral made him think a lot about her. It made him miss her."

"Was every funeral sad?"

"I'm sure every funeral was sad for some people who were there, but there were lots of funerals that gave Wolf things to be happy about, too."

Eve nodded. "What other kind of funerals did he go to?" she asked as she flipped through several pages.

"All kinds. He went to big ones and small ones. He went to funerals at churches and others that were just at the cemetery. He went to one that was held at the Greek Orthodox Church that was conducted by three priests who only spoke Greek during the whole ceremony."

"What did Wolf learn from that one?"

"He learned that he needed to take some Greek lessons before he went to another funeral at that church," he responded with a laugh.

"Did everyone else understand?"

Paul shook his head. "Wolf was pretty sure only a few of them did, mostly just the older people."

"What do people get out of a funeral if they can't understand the language?" asked Rachel.

"Well, the church was beautiful, with all the stained glass windows, and the music, even though it was in Greek—was beautiful, too. He learned that you might need to grow up in some cultures in order to understand all of the rituals and rites. Wolf sat in the back row at that one, not knowing what to expect and hoping to stay out of the way and not draw any attention to himself. But had he been aware of some of the traditions, he might have chosen another funeral."

"Why? What happened?"

Paul laughed to himself. "He thought he might die at the end of the funeral when the ushers started at the back of the church and escorted all of the guests forward to pay their final respects to the woman who had died."

"What was so awkward about that?"

BLESSED IS THE INFLUENCE OF ONE, TRUE LIVING SOUL ON ANOTHER - GEORGE ELIOT

"Well, to begin with, Wolf very quickly recognized that he stuck out like a sore thumb."

"Why?"

"Because he was the only one in the whole church who was not wearing black from head to toe, but that was only the beginning. The guests were supposed to kiss an icon that the priests had placed on the open casket. Then they were to kiss the dead woman goodbye, and cross themselves." Paul laughed. "Wolf just about had a heart attack right there. As he watched the three people in front of him, he knew there was no way he could do any of it without making it known that he was far more "geek" than Greek, and was an impostor."

"So what did he do?" Rachel asked, smiling broadly.

"Well, he had about ten seconds to decide what to do. He tried to imagine the best case scenario but was afraid that if he tried to look authentic, he would likely knock the icon on the floor. He figured the casket lid would probably fall on his head when he tried to kiss the woman's cheek, and on top of that, he had absolutely no idea how to cross himself. So, he did the most respectful thing he felt like he could do."

"What was that?"

"He nodded to the woman and her family seated on the front row and got the heck out of there."

"Did anybody say anything?"

"Wolf didn't stick around long enough to find out. As soon as he hit the church doors, he sprinted down the steps and didn't stop running until he was a block away. That funeral put a halt to his funeral crashing for almost two weeks."

Rachel shook her head, but her smile was brighter than it had been all day. "I don't think I could ever go to another funeral after something like that. Why did he start going again?"

"Because the newspaper was full of people with compelling stories. And he still had lots of questions, maybe more than he'd ever had."

A man searches the world over for what he needs, and then returns home to find it.
-George Moore

Perspective is a lovely hand to hold

Death is not extinguishing the light; it is putting out the lamp because the dawn has come.
-Rabindranath Tagore-

We are each of us angels with only one wing, and we can only fly by embracing each other.
- Luciano De Crescenzo

Do not fear going forward slowly— fear only standing still.
-Chinese proverb

-Chapter 11-
Eulogy For A Boy Named Wolf

You only live once, but if you do it right, once is enough.
—Mae West

"Daddy, what's this?" Eve said, pointing to top of a page. The title at the top of the page was ornate and much more intricate that anything she had seen in the book to that point.

Paul leaned in to take a closer look. "What does it say?"

"I don't know. I can't read that language," she said pointing at the first word.

"That's actually an English word."

"It is? I've never seen it before."

"No, I suppose you probably wouldn't."

"How do you say it? EEE-ooh-low-guy," she said, trying it out.

"Not bad. That is a silent 'E'," he said, pointing to the E.

"Ooo-lo-guy?" she said, trying again.

"Close. It's pronounced 'you-la-gee.'"

"That's a funny word. What does it mean?"

"Well, a eulogy is like an honor or a tribute to someone who has died. Lots of times, you hear a eulogy at a funeral. It kind of tells a person's life story."

Eve looked down at the journal. She pointed her index finger at the title, reading it in its entirety. "You-la-gee for a boy named Wolf." She looked up, looking confused. "So, did Wolf die?"

"Eve, would that be a very good story if he did?" Paul teased.

"No, but I thought you said that you-la-gee means …"

"It does," he said, feeling a little nervous that reading any further would enable her to realize Wolf's true identity. "Let me tell you about it." Paul reached for the book before turning his head toward the front, stretching his neck. "Wolf wrote this one after he had only been to a few funerals."

"This one?" asked Rachel. "How many did he write?"

"I'm not sure. Probably at least ten during the year he was attending funerals."

"Why?"

Paul shrugged. "I think he must have wanted to make sure to put down the important things he was learning."

"But didn't writing eulogies for himself keep him thinking about dying? I'd think he'd want to be more worried about living."

"He was worried about living, that's why he wrote so many eulogies for himself."

"Huh?"

"Remember how I said that Wolf learned that in order to have a really good funeral, you had to live a really good life?"

"Yeah."

"Well, Wolf wrote these eulogies to help him remember that. He wrote down the things he believed were part of living a great life. The eulogies he wrote didn't keep him thinking about death as much as they kept him thinking about life—about his life. I think that the world would be a much different place if every twenty-six-year-old man spent a little more time thinking about the things he hoped might be said about him at his funeral."

Rachel nodded thoughtfully.

"So, what did he write, Daddy?"

Paul turned back to Eve and smiled. "Would you like me to read it?"

"Yeah."

"Okay," he said, turning back to the open book.

WOLF WAS BORN IN ADAMS-FRIENDSHIP, WISCONSIN. FROM THE TIME HE WAS A CHILD HE LEARNED TO WORK HARD, BOTH IN SCHOOL AND FOR HIS EMPLOYERS. THIS BECAME A PATTERN FOR HIS LIFE AND SOMETHING HE TAUGHT HIS CHILDREN. WOLF WAS A FAMILY MAN AND SPENT AS MUCH TIME AS HE COULD WITH THE PEOPLE HE LOVED THE MOST. HE WAS A GOOD FRIEND, A TERRIFIC HUSBAND, AND A WONDERFUL FATHER AND GRANDFATHER. HIS FAMILY WILL ALWAYS REMEMBER THE FUN-FILLED VACATIONS TO PLACES AROUND THE WORLD AND THE TIME HE SPENT WITH THEM. WOLF HAD A GREAT SENSE OF HUMOR AND WAS QUICK TO LAUGH AT HIMSELF. HE WILL BE GREATLY MISSED.

"He sounds like a nice guy," Eve offered.

"Good. That's what he was hoping for. But remember that this was the same guy, who just a few weeks earlier, had tried to end his life because he couldn't think of any reason to live."

Eve nodded slowly.

"The eulogies that he wrote in this journal became the goals and dreams he hoped to achieve by the time he died, and writing them down made him feel responsible for the person he was becoming. It made him feel like he could design his own life and then become whatever he designed."

Paul flipped several pages, remembering a poem that he'd once been so impressed with that he'd stapled it into the journal. He found it about a third of the way into the journal. The corner of the page had been dog-eared, and he smiled to himself as he looked over the poem that had been typed on the back of a funeral program. It was the first poem he'd ever committed to memory, at least since he'd tackled Clement Clarke Moore's "The Night Before Christmas" in the fourth grade.

"What is it?" asked Rachel.

"Invictus."

"What's that?"

"I am the master of my fate: I am the captain of my soul."

"You used to say that all the time."

INVICTUS

Out of the night that covers me,
Black as the Pit from pole to pole,
I thank whatever gods may be
For my unconquerable soul.

In the fell clutch of circumstance
I have not winced nor cried aloud.
Under the bludgeonings of chance
My head is bloody, but unbowed.

Beyond this place of wrath and tears
Looms but the Horror of the shade,
And yet the menace of the years
Finds, and shall find, me unafraid.

It matters not how strait the gate,
How charged with punishments the scroll.
I am the master of my fate:
I am the captain of my soul.

-William Ernest Henley

"I know. I suppose I still do."

"Why?"

"Because it was a harbinger of change, and when I repeat it, it still is."

"What is a harbinger?" asked Eve.

Paul paused, thinking of how he might describe the word in a way a seven-year-old could understand. "I guess it's kind of like a turning point."

"It sounds like Wolf had a lot of turning points," she responded.

Rachel smiled at her daughter through the rearview mirror.

"You're right. He did. But each one was important and each one brought him closer to the treasure. There were many times that it felt to Wolf like he needed to be in a certain place at a certain time in order for him to hear the things he needed to learn. This was one of those times. He needed to hear about this woman," he said, turning back to the page with the picture of a white-haired woman with a gentle smile.

"Why did he go to her funeral?" asked Rachel, peering at the photograph.

"Because of her obituary."

"What about it?"

"She led a very interesting life and had to deal with a lot of disappointments and heartaches, but she still found a way to smile. I guess it was that smile that most interested Wolf. She was still smiling after all she had gone through."

"What happened to her?" asked Eve, leaning forward to take a closer look at the picture.

"Let me read it," he responded.

SYLVIA WAS BORN IN GERMANY AT A VERY DIFFICULT TIME. HER FATHER WAS GERMAN, BUT HER MOTHER WAS POLISH. AND UNBEKNOWNST TO HER, HER GREAT-GRANDFATHER WAS A JEW. WHEN SHE WAS ONLY EIGHT YEARS OLD, SYLVIA'S FATHER WAS FORCED INTO THE MILITARY. SHE AND HER MOTHER WERE LEFT IN THE CARE OF A NEIGHBOR WHO QUICKLY TURNED THEM OVER TO THE POLICE. SHE WAS SENT TO A CONCENTRATION CAMP WITH HER MOTHER AND BABY BROTHER IN THE MIDDLE OF WINTER. HER BROTHER DIED ON THE OVERCROWDED TRAIN ON THE WAY THERE, AND HER MOTHER DIED A WEEK LATER OF TUBERCULOSIS. SHE WAS FORCED TO WORK IN A KITCHEN, HELPING TO PREPARE MEALS FOR THE VERY MEN WHO HAD DESTROYED HER FAMILY. SHE WAS THERE FOR OVER A YEAR BEFORE SHE ESCAPED FROM THE CAMP WITH ONLY THE RAGS SHE WORE. IN THE COLD OF WINTER HER FINGERS AND TOES WERE FROZEN, BUT SHE KEPT MOVING, MAKING HER WAY TO FRANCE WHERE SHE WAS TAKEN IN BY A FARMER WHO HAD TO REMOVE ALL OF HER TOES AND THREE OF HER FINGERS WITH A SAW IN ORDER TO SAVE HER LIFE.

"I don't like this story, Daddy."

"I didn't either, Baby. It's one of those stories that really hurts to hear. But like all of the stories I've ever told you, things got better for Sylvia, even without her toes."

Eve looked back with challenging eyes. "How?"

"Can I read you what Wolf wrote?"

"Is it happy?"

"I think so. I'll let you decide." He scanned the page until he found the place where he left off.

While I was listening to all the awful things that happened to Sylvia, most of which happened before she was even twelve years old, I found myself wondering how someone can go on after so much tragedy. But I learned many things today. There seems to be within each of us a potentially unconquerable spirit.

It was inspiring to hear how she learned to play the violin from the farmer who took her in. She couldn't do everything, but by focusing on the things she could do, she was able to do most things. A series of fortunate circumstances brought her to New York to perform at Carnegie Hall when she was only fifteen. She stayed and studied in New York and Boston where she met James Robbins, a musician from Chicago, who was finishing his studies. They married when she was only eighteen and they later had five children and twenty-three grandchildren. I realize that none of these things could have happened to her if she had given up. Few people would have faulted her if she had. But something kept her going despite her trials and tragedies.

The funeral was held at the Clarkston Funeral Home. Two of her sons gave speeches, talking about how their mother

never allowed them to feel sorry for themselves, no matter what. "To feel sorry for yourself is to lose the battle," she told them, and "We're never really defeated until we give up trying." Her sons are both successful businessmen. Her three daughters are also successful— two musicians and one doctor. Each of them was proud of the way their mother raised them to believe that everybody has at least one unique gift that needs to be shared with this world, regardless of one's challenges.

This poem, "Invictus," was the motto she lived by. She was inspired by the man who wrote it, William Henley, who had his foot amputated after a long illness. But he never allowed the sadness and challenge of his circumstances to determine who he was or what he accomplished in life. Neither Sylvia nor Mr. Henley gave up when the reality they had to deal with could have swallowed them whole.

I have found myself thinking about this all day. Am I the master of my fate? Am I the captain of my soul? I am ashamed with the reality that I have been neither. Despite my capable body and reasonably capable mind, I have allowed my childhood and the tragedy that is my family to stand in the way of who and what I am and what I am becoming. Today I recognized that I've had a problem with perspective.

If pain doesn't lead to humility, you have wasted your suffering. –Katerina Stoykova Klemer

I am twenty-six years old, and I am still allowing my father and the choices he made when I was a child to affect my life. He ruined his own life, and our family, and I have allowed him to continue to hurt me by holding onto the pain. I hate that about myself. I have wasted the last ten years or more of my life believing that I could be no better than my father. I have allowed the sorrow of poverty, abuse and neglect to define who I am. I have bought into the idea that life has been unfair for me. What a waste of time. What a waste of effort. In many ways, I am no better off than I was when I was fifteen. I am angry with myself for allowing someone else to pilot my destiny. This funeral today has taught me that I need to be done with my excuses. I need to "man-up" and figure out the rest of my life. I need to become something more. I need to figure out what my gift is to this world.

Today I am a pizza boy—a life that has been reasonably good to me. But I did not choose this life deliberately. I fell into it with very little effort on my part. Tonight I realize that for the past ten years I have been stuck in a rut. It is reasonably comfortable, and I have pretended to be satisfied, but I am not. There may be some people who can make a difference in the world by being a pizza boy. But tonight, for the first time since

I MADE MY FIRST PIZZA, I KNOW I NEED TO DO SOMETHING MORE. I FEEL LIKE IF I'M A PIZZA BOY A YEAR FROM NOW I WILL HAVE FAILED AGAIN. THE STORIES FROM SYLVIA'S LIFE LIT A FIRE INSIDE ME. I'M TIRED OF MAKING EXCUSES FOR THE DREAMS I'VE NEVER PURSUED. I HAVE ALLOWED FEAR TO HOLD ME BACK, TO PARALYZE MY PROGRESS. I FEEL LIKE I AM READY TO TAKE IT ALL BACK. I AM READY TO BECOME THE CAPTAIN OF MY SOUL.

Paul set the book down in his lap and looked up, smiling. More than twelve years had passed since he'd written those words. He had no way of knowing at the time how the repercussions of that line of thinking would affect him—how they would change his future. He looked at the picture of the woman again, running the tip of his index finger over her name.

SYLVIA RAUSCH ROBBINS

By most standards, she was a stranger to him. But this stranger, and the truths he'd been given by attending her funeral were truths that had profoundly changed him. Paul recognized that his decision to embrace those truths—to become the captain of his soul—had changed everything for him—everything! He had wanted to make his mark on the world—wanted to give his gift to the world. And that desire had led him to expand his horizons in search of opportunities to stretch and be bigger than he believed he was. In the process of stretching, he'd broken away from the small ideas that had held him back and inhibited his growth.

The oft-repeated mantra, "I am the master of my fate: I am the captain of my soul," had kept him from becoming stagnant. It kept him growing, reaching higher and expecting more of himself. There had been many times over the course of the last decade where he had wondered where he might be if these changes had not come. Would he still be making pizzas? Would he ever have gotten married? Hearing these truths at Sylvia's funeral had come at a critical time, but it was what he'd done with those truths that had made all the difference in his world.

AND GOD SHALL WIPE AWAY ALL THE TEARS FROM THEIR EYES; AND THERE SHALL BE NO MORE DEATH, NEITHER SORROW, NOR CRYING, NEITHER SHALL THERE BE ANY MORE PAIN ... BEHOLD, I WILL MAKE ALL THINGS NEW.
—REVELATION 21: 4–5

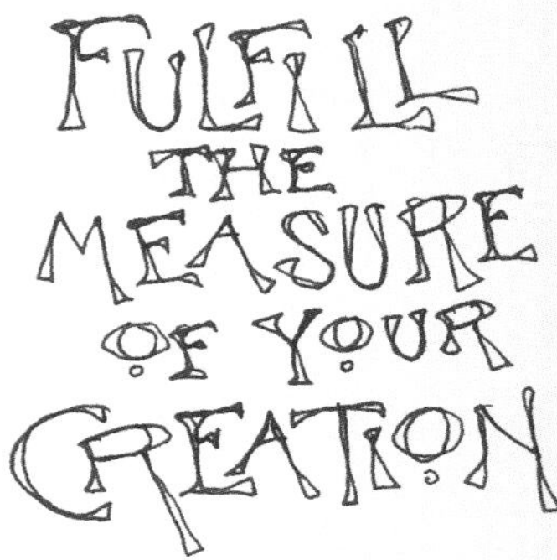

AND WHERE DOES THE POWER COME FROM, TO SEE THE RACE TO ITS END? FROM WITHIN. JESUS SAID, "BEHOLD THE KINGDOM OF GOD IS WITHIN YOU. IF, WITH ALL YOUR HEARTS, YOU TRULY SEEK ME, YOU SHALL EVER SURELY FIND ME." IF YOU COMMIT YOURSELF TO THE LOVE OF CHRIST, THEN THAT IS HOW YOU RUN A STRAIGHT RACE.
—ERIC LIDDELL

-Chapter 12-
A Six-Month Decade

For the truly faithful, no miracle is necessary. For those who doubt, no miracle is sufficient.
—Nancy Gibbs

"That was a good thing for Wolf to learn, huh?" Eve said, interrupting Paul's thoughts and pulling him back into the present.

"Yes," he said softly, struggling to focus. "It was that kind of stuff that made all the difference for Wolf. It picked him up, dusted him off, and set him on a new course."

"Is that why he decided to become a paramedic?" Rachel asked.

"I'm sure that was a big part of it. Before then it had never really occurred to Wolf that he might have something to give the world."

"You mean besides yummy pizzas?" asked Eve.

"Yeah, besides pizzas. He must have been a pretty selfish guy before that. I'm sure he didn't spend much time thinking about other people. But not long after that funeral, he was on his way home from work late one night, and witnessed a terrible accident. He was stopped at a stop sign when a car coming the opposite direction didn't stop. The driver was drunk and probably half-asleep and T-boned another car as it passed through the intersection, just inches away from Wolf."

"What did Wolf do?" asked Eve, a look of concern on her face.

"He panicked. He'd never been so close to an accident before. He got out of his car with adrenaline coursing through his whole body. A woman came out of her house to say she would call 911 while Wolf tried to help the people in the cars. The drunk man broke his nose when his face hit the steering wheel, but he was well enough to be screaming and cursing, so Wolf went to check on the other man. The side window had broken when the man's head hit the glass and he was bleeding from the side of his neck and face. Wolf thought he might be dead and he was afraid to touch him if he wasn't, knowing he could do more damage."

"So, what did he do?" Eve persisted.

"He took off his shirt and held it against the man's face to try and stop the bleeding. And he said a hundred silent prayers that the ambulance would hurry and that the man would live."

"Did he?"

"Wolf looked for the man's picture in the obituaries for several days, wondering if he'd died. He didn't find out until he got a phone call from a woman who said she was the man's wife. She'd gotten Wolf's number from the police report and called to thank him for helping to save her husband's life. He knew he hadn't done very much, but she made him feel like a hero. He liked the way that felt. I think it was probably that week that he started looking into becoming an EMT. And once he started, he felt like he was on the right track for the first time in his whole life."

"Did he learn how to save people's lives, like you do?" asked Eve.

Paul nodded. "Yes." He turned back to the journal, looking distracted, and flipped through a dozen pages before smiling to himself.

"What did you find?" asked Rachel.

He looked up, a curious grin on his face. "It's here. In the back of my mind I knew it would be, but it feels good to see it."

"What? What is it?"

"It's … it's an entry from a very important day."

"What day is that?"

"June 25, 1999."

"What is so important about that day?"

He looked back to the journal before responding. "Maybe it's not so much the day that's important as it is where he was and what he was thinking. Maybe I should just read it."

"Yeah, let's hear it," Rachel said.

June 25, 1999

I TOOK THE WHOLE DAY OFF TODAY, SO I COULD SPEND SOME TIME THINKING. IT WAS A GOOD THING TO DO. IT HAS LEFT ME WITH A SENSE OF DIRECTION AND CLARITY THAT I HAVEN'T HAD BEFORE.

SIX MONTHS—IN MANY WAYS, IT FEELS LIKE IT'S BEEN A DECADE. NOT A DAY HAS GONE BY THAT I HAVEN'T THOUGHT ABOUT THE NIGHT I NEARLY DIED. I CAME BACK TODAY FOR THE FIRST TIME SINCE THEN, BACK TO THE PARK, BACK TO THE LAKE, BACK TO THE BENCH. I REALIZE THAT I'M A DIFFERENT PERSON TODAY THAN I WAS SIX MONTHS AGO. IT'S HARD FOR ME TO REMEMBER THE GUY INSIDE ME WHO COULDN'T THINK OF ANY REASON TO LIVE. TODAY I FEEL LIKE I HAVE NEVER BEEN MORE ALIVE. I FEEL LIKE I'VE NEVER HAD MORE PASSION TO LIVE. THE ONLY THING THAT IS LEFT OF THAT PERSON ARE THE MEDICAL BILLS HE LEFT BEHIND, BUT I AM WORKING ON THAT AND HOPE TO HAVE THEM PAID OFF IN ANOTHER SIX MONTHS. THANK GOD FOR INSURANCE. I'M NOT SURE HOW HOPEFUL I'D BE IF THE MOUNTAIN OF BILLS WAS ANY LARGER, BUT IT FEELS GOOD TO BE TAKING RESPONSIBILITY FOR MYSELF. I AM ALMOST 27 YEARS OLD, AND I AM JUST BEGINNING TO FEEL LIKE AN ADULT.

I wondered how it would be, coming back to this place. I have avoided coming here—worried that some of the old feelings might still be here. But I didn't need to worry. The day is beautiful; the sun is bright, and big puffy white clouds are racing over the lake a little slower than the sailboats. The park is filled with people: children making sandcastles, college students playing Frisbee, families flying kites, fishermen out on the pier. The world is alive, and so am I.

I called Katie today to ask her to dinner. She has to work tonight, so we are meeting at the diner just around the corner from the hospital during her break at 8. I am excited to tell her about the things I've learned over these six months and show her what has become of her journal. I am grateful to her for the challenge she has given me to fill it with interesting stories. I doubt she could have imagined what I would do with it when she gave it to me. I have spoken to her several times over the past months, but I've never mentioned this project. I don't know how she'll take it, but it has been everything I hoped it would be and more. In many ways, the gift of this journal has been like giving me a car with a bottomless tank of gas and telling me to discover the world around me.

As I flip through the pages of this

journal I am surprised at how many people I have met and how many have inspired me. So far I've been to 28 funerals. I still laugh when I think of some of them—the Greek Orthodox woman who made me panic. The man who cheated on his diet by using the Weight Watchers point system reserved for pregnant women. The woman who woke up every morning to the sound of her 28 cuckoo clocks. It sounds crazy, but over the past six months I have laughed and cried numerous times at the funerals of total strangers. I hold in my hands a unique collection of friends. These people have taught me many lessons I doubt I could have learned any other way. I have come to their funerals hungry and thirsty for understanding, and I have gone away fed but also hungry for more.

There have been many lessons from these funerals that have repeated themselves again and again, and if I had to find one commonality among them all, I would have to say it's love. Some of my new friends were obviously better at that than others, but I've thought many times how each of their stories is a love story. Some have struggled their whole lives to find it. Some have been in love with themselves and have died wanting it. Some have found love and lost it. But a handful of the lucky ones have defined it for me. I can't say that I know what love is—not exactly, but I'm miles closer than I was just six months ago. Love is healing. It is caring. It is unselfish. It is fun. It makes life worth living, even the very hope of it.

I told myself six months ago that I needed to figure out my life before I began dating again. I am glad I did. I'm not sure I could have learned the things I have in these months if I had been dating someone. My time would have been divided, and I might have missed out on some of the things I am learning. I hope that when I begin dating again I will have learned the things I need to learn. These six months have taught me so much about all the things I don't know about love and life. But it has given me hope and a chance to learn. I hope that when I love again I will be able to love better. I hope that I will have the understanding that I need to become a better man and eventually a better husband and father.

I just read what I wrote and had to laugh at myself. So many things have changed over the past few months. When Emily left I swore off marriage and family all together, but I don't think I can do that anymore. There is no one I am even interested in dating right now, but from all that I've learned from the funerals, marriage and family, having someone to love, is a critical ingredient to happiness. It may be years before I get

MARRIED. AND IF THAT'S THE CASE, IT WILL BE OKAY. I'VE GOT A LOT OF THINGS TO FIGURE OUT.

FOR THE PAST TWO WEEKS, SINCE WITNESSING THAT ACCIDENT, I'VE BEEN THINKING A LOT ABOUT BECOMING A PARAMEDIC. I WAS INSPIRED BY WATCHING THE AMBULANCE CREWS WORK ON THOSE MEN, AND I DID SOME RESEARCH ON WHAT WOULD BE REQUIRED TO BECOME AN EMT. 120 HOURS WORTH OF COURSE WORK AND ANOTHER 10 HOURS FOR AN INTERNSHIP TO GET AN EMT CERTIFICATE. THEN MORE TRAINING AFTER THAT TO BECOME A PARAMEDIC IF I WANT TO. THERE IS A COURSE STARTING IN TWO WEEKS AND I'VE DECIDED TODAY THAT I NEED TO DO IT. I THINK THAT BY WORKING AROUND MY SCHEDULE AT THE RESTAURANT I COULD BE AN EMT IN SIX MONTHS, MAYBE LESS. I'M EXCITED TO DO THIS. I'M EXCITED TO DO SOMETHING THAT WILL BE GIVING BACK TO THE WORLD. I WONDER WHAT KATIE WILL SAY.

IT FEELS A LITTLE STRANGE TO ADMIT THIS, BUT OVER THE COURSE OF THE LAST FEW MONTHS, I'VE DECIDED TO START PRAYING. I'M NOT SURE WHY I HAVEN'T MENTIONED IT BEFORE, BUT NOW SEEMS AS GOOD A TIME AS ANY. AS I'VE READ AND REREAD MY NOTES FROM THESE FUNERALS, I HAVE NOTICED SOME COMMONALITIES. THE PEOPLE WHO SEEM TO HAVE LED THE HAPPIEST LIVES, HAD THE BEST MARRIAGES AND THE STRONGEST FAMILIES, ALL SHARE A SIMILARITY IN THAT THEY HAVE

A connection to God. One of last week's funerals, Jerry Grimshaw's, inspired me to take a closer look at my notes and make this connection. His funeral was held at the Golden Pines Funeral Home. It had been a couple of months since I'd been to a funeral that wasn't at a church. It was a disappointment, but it also opened my eyes. Jerry was only 55 years old. He was never lucky in love. He never married or had any children, so he decided he'd be a favorite uncle instead. I have no doubt that he succeeded—several of his nieces and nephews gave speeches about him, but there was something missing—something big. There was no mention of God or Jesus, and all of the speeches seemed fairly shallow, almost immature. I left feeling empty—even sad. There was no hope for a brighter future, nor any sense of understanding of the purpose or meaning of this life. It almost seemed like they were doing all they could to avoid any talk of the things I've spent the last six months seeking out—those good feelings. There was none of that there. It left me feeling so empty that I went home and started looking for another funeral to go to. I'm glad I did. The funeral I went to the next day for Albert Hafen was exactly what I was looking for.

I'VE SPENT SOME TIME, TODAY TRYING TO DISCERN THE DIFFERENCES BETWEEN THE FUNERALS, AND I HAVE COME TO THE CONCLUSION THAT LIFE WITHOUT SOME SENSE OF CONNECTION TO DEITY IS DRUDGERY. IT IS LIMITED AND FINITE. IT IS HOPELESSNESS. I DON'T DOUBT THAT PEOPLE CAN LIVE GOOD AND PRODUCTIVE LIVES WITHOUT AN UNDERSTANDING OF GOD, BUT HAVING BEEN THERE AND TRIED IT MYSELF—AND NOW HAVING EXPERIENCED THE HOPE AND UNDERSTANDING THAT FAITH PROVIDES, I SEE THAT FAITH IN GOD GIVES LIFE ANOTHER DIMENSION. IT OFFERS HOPE AND MEANING AND UNDERSTANDING. IT MAKES ME FEEL LIKE THE DAILY STRUGGLES ARE WORTH IT, AND I AM FINDING MEANING IN THEM AS WELL AS A HUMILITY I NEVER KNEW BEFORE ALL OF THIS. I WOULD LIKE TO SAY IT OFFERS ANSWERS, AND I KNOW IT DOES, BUT I HAVE MORE QUESTIONS NOW THAN I'VE EVER HAD BEFORE.

AND I GUESS THIS IS WHY I STARTED PRAYING—I WAS LOOKING FOR ANSWERS, MEANING AND UNDERSTANDING. AND ALL THOSE THINGS HAVE COME. I WISH I COULD SAY THAT I KNOW EXACTLY WHAT I AM DOING AND THAT LIFE MAKES PERFECT SENSE TO ME ALL THE TIME, BUT I'D BE LYING. ANSWERS HAVE COME SLOWLY AND VERY RARELY IN THE WAY I EXPECT. THE NIGHT I PRAYED FOR THE FIRST TIME, I DECIDED TO STAY ON MY KNEES UNTIL I FELT LIKE AN ANSWER CAME. I'M NOT SURE WHAT I WAS WAITING FOR, BUT I WOKE UP THE NEXT MORNING ON MY KNEES, FEELING LIKE I'D BEEN run over by a truck. It took me a few days, but the answer came, and when I finally heard it, it was almost as if I'd always known the answer. I feel like prayer has become an important part of my life, but even more important than prayer, at least for me, is the act of listening. I have never thought much about mysticism, but I have begun wondering if there isn't some mystic connection to whatever it is that lies beyond; almost like the universe is waiting for us to ask before it is allowed to show us all its secrets.

If you had asked me a year ago if there was a God, I might have argued that there couldn't be because I'd never seen him. But today, six months after attempting suicide, I have to say I know there is something there. I don't know how to define it or describe what it looks like, but I do know what it feels like. There is a warmth and a strength that oozes with positive feelings and a sense of endless possibilities.

I'm quite sure I didn't understand the perils of hopelessness until I began to understand the possibilities of light. Sitting on this bench has reminded me of that stark contrast and reality. In the past months I have dreamed many times of the woman in the white dress. She has continued to bring me hope. Those

DREAMS HAVE GIVEN ME A SENSE OF WORTH THAT I NEVER KNEW BEFORE. I STILL HAVE BAD DAYS AND HARD TIMES. I CONTINUALLY WONDER WHY I WAS ALLOWED TO LIVE AND I'VE STRUGGLED AS I'VE LOOKED FOR THE MEANING AND UNDERSTANDING OF LIFE. BUT I'M ALIVE! THROUGH THE STRUGGLE, THE ANSWERS HAVE COME AND THEY HAVE BOTH SATISFIED ME AND ENCOURAGED ME TO CONTINUE TO SEEK. WITH NEARLY EVERY FUNERAL I ATTEND, I FEEL AS IF I COME CLOSER TO UNDERSTANDING WHAT LIFE IS ALL ABOUT. TODAY, FOR ME, IT ALL HINGES ON THREE THINGS: LEARNING HOW TO LOVE, SEEKING JOY, AND LEARNING TO KNOW GOD. AND PERHAPS, WHEN IT COMES RIGHT DOWN TO IT, THEY ARE ALL THE SAME THING. I'M NOT SURE IF ONE CAN TRULY LOVE WITHOUT KNOWING GOD AND I'M CERTAIN WE CAN'T TRULY KNOW GOD WITHOUT LOVE IN OUR HEARTS. AND I'M NOT SURE ANYONE CAN EXPERIENCE JOY WITHOUT THOSE THINGS.

TELL YOUR CHILDREN WHEN YOU ARE PROUD OF THEM.

DON'T WORRY- BE HAPPY.

WHEN I GO BALD, I WANT TO GO BALD WITH DIGNITY—SAY NO TO TOUPEES!!

FUNERAL THOUGHTS

"DON'T BE AFRAID OF SAYING 'I LOVE YOU.'"

"GET OUT OF YOUR OWN WAY." –BB

"WHEN SHE SPOKE, HER WORDS WERE WORTH LISTENING TO."

"SHE HAD A REAL TALENT FOR TURNING STYROFOAM INTO THINGS OF BEAUTY."

"I MADE THE LIVING, BUT BETTY MADE ME—AND THE LIVING WORTHWHILE."

"SHE WAS CONVINCED THAT YOU DON'T HAVE TO BEAR CHILDREN TO SERVE AS A MOTHER OR FATHER."

"I LOVE YOU, LET'S ALWAYS BE CLOSE."

"LEAVE TREASURES FOR YOUR KIDS TO FIND AFTER YOU ARE GONE."

"MAKE GOOD USE OF YOUR TIME."

"CHASE YOUR DREAMS."

"CELEBRATE YOUR BIRTHDAY ALL MONTH LONG."

Take time to feed the ducks. You may never know when you will need their help. –BB

LEARN TO WRITE LETTERS. PEOPLE KEEP THEM.

* CHAPTER 13 *
THE ARMADILLO AND THE RAVEN

BEAUTIFUL LIGHT IS BORN OF DARKNESS,
SO THE FAITH THAT SPRINGS FROM CONFLICT
IS OFTEN THE STRONGEST AND THE BEST.
—R. TURNBULL

Paul looked up from the journal and into Rachel's eyes. She looked tired, but her eyes were also filled with compassion.

"I'm so sorry," she said, reaching out to take his hand.

"For what?"

"For not listening. I'm sorry I thought the woman in the long, white dress was some kind of secret fantasy. I'm sorry I never let you tell me your story."

He turned his head to the back seat quickly.

"She's asleep," Rachel said, reassuringly. "She dozed off a few minutes ago. We stayed up late last night watching a movie waiting for you to get home."

"Do you want me to drive?"

Rachel shook her head. "No, I want you to talk to me."

"Sure, about what?"

"I want you to tell me about that bench. Is that the same bench where you asked me to marry you?"

"Yes."

She squeezed his hand as a tear rolled down her cheek. "I'm sorry," she repeated, shaking her head. "I'm sorry I couldn't hear you then."

"It's okay."

"No, it's not." Her words came out softly, almost a whisper. "You've taken me back to that bench every time we've been in Kenosha, and I've never been able to hear you, have I?" She looked him in the eyes before turning back to the road, a look of disappointment on her face.

"No," he finally said.

Tears began to fall freely as she looked out on the road. "I'm so sorry," she whispered again.

"I'm sorry I couldn't find a better way to tell you. I guess I … I always hoped I could. I never stopped praying that when I told you, you could hear me, that you could understand."

She shook her head again. "I'm sorry."

Paul wiped a tear from her cheek with the back of his hand. "I love you," he whispered.

"Even after I was so close-minded?"

"Yeah," he said, assuringly, squeezing her hand again.

"I've been so selfish."

"What do you mean?"

"You've needed to talk, and I've shut you down."

Paul was silent. She was right. So many times he'd tried. So many times he'd been disappointed that she couldn't or wouldn't hear him.

"I realized when you started talking about the bench that you have been trying to tell me this story ever since … ever since the beginning, haven't you?"

Paul nodded. "I never wanted to keep anything from you. I wanted you to know what you were getting yourself into from the very beginning. I felt like you deserved to know."

"And I shut you down."

"Hey, I can't imagine it being very easy to hear that the guy you were falling in love with tried to commit suicide. It has never been anything I was proud of. I tried to tell you early on because I felt like you deserved to know, and I wanted to give you a way out if you wanted one."

Rachel shook her head. "I never would have wanted out. You tried, which is way more than ..." She stopped herself and looked away.

"Which is way more than …?" he repeated.

A long pause followed. Finally, she shook her head. "I'm sorry, I can't."

Paul looked away, trying not to feel hurt.

"I'm sorry, Paul, I'm just not ready to talk about it."

"Rachel, you know you can tell me anything. I'm right here. I always will be. I'm not going anywhere."

"I know." Tears continued to fall and Paul waited patiently, quietly. "I will tell you," she whispered, "but not now. I don't want Eve to know. I've protected her from my history for this long, and maybe there will come a day when I'll tell her everything. But I hope there will never come a time that I have to."

"Why do you think I changed my name?"

She looked at him, surprised.

"I've tried for the past seven years to protect her from the person I once was. There is a lot about me that you don't know, like most of my first twenty-six years. I started going by my middle name a few months before we met, when I began imagining a time I could tell my children about a boy named Wolf. I imagined it might be the easiest way."

"Has it been?"

"I don't know. I've imagined it a thousand times over the past ten years—trying to play it out in dozens of different scenarios." He smiled to himself, shaking his head. "I don't think I ever could have imagined it playing out this way. I never figured I would see this book again." He rolled his neck and tried to massage his shoulders. "I never thought it would come out on a road trip where I'd spend half the trip looking backwards."

"But we always do, don't we, no matter how hard we try."

"What do you mean?"

"We spend our time looking backwards."

"Hmm. Yeah, I guess we do. As much as we try to live in the present and plan to make the future even brighter, we still can't shake our past. I can't think of any way to get around that, can you?"

She shook her head. "You have no idea how many times I've wished I could change my past. There's so much I wish I could undo, or at least redo. That's one of the reasons I'm most grateful for Eve."

"Why?"

"Because it gives me a chance to remake the world—to hopefully give her a better childhood than I had."

"I know. I've had the same thoughts," Paul responded.

Rachel nodded her head, but kept her eyes on the road. "I know."

"How do you know?"

"Because I've spent the last seven years listening to the stories you've told her, trying to put together the bits and pieces of truth that you sprinkle in with your adventures of she-bears and armadillos."

Paul grinned. "Were they that transparent?"

"Hey, I'm a writer, remember, give me some credit. I know the language of metaphor."

Paul smiled, but the confused look on his face betrayed him.

"Writers write what they know, and storytellers tell stories about what they know the best."

"Oh, you mean like when Bob the Armadillo made friends with Chucky the Chipmunk," he said sarcastically.

"No, not exactly. More like when Bob the Armadillo went ice fishing with his friend George the Beaver and fell through the ice and would have drowned if it wasn't for Alex the Goose."

"I guess I am that transparent."

"Yes you are, Bob, the Armadillo—an animal with a tough shell that protects his soft heart."

"Wow, it sounds like you've got me figured out."

"IF YOU'RE GOING TO DO THE JOB, DO A JOB YOU CAN BE PROUD OF."

"Pretty much. But I've always wondered why you made me Susie the Raven."

Paul smiled. "You're not always Susie the Raven. Sometimes you're Polly the Porcupine."

"I am?"

"Yep. And occasionally you're Charlotte, the Crocodile."

"What? I never got those. What are those supposed to mean?"

"You want me to give away all my secrets?"

"Isn't that what this is about?"

"I guess you're right. I suppose the porcupine is pretty similar to the armadillo—a prickly shell protecting a very soft heart."

"Are you calling me prickly?"

"Not necessarily, but sometimes you bristle to make yourself look a little more fierce. Then you usually walk away when anyone calls your bluff. You want to be tough, but underneath it all you're soft and harmless."

"Interesting. And the Raven?"

"I read a story once when I was a kid about a raven that lived in a church tower, and its nest was filled with all sorts of shiny treasures that it guarded passionately, plucking out the eyeballs of any intruder."

" And the crocodile?"

"Well, that's kind of a new one."

"And?"

"I'm not so sure you'll like it."

"Why not?"

"Because its about … it's about how crocodiles like to chomp on the legs of anyone who gets too close to their territory, especially if anyone comes near their nest."

"And how does that symbolize me?" she asked, one eyebrow raised.

Paul laughed, trying to release the sudden swell of tension. "I knew you wouldn't like it, but you're a very protective mom, you know. That's a good thing. Eve is lucky to have you. You're a much more attentive mom than I ever had."

"Do you think I'm too protective?"

"I don't think I want to take that loaded question."

"Paul?"

He squirmed. "If Eve were a boy, I'd worry a bit, but no. A crocodile is not a bad thing. It's fiercely loyal and protective, and those are positive attributes, right?"

"Yeah, I guess, but there was something else you said—something about chomping on legs, or getting too close to its territory. What does that mean?"

Paul looked out the window and was slow to respond, trying to find the right words. She had him in a corner, but he knew he had to be sensitive. He was sorry he even mentioned the crocodile, or the porcupine, but he had. In their ten years of marriage, this discussion had already come closer to unlocking the door to the unmentionable past than any discussion they'd ever had. Rachel had always been so protective, shielding what was obviously a very sensitive matter. "I don't know what to say," he finally muttered. "I just want you to know that when you finally decide to open up and share the things you've been hiding in your nest, I'm ready to listen, and I'll always love you."

She took a deep breath and nodded. "What else is in that book of yours?"

He turned back to the book, feeling disappointed that the subject he'd hoped to talk about for the better part of eleven years was being changed again, but he knew from experience that he shouldn't push it. He knew he had to continue to be patient. It was better than having his eyeballs plucked out of his head. But he knew the Raven was still not ready to share with him the contents of her nest. He wondered if she ever would be.

PLAN PARTIES AT OTHER PEOPLE'S HOUSES.

-CHAPTER 14-
MOVING ON

I DO NOT SEEK TO UNDERSTAND THAT I MAY BELIEVE, BUT I BELIEVE THAT I MAY UNDERSTAND: FOR THIS I ALSO BELIEVE, THAT UNLESS I BELIEVE I WILL NOT UNDERSTAND.
—ANSELM OF CANTERBURY

Paul opened the journal again. He turned past one page, then another, stopping at the third.

"Who's that?" Rachel asked, stealing a peak.

Paul moved the journal closer so she could see. "It says his name is Roger Curly."

"That's kind of a funny name for a bald guy. Why did you go to his funeral?"

"I'm not sure. I can't remember"

"What does it say?"

"Would you like me to read it?"

"Sure."

Paul began.

ALWAYS BRUSH YOUR TEETH.

July 16, 1999 2:35 p.m.,
the bench at Eichelman Park.

I'm back at the bench after a really great funeral. The music was beautiful, the pastor gave a great speech, and I was inspired by the things I heard and felt. Before the services even started, I was inspired by the feeling that was there as his children and grandchildren walked down the aisle with Mr. Curly's widow. He died of cancer, after being diagnosed only one month ago. He was only 72. I used to think that 70 was super old, but trying to look at it from his wife's perspective, I would have to say that he died too young. His wife could live for another 20 years or more. That's a long time to be alone. There was obviously a deep love between them, and I have found myself thinking about that love for the past few hours.

They were married when he was 19 and she was 18, and they just celebrated 53 years of marriage. His three boys looked very much like their dad, each of them inheriting his hairline. He also had three daughters who were fortunate to look much more like their mother. He must have had at least 20 grandkids. Everyone was obviously sad to see their father and grandfather go before they were ready.

Maybe that's kind of a strange concept – to be ready to say goodbye. The funeral that I went to at the Mormon church a while back, that woman was almost a hundred years old. Her family seemed much more ready to let her go than this man's family was. What happens after the age of 85 that makes death more acceptable? It's almost as if we expect it and wait for death after people reach those older ages. But it comes as a shock and a tragedy when the same illness inflicts someone twenty years younger.

It has made me think a lot about my own father. So many of my memories of him feel heavy and depressing. I have tried hard in these past months, since I gave up alcohol, to forget those negative memories. I know they have done nothing good for me. Today, as I listened to the funeral and even more as I sit here on this bench, I have come to the realization that we have very little control over how we are loved by the people who are supposed to love us. We can't make anyone love us, but we do have total control over how we love. And it seems that how we love tends to determine the success of every relationship we have in life. And maybe it's those relationships that matter most. Those are the relationships that bring us the greatest joy in life; the ones in which we invest the greatest portions of ourselves.

This man, Roger Curly, the last month of his life was a living hell as his body fell apart and the cancer overtook him. I can't imagine it was a pleasant thing for any of his kids to watch, but they were all there, loving him, helping him use the toilet, helping him manage his pain, and sharing stories and love. His family reminded me a lot of Dr. Dinglebottom's family. They didn't care what their father looked like or smelled like. They loved him till the end because he had spent his life loving them. To witness the sincere expressions of love that come from those who have been loved—I don't know if there can be a purer form of joy than that. I am sure they prayed for a miracle, and though their father died, I'm not convinced that they missed out on the miracle. Love is the miracle!

With the realization that I have no control over how I was loved as a child also comes the recognition that I have no control over how people choose to love me today. But I do have control over how I love, and maybe that's all that really matters. There is nothing I can do to change the past. No amount of wishing things were different will ever change the way things were, but I can influence the future by how I love today. If I can focus on that, I will likely be too busy to think about the past.

MY EMT CLASSES BEGIN NEXT MONDAY. I HAVE ARRANGED MY WORK SCHEDULE TO FIT MY CLASSES, AND I AM ANXIOUS TO GET MOVING FORWARD. I KNOW THIS IS THE RIGHT THING FOR ME TO DO.

Paul looked up to find Rachel smiling. "What are you thinking about?" he asked.

"About what you just said."

"Which part?"

"That part about love, that the only part of love we can control is the way we love."

Paul nodded.

"You've told me that before, but I'm not sure if I understood it."

"No?"

She shook her head. "I mean, it's obvious, right? We can't control our parents. We can't force them to love us the way we need to be loved, or do anything about the way we were loved. The way we are loved determines so much of who we become, and the way we in turn love other people."

Paul nodded, encouraging her to continue.

"How many things would be different in this world if people didn't have to spend so much of their lives sorting through the baggage they accumulated in their childhood? It's too bad we can't leave it all behind as we move into adulthood—that we can't sort through all the garbage to pick out the good things, and then throw the rest away."

"Isn't that what we've tried to do?"

"Yeah, but does it work—does any of it ever really work? I mean, we try not to repeat the stupid things our parents did, but on the way, aren't we making our own set of stupid choices? As hard as we try to be smart and sensitive, sometimes I find myself wondering if I'm not giving Eve her own set of baggage that she'll have to sort through for the rest of her life."

Paul nodded again. "So, how are we doing?"

"What do you mean?"

"I mean, what kind of stuff are we putting in that baggage? I don't know about you, but I feel like we've been pretty conscientious about the way we've raised her. We're teaching her responsibility and love and compassion for others. You heard her talk about her friend, Carter. How many other seven-year-olds do you know who know how to love like that? I have no doubt that we've made plenty of mistakes and that we're going to make plenty more, but I like to think that my daughter—that our daughter—is going to have a much different life than I did. I like to believe that she's growing up knowing that she's loved and adored, that she's an important part of our family. Isn't that what we always wanted for her?"

Rachel nodded.

"What's bothering you?" Paul asked after a long lull in the conversation.

"I don't know. Maybe it's just the fact that we're going home, that tonight we're going to be sleeping in the same room I grew up in, on the same bed where I cried myself to sleep too many times, feeling like I was more of a burden to my mom than I was a blessing."

"Do you still feel that way?"

"No, of course not, but there were lots of times that I did after Dad left. It's hard to feel love in a house where your parents don't love each other and your world is falling apart."

Paul nodded, knowingly. "Listen, I know there's nothing we can do to change that, but I do find comfort in knowing Eve has never cried herself to sleep feeling unloved or unwanted. The only thing we can change is the future, and I feel like we're doing a pretty good job at that, don't you?"

Rachel nodded. "I'm not saying that we're not trying our best. I guess I just wonder if our best is good enough. I mean, Mom tried hard to make life good for us, but I still grew up feeling—knowing I was a burden."

"I'm not sure there's any way to totally avoid that, do you?"

"What do you mean?"

"I mean, last I checked, we're human, and because of that we're naturally at least a little bit selfish. It seems to me that any time we have to worry about someone else's interest, they become a burden. I mean isn't that the definition of a burden—that we have to stop thinking about ourselves for a time and worry about the welfare of someone else?"

"I guess, but …"

"All I'm saying is that it seems that it's the burden of caring for others that makes us better humans. It lifts us out of our own fallen state and inspires us to be better—to be someone's hero—to give a better name to the human race by inspiring the next generation. You can't tell me you don't hope for that every time you look at our daughter."

Rachel took a deep breath and exhaled slowly, staring straight forward at the road ahead, but she nodded in agreement. "So, how are we doing?"

He put his hand on Rachel's arm, prompting her to turn and look at him. "The fact that we're asking that question suggests to me that we're trying to remain conscious of what we're doing as partners in raising a child. Just look at her!" he said, turning to the back seat. "In every way, she's beautiful."

Rachel looked in the rearview mirror. The tent Eve had constructed with blankets and pillows before they left was sagging now, but inside the cocoon was a beautiful little girl, propped up on either side by her favorite stuffed animals. Her hand was still clutching a bouquet of colored pencils with her pigtails framing her angelic face.

"We're doing the best we can," Paul whispered. "I have no doubt that we're going to make a boatload of mistakes along the way, but we're choosing everyday to love her. And that's what matters most. It will be enough."

NO MAN SHOULD BE AFRAID TO DIE WHO HATH UNDERSTOOD WHAT IT IS TO LIVE.
—THOMAS FULLER

» CHAPTER 15 «
SEARCHING FOR DINGLEDODIES

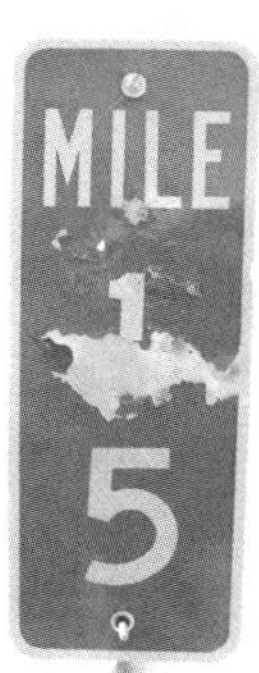

WE UNDERSTAND WHY CHILDREN ARE AFRAID OF DARKNESS ... BUT WHY ARE MEN AFRAID OF LIGHT? –PLATO

The journal drew Paul's attention again and he flipped through several pages before stopping at a funeral program that he'd stapled to the page. He smiled to himself as he read the quote on the backside.

"What are you looking at?" Rachel asked.

Paul turned to her and read it aloud.

She smiled. "That was what you were after, wasn't it? I guess I've never really understood until today, but

IN LOVING MEMORY OF
JOHN THOMAS SUMMERFIELD

But then they danced down the street like dingledodies, and I shambled after as I've been doing all my life after people who interest me, because the only people for me are the mad ones, the ones who are mad to live, mad to talk, mad to be saved, desirous of everything at the same time, the ones who never yawn or say a commonplace thing, but burn, burn, burn, like fabulous yellow roman candles exploding like spiders across the stars…
- Jack Karouac

you've been doing that for at least as long as I've known you—chasing dingledodies. I thought you made up that term."

Paul shook his head. "I don't know how much more of this book I should share with you."

"Why?"

"Because you'll find out I'm not as original as you think I am. You'll find out that all my best lines are borrowed, and all the wisdom that I have, if I have any at all, really belongs to someone else."

"Like what?"

"Like making sure we go out on dates regularly, and not arguing about anything that's more than two weeks old."

Rachel looked a little surprised. "Those weren't your ideas?"

Paul shook his head sheepishly. "I heard about those things by going to funerals."

Rachel smiled. "And making jam? That came from funerals, too?"

"Yep," he responded sheepishly.

"There's something about smashing fruit between your fingers that brings a family closer together. That wasn't your line?"

Paul shook his head again. "I made it my line, but no …"

"You're kidding me, right? That totally fits your personality."

"Sometimes you have to fake it to make it."

"What do you mean?"

"Rachel, after I got my second chance, I realized I had a unique opportunity to reinvent myself—to become a new person. I never made jam before that, and I certainly didn't save my change for vacation. To be honest, I'm not even sure who I was before … and I'm certain I wasn't nearly as funny or interesting. I went chasing dingledodies because I was attracted to people with passion, people that knew how to live, even though most of them, by the time I met them, were dead."

"I was just going to ask why you didn't tell me, but I never let you, did I?"

Paul shook his head. "Ya know, the funny thing is, I'm pretty sure you never would have liked Wolf."

"Some men are about as romantic as a fence post."

"Why do you say that?"

"Trust me. He was a totally different person; selfish, ignorant … lost. I didn't even like myself back then. I went chasing dingledodies and in the process, I reinvented myself, picking up a piece here and a piece there, scrapping together anything that made sense and felt right. I tried on a lot of different hats, trying to figure out which ones fit. I suppose I'm still chasing dingledodies. I hope I always will."

"I guess a lot of things make more sense to me now."

"Really? Like what?"

"Like why you read the obituaries every morning, and why you listen to radio programs like "This American Life" and "A Prairie Home Companion." It makes sense to me why you befriended Mr. Miller, and why the guys at the station all tell me you've helped them work through their problems. I understand why your bedside table is stacked with books by Transcendentalists and philosophers. And I suppose I can understand a little bit better why you can't sit still, why you always have to be doing something to sharpen your mind. That's why you hate TV isn't it? You'd rather be chasing dingledodies and sucking the marrow out of life."

Paul shrugged, then nodded. "I think one of the most important things I learned from my year of funerals is that none of us knows how much time we have left. We are born and someday each of us will die, but that dash that's carved into our headstones between the two dates ought to mean something no matter how many years that dash represents. When I meet the woman in the long, white dress again, I want to see a smile on her face. I want her to welcome me into the next life. I want to be able to look her in the eyes and thank her for a second chance to figure it out. I have spent the last decade of my life afraid of wasting a single minute."

"I love that about you. I love your passion for life. And I love that our daughter has inherited some of that same passion."

"I'm sorry that it overwhelms you sometimes."

"You do make me tired," she said, smiling, "but I guess that's the price of passion."

Paul squeezed her hand.

"So, what other stories do you have in that book of yours? Tell me about that guy," she said pointing to the funeral program he'd just read from.

"His name was John Thomas Summerfield."

"Tell me his story."

Paul smiled at the request. "John started an opera company because he loved to sing and to be around other people who had a passion for music."

"How do you start an opera company?" Rachel asked, looking both impressed and a little bit doubtful.

Paul chuckled. "I'm not sure, but I think that when you have a passion, you don't let anything get in the way of the things you want to do."

"Is that what he did for a living?"

"Yes and no."

"What do you mean?"

"I think it was Winston Churchill who said that we make a living by what we get, but we make a life from what we give. I don't know if he ever made much, as far as money goes, but he had so many friends, and his family adored him. Music was one of the things that made his life worth living, but his job was in the printing industry. Maybe it would be better if I just read what I wrote."

"Sure."

Paul looked for a minute, trying to find a logical starting point.

"YOU DON'T ALWAYS NEED A RECIPE."

... I'VE BEEN TO MORE THAN THIRTY FUNERALS SO FAR, BUT THIS WAS ONE OF THE BEST. BEYOND HIS LOVE OF MUSIC AND FAMILY AND BURNT ALMOND FUDGE ICE CREAM, MR. SUMMERFIELD WAS A MAN OF FAITH AND compassion. Before he died, he asked his children, all eight of them, if they would speak at his funeral and each one did, telling beautiful stories. One daughter talked about how her father taught all of them that the only way to actively love God is to care for His children; that God gives each of us errands that only we can perform. He taught them that with grace and wisdom, we can share the blessings we have with those who have less. He taught them that where much is given, much will be required.

One of his sons said his father believed it was necessary to be in a hurry in order to accomplish all the important things in life. They all said they'd miss his great belly-laugh that was quick and generous, making everyone feel welcome in their home. In fact, many of his children said their friends felt more comfortable in the Summerfield home than they did in their own homes. He was patient and kind, and the only time they ever heard him curse was when he was golfing. There were lots of reasons to be impressed with Mr. Summerfield. He was a man of both passion and wisdom. Like the funeral I went to a few weeks ago for Mr. Curly, his children all believed he died too soon. He was only 75 years old.

I've been trying to decide why this funeral was so good. There was a good feeling there. The stories were fun and engaging. He was a man who used humor to brighten the lives of those who loved him. He was a spiritual and humble man who seemed to have his priorities in order; always putting family first. As I listened to his children, I found myself feeling envious. There have been thousands of times over the years that I've wished my dad could have been more like this man. I hope that someday I can be the kind of dad I wanted. I want my kids to be happy to be around me. I want to have a relationship with each of them where they can count me as not just their dad, but as one of their best friends.

Writing this, I recognize that those kind of relationships don't come easily. If I had not seen this family today, I probably would have doubted such a relationship could be possible. Seeing their family—how they interacted with each other, how they loved each other, hearing how they loved spending time together as a family—it was awesome. His house was modest and his cars were old, but he has to be one of the richest men I've ever met. He had eight kids and their spouses, twenty-something grandkids and a wife who adored him and misses him. They all want to live the best lives they can so they can have the kind of family he had. I can't think of anything that would be better.

In contrast, I'm reminded of one of the first funerals I went to, back in January or February. I just looked for his picture, and it doesn't look like I kept it— his funeral was that depressing. I don't even remember his name and apparently didn't even write about him. He had three children before he divorced their mother. If I remember right, he owned a car dealership somewhere out on State Highway 97. He made a lot of money but lost his family in the process. The funeral lasted all of twenty minutes, and it was painfully long at that, with the funeral director trying to scrap together something meaningful. There was only a handful of people who came, and I was so depressed by it that I snuck out early. I knew there had to be more to life than that, and I'm glad I didn't give up in my search. I would have missed out on this one today and so many others that have helped and inspired me and given me something to aspire to. God bless John Thomas Summerfield and his family.

Do something everyday to improve your mind.

"My father was the most honorable man I have ever known."

-CHAPTER 16-
TRUST

IF I HAD EIGHT HOURS TO CHOP DOWN A TREE,
I'D SPEND SIX HOURS SHARPENING MY AXE.
—ABRAHAM LINCOLN

Paul set the book down in his lap and looked at Rachel, surprised to find her looking upset. "What's wrong?"

She shook her head, but said nothing.

"Honey, what's wrong?"

"Paul, we'll never have that kind of family."

"What do you mean?" he asked, feeling a sense of tension.

"I know you wanted a bigger family. I did too. But unless …"

"Rachel, I never wanted eight children. Where in the world would we put them?" he asked, trying to lighten the mood.

"But you wanted more than one."

"Yeah, I did. So did you. But you know, Rach, there are lots of things in life that we don't get to plan, that we don't get to decide."

She shook her head as if she didn't want to hear it.

"Rachel, I know things didn't happen the way either of us hoped or expected, but look at us, look at our family. There were lots of years I never even wanted a family, that I never wanted to risk passing on my genes to another generation. Remember those conversations, back when we first got engaged when we considered not having any children

MAN PLANS, GOD LAUGHS. – YIDDISH PROVERB

at all? I'm grateful we came to our senses. I don't know about you, but there's not a lot in my life that's worked out the way I dreamed it would, and I'm grateful for that. Things aren't the way I thought they would be, but they're way better than I imagined."

Rachel let out a long, exasperated breath. "I know life isn't fair," she finally said, "but sometimes, don't you wish it would be more fair? Don't you ever wish things would work out better—that things would be at least a little bit closer to the way we planned?"

Paul nodded.

"I mean, take my boss, Pauline, for example. She's fifty-six years old. She's beautiful and intelligent and insanely funny. She dated a lot of different guys through high school and college. She was even proposed to a couple of times, and even though she was voted most likely to have the most children, she's never been married. She's never had the opportunity to have children. She did everything right. She got her education. She has a good job. She's outgoing and attractive. I know she would love to be married—to have a family. She could have grandkids by now, but unless she marries someone who already has kids, she'll probably never have that opportunity. How is that fair?"

Paul had no answer. He wasn't even sure if there was one.

"I understand what you're saying—that life is probably at it's best when we can grow up, get married, have a perfect family, and live happily ever after. But what about the rest of the world? What about the people who only have a piece of that happy scenario? What about the people who have to deal with disappointment or illness their whole lives? What happens to them? And don't get me started about the people who screw up their lives with a couple of stupid choices when they're young and naive, or those people who have to spend their whole lives dealing with the stupid choices someone else made. What about that guy in your story who was hit by the drunk driver and probably is still dealing with the consequences of being at the wrong place at the wrong time? How is any of that fair?"

Paul sat silent for nearly a minute, wondering what he'd said that had triggered Rachel's strong emotions. She was right on all counts—life was definitely not fair. If there was an answer to Rachel's questions, he didn't know what it was. Before he could respond, Rachel spoke again.

"Sometimes I wonder about God. Sometimes I wonder how your faith remains constant when the world is full of questions that don't make any sense—that don't seem to have an answer."

"You don't think I have my doubts?"

"I don't know. I'm sure you probably do, but ..."

"Sometimes you have to fake it to make it," he responded when she didn't finish.

She gave him a funny look. "How does that apply here?"

"Rachel, I feel like faith is still a new concept for me. I spent the first twenty-six years of my life without it, trying to make sense of my world by avoiding even the mention of God." He flipped through the journal, stopping at a page with ornate words drawn across the paper. "I'm not sure I could have changed without the visits from the lady in the long, white dress and the steady reminder it gave me that something was out there." He pointed to the page and read what he had written more than a decade earlier.

"The sting of death is soothed by faith."

ALL I HAVE TEACHES ME TO TRUST THE CREATOR FOR ALL I HAVE NOT SEEN.
-RALPH WALDO EMERSON

Rachel looked at the words, reading them silently again. "What does that mean to you?" she asked after a moment's thought.

"In a word, everything!"

She looked at him as if she were trying to decide if he was serious. "Why?"

"Because it made me open my heart and mind to the possibility of the unseen."

Rachel nodded.

"There is a sense of responsibility that comes when you get a second chance at life that I'm not sure you can get any other way, at least that's the way it was for me. I think it's probably humbling for anyone to recognize how fragile life can be, but especially when you're the one who's conducted the fragility test, and you know how easy it can be to end it all. It made me ask questions I'd never asked before. It made me think about life differently. It's hard for me to admit, but it wasn't until I almost died that I first considered that there really could be a purpose to my existence beyond fulfilling my own selfish impulses.

"I know life isn't fair. I have a keen understanding of that reality. My family, the family I grew up in, taught me that." He shook his head, smiling. "I learned that the hard way, every day of my life. Holding onto that idea didn't make me any happier, and it definitely didn't give me any answers. It only turned me into a cynic."

"So what was it that changed things for you?"

He pointed to the words he'd written years before. "I learned to trust the Creator for all the things I couldn't see or understand. I already knew from my dream that there was a parallel world I couldn't see, but one of the funerals I went to early on gave me another idea." He flipped through the early pages, stopping at each of the pictures. He tried to remember who had inspired the idea that had shaped so much of his faith and eventually given him the insight that freed him from his cynicism. Recognizing the face of the woman who had inspired these thoughts, he stopped and began to read.

I HEARD SOMETHING AT THE FUNERAL YESTERDAY THAT MAKES A LOT OF SENSE TO ME, OR AT LEAST IT HAS THE MORE I'VE THOUGHT ABOUT IT. TO BE HONEST, IT SOUNDED LIKE A COP-OUT AT FIRST, BUT I HAVE TO ADMIT THERE SEEMS TO BE A LOT OF wisdom in it. Mrs. Garbett was diagnosed with polio when she was twenty-five years old and spent the rest of her life either in a wheelchair or struggling with the crutches and heavy braces that allowed her some limited mobility. She could have let that ruin her, but she didn't let her troubles get in her way. She already had two children when she was diagnosed, but she and her husband had three more children after that. Almost 60 years in a wheelchair! I don't know if I could do it and maintain the faith her family said she had.

One of her daughters talked about that specifically—how do you maintain your faith when there are so many questions that don't seem to have answers? She said her mom had an imaginary jar filled with all the questions she couldn't answer. Over different periods of time in her life, that jar could have hundreds of questions inside, or only several dozen, but she believed that even though she didn't have an answer to each of the questions, she always believed there was one. Her daughter said it took their mom her whole life, but at the end of it, she only had a few questions left, and those she believed would likely be easily answered in the next life. All of her children, as well as their pastor talked about her faith, how she believed it was important to have a faith that was both solid and flexible—solid enough to continue to ask God good questions, and flexible enough to accept whatever answers came.

When I first heard this, I wasn't very impressed. The whole idea of just putting your unanswered question in an imaginary jar and waiting for the answer to show up like the Easter Bunny???? Give me a break! But maybe there's something to it. I can think of at least a dozen questions today that I don't have an answer for—questions that would make faith difficult if that was all I ever thought about. But what if I could set those aside and practice believing? Maybe the answers wouldn't come tomorrow and maybe not even next year, but how would my life be better if I believed the answers would come? How would it be different if I could practice some patience and faith?

I have sat here for the past twenty minutes, and looked at what I just wrote and I think the answer has come. I remember watching the construction of the new gym at the high school, ten or eleven years ago. It seemed like it took five months for them to even get out of the ground after they dug the hole. It was hard to watch, waiting—rather impatiently, I'm sure, for the men to cut and tie the rebar together, build the concrete forms, and then pour the footings and foundation. It was only after they had done all that and poured the floor that they could build the walls and put on the roof. I remember thinking as I walked past the hole in the ground everyday that I'd be in college by the time the gym was finished. But I really didn't need to worry. It was amazing to see how fast things progressed once the timing was right and the foundation was complete. It seems like the walls went up in one day, and the roof was on three days later.

Maybe it's the same way with life and faith. Maybe the part of the building that we don't see, the foundation, maybe that's at least as important as the part we live in. You rarely see it and you probably never think about it, but if the foundation wasn't there, you'd know about it in a hurry. I've spent the last 26 years trying to make sense of life, but I don't remember giving any thought to spending time working on a foundation. I was so busy trying to survive and build whatever I could that I'm sad to admit I've been ignorant and impatient. I started building before I had a foundation, or even a plan, and my house turned out to be quite a mess.

So, maybe there is wisdom in the idea of Mrs. Garbett's imaginary jar full of unanswered questions. If I don't ask the

QUESTIONS AT ALL, IT SEEMS UNLIKELY THAT I'LL EVER GET AN ANSWER. BUT IF I GET HIGH-CENTERED ON THE THINGS I CAN'T FIGURE OUT, LIKE I HAVE SO MANY TIMES BEFORE, IT SEEMS MY PROGRESS WILL BE LIMITED AND MY GROWTH—STUNTED. I FEEL LIKE IT WOULD BE A GOOD IDEA TO FOCUS MY ENERGY ON BUILDING A FOUNDATION, AND SET ASIDE THE PERSISTENT QUESTIONS FOR ANOTHER DAY. I KNOW THERE IS SOMETHING OUT THERE. MAYBE IT'S TIME TO LEARN HOW TO EXERCISE FAITH AND START WORKING ON A FOUNDATION ON WHICH I CAN BUILD A BETTER LIFE.

He set the journal down on his lap and looked up to find Rachel's demeanor had changed. Her posture was more relaxed and blood had returned to the knuckles in her hands.

"An imaginary jar, huh?" She smiled coyly.

"Rach, we all have to deal with things our own way. I don't know if faith is easy for anyone. It seems like faith is a series of questions and hopes, and I think most of those are good for us to exercise. They make us think, but more than that, they make us look for answers."

"But you could go mad and spend your whole life looking for answers and never get anywhere."

"Yeah, and I suppose a lot of people do, but I have to believe there is a better way. I don't know the Bible very well, but I've been through it a couple of times, and I've noticed something that gets repeated a lot. It's the suggestion of asking with the hope that we can receive and knocking, so the doors can be opened for us. I think God designed each of us to be curious, to ask questions, and to look for answers. But it seems to me that in order to get the best answers, we probably need to ask the best sources."

"Go on."

"Take our tree house for an example. I needed a lot of help. Mr.

Miller wasn't a builder either, but he had some tools that made the project a lot easier and some answers that steered me in a much better direction."

"Yeah, okay."

"Things worked out pretty well, at least for a tree house. It's definitely not the best work in the world, but it's still standing. Eve loves it, and it's serving its purpose. Asking Mr. Miller for advice worked for a tree house, but all the advice he could give me would probably never be enough to help me build a home, or a skyscraper."

Rachel snickered. "I would have to agree. I love you, but I hope you never have to build us a house."

"Why not?"

Rachel looked surprised, like the answer to the question was beyond obvious. "Honey, you're a great fireman, but you're no builder. I think it's important to know your limitations."

"I couldn't have said it better myself."

"What do you mean?"

"I think the same rules apply to life's persistent questions. You said it—it's important to know your limitations. For the things that are beyond our limitations, it seems we have only a few options: we can either seek out someone who knows better than we do or we can get frustrated and sit around and stew about the problem until we turn blue in the face."

"Or you can try to ignore the problem all together and hope it goes away," she suggested with a smile.

"And there's always that. The problem—as I see it—is that most of us choose either your option or the blue-faced option."

Rachel looked pensive. "That's kind of silly, isn't it?" she said after a moment.

"Which part?"

"That we don't—like you said—seek out someone who knows better than we do."

"Yeah, instead we seem to hunker down into our mess and curse the world and the gods. And if we seek council at all, it's usually from fools

"I've been sideswiped by a geriatric conspiracy."

who are happy to make room in the boggy mire for one more."

Rachel laughed. "It sounds just like the clubbing scene."

"How so?"

"You remember how it was. You feel lonely and wanna find some new friends, so you go hang out at the bar with a bunch of other lonely people who drink too much and make dumb jokes, not to mention dumb choices. And you wake up with a hangover the next day, wondering why you can't, for the life of you, meet some nice, sober person who is emotionally mature and a contributing member of society. It's kind of a vicious cycle."

Paul shook his head, but smiled. "That sounds about right! Unfortunately that cycle seems to repeat itself in every aspect of life, doesn't it?"

"How do you mean?"

"Like Larry, ya know, from the station? His marriage was suffering, but instead of trying to find a counselor who could work with them, they both started talking to all the people they knew who were divorced."

"Oh yeah, I meant to ask you how that worked out."

"It didn't. I think their divorce will be final in the next few weeks, and they're both fighting for custody of the kids. It's a mess."

"You know his wife. Do you think they could have worked it out?"

Paul shrugged. "Yeah, if they were both willing to stop being stupid. But the sad truth is, it's usually a lot easier, once you've been stupid, to stay on the path to hell than it is to open your eyes, acknowledge your stupidity and change course. I think most of us, if we're not careful, spend far more time than necessary on a collision course with hell."

Rachel let out a long breath. "Isn't it depressing that so much of who we are—who and what we become, usually hinges on just a handful of choices?"

"They don't really tell you that in school, do they?"

She shook her head.

"What do you wish you would have known when you were … say … sixteen years old that would have changed your life if you'd known it?"

Rachel glanced at Paul, then back through the windshield, leaving the question unanswered. After thirty seconds, the silence became strangely uncomfortable.

"Are you okay?" Paul asked, resting his hand on her arm.

"Yeah, I'm just really tired. Do you mind driving for a while?"

"No, sure."

As she slowed and pulled to the shoulder, Paul found himself wondering if he had said too much or asked too many questions. As he'd experienced so many times before when broaching the topic of her past, Rachel had clammed up. Today, she had let him in further than she ever had before. But like every other time, Paul feared the door was closing again.

"Let's try not to wake Eve," she said when the car had come to a stop. "I'd like to keep talking."

Paul looked at her, surprised, but nodded as he quietly opened the door, sincerely hoping that this rare conversation might continue.

NEVER SET UP CAMP IN A SWAMP

-Chapter 17-
Seeds of Hope

A man can no more diminish God's glory by refusing to worship Him than a lunatic can put out the sun by scribbling the word, 'darkness' on the walls of his cell. —C. S. Lewis

As the car reached cruising speed again, and Paul merged back onto the interstate, Rachel reached for the journal he'd left on the dashboard. It was the first time she'd touched the book, and Paul watched her out of the corner of his eye as she flipped through the pages, stopping here and there to look at the different photos and scraps of paper that had been taped and stapled, becoming integral parts of the artifact.

"How many funerals did you say you went to?" she asked, breaking the silence as she neared the end of the book.

"Almost sixty, I think."

She smiled and shook her head. "And you really didn't know any of the people before hand?"

"No."

"What were you looking for, I mean besides dingledodies?"

"The meaning of life."

Rachel laughed softly. "Isn't that the question that has led men to philosophizing throughout the history of time?"

Paul nodded. "It's not a very easy question to answer, especially for the uninspired. Unfortunately, most of us who seek the answer to that question believe we have to both reinvent the wheel and kindle fire from nothing before we can even begin to find the answer to that question."

"How were you any different?"

Paul smiled. "I started my search with hope and a dream."

"Are you talking about the lady in the long, white dress?"

"Yes. I have to think that philosophers across history might have come up with different answers if they'd begun their quest with a dream of the world beyond. They may not have come up with the same answers I did, but it would have had to inform their thoughts and outcomes. I have to believe that starting out in a place of hope instead of despair could change the outcome for everyone who ever sought understanding."

"But isn't it despair that turns men into philosophers? Wasn't it despair that led you to the lake that night?"

Paul nodded thoughtfully. "It's a sad truth that most of us have to hit our faces on the bottom of the deep end of the pool before we can look up and realize we've been swimming the wrong direction in our quest for a breath of fresh air. It's unfortunate that most of us have to indulge in the bitter before we can appreciate the sweet."

"I guess that's what I mean. How else does change take place? Don't we all have to reach a point of discomfort before we're willing to change our course?"

"I think that's the way it usually is. But experience is expensive and often painful, and I want to believe that some, if not most of that, can be avoided if we can use wisdom to light our path."

"But how do you obtain wisdom without painful experience?"

"You open your eyes and look around and pray for direction along the way."

"But how do you pray for direction if you don't have faith?" Rachel argued.

"You usually don't, which often leads you back to the deep end of the pool on a dark and stormy night."

"That's really positive. You make it sound like life is a hopelessly broken record."

"Maybe that's the definition of despair: rotating through, again and again without the hope of moving forward."

"So, how do you get off that cycle?"

"I'm afraid a lot of people don't." He reached for the journal, flipping nearly to the last page where he'd written several quotes. He pointed to one, reciting the line without having to look at it.

MOST MEN LEAD LIVES OF QUIET DESPERATION AND GO TO THE GRAVE WITH THEIR SONG STILL IN THEM.
– HENRY DAVID THOREAU

"You think Thoreau was talking about the cycle of despair?"

Paul shrugged. "I'm not sure, but it certainly seems plausible. Aren't we all on some part of that spectrum? I want to believe, like Thoreau suggests, that we all have a song to sing; that we all have something amazing to give to this world. But fear and despair keep us from it—keep us feeling lost and in the dark. If we want to get off the cycle, it seems the only way is to consciously slow down, get off the train to nowhere, and find a better way."

Rachel looked thoughtful for a long moment as she considered the things Paul had said.

"So that's what this is about, isn't it?" she said, hefting the journal. "This was your attempt to get off the cycle of despair and find a better way."

Paul nodded. "But I'd like to think of it as more than just an attempt," he said, smiling. "This, like I was telling Eve, is the treasure map that led me away from despair and towards happiness."

Rachel pursed her lips, looking down again at the journal. "Do you believe faith is the only way out of despair and desperation?" she asked after a long silence.

He turned and looked at her, ignoring the road for a moment as he looked into her eyes. They had had at least a dozen discussions about faith over the years, but this was the most pointed question she'd ever asked. He knew she had struggled with faith—that it had never come easy. There were many of her questions that he couldn't answer, but this one was easy. "Yes," he said softly.

She looked back at the journal. "What about the rest of the world?" she asked after another stretch of silence. "How do they get out of despair?"

Paul carefully considered her question, knowing this was more of a time for understanding than it was for preaching. He took a deep breath before repeating Thoreau's words, more softly and slowly than he had before. "Most men lead lives of quiet desperation and go to the grave with their song still in them."

"Do you really believe most of us are in a lost and fallen state?"

"No, I believe we all are."

"Really?"

"Rachel, I know I can't speak for everyone. I don't know what's in the hearts of other people, but it seems to me, when I watch the people who cross my path, that most of us are struggling, trying to find our footing. We are all trying to make sense of the nonsense that surrounds us. I don't want to pretend that I have all the answers because there are plenty of times when I don't feel like I have any at all. But as I said before, I've learned that most questions have answers, and I believe there is a God who is anxious to teach us if we're willing to listen—if we're willing to admit we need some help—if we're willing to change."

"Maybe that's the part I least understand."

"What do you mean?"

"I've never been able to wrap my head around the idea that the death of a carpenter, two thousand years ago, can somehow buy my salvation if I'll jump on the Christian bandwagon and decide to believe. Don't get me wrong, I like the idea of mercy, but I'm fairly sure I've done nothing to deserve it."

"I don't know if any of us have."

COMFORT RETARDS GROWTH

"What do you mean?"

"Rachel, I'm not an expert at this … I … "

"I know." she said, cutting him off, "That's why I asked you. I don't want some canned, expert answer. I want to know why you believe."

Paul stared out at the road in front of him. He knew the answer, but he wasn't sure if Rachel could or would hear him. He'd tried so many times to have this conversation, but the time and place had never been right. Now that it was here, he wasn't sure if he was ready. He felt nervous and anxious.

"Listen, just because I exercise some faith in this doesn't mean I understand any better than you do how it works."

"Then why believe in it?"

"Rachel, I don't understand how it works, but I know my ignorance doesn't keep it from working."

"Isn't that kind of a cop-out?"

"I don't know, maybe, but there are lots of things I don't understand that still work, regardless of my ignorance. Right now we're traveling down the road at seventy miles an hour, and I'm pretty sure it's not just because we put gas in the tank. I could probably take this whole car apart, one piece at a time and still not understand how it works. Do you know how the TV works, or the microwave, or your laptop?"

"Well, no, not exactly."

Paul raised one eyebrow. "Not exactly?"

She smiled. "Okay, beyond plugging them into the outlet, I guess I don't have a clue."

"But despite your ignorance, they still work, don't they."

"Most of the time, yes."

"Do you know how your heart beats, or how an insect flies, or why the seeds of a strawberry are on the outside?"

Rachel laughed. "The seeds of a strawberry?"

"Answer my question," he chided.

"No, I guess I don't have an answer for any of those questions."

"Honey, I don't know why strawberries wear their seeds on the

"DON'T BE AFRAID TO LOOK DORKY FOR A LAUGH."

outside either, but for whatever reason, they do. I could spend my whole life trying to figure it out, or I could eat my strawberries before they go bad and thank the heavens for them."

"That's enough for you? Really?"

"Come to think of it, no. Those strawberries have actually made me very curious. I've never thought about it before just now, but I can't think of any other fruit that wears it's seeds on the outside. Can you?"

Rachel rolled her eyes, ignoring his teasing.

"I guess I'll have to put that on my list of things to ask God, if I ever get the chance."

She put her hand on his knee until he turned to look at her. "It's not that I don't want to believe; it's just that I don't know how."

He set his own hand on top of her's, reassuringly. "Rachel, I promise it's not as hard as you might think. I believe God plants a seed of hope in every person's heart. If we can shelter that hope from doubt and cynicism, and surround ourselves with true things, the warmth of truth will incubate that seed, encouraging it to sprout and begin to grow. And if we nurture that hope with faith, it can blossom and flourish, mature and prosper."

Rachel took a deep breath and exhaled slowly. "I don't know, Paul. I just don't know."

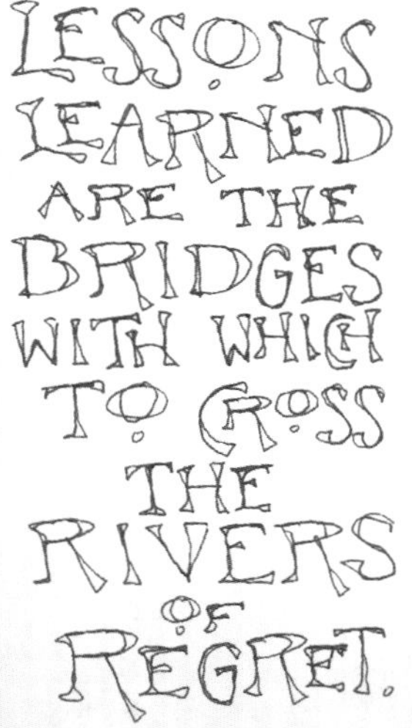

"THE ONLY WAY TO TAKE SORROW OUT OF DEATH IS TO TAKE LOVE OUT OF LIFE."

-CHAPTER 18-
ALMOST THERE

COINCIDENCE IS GOD'S WAY OF REMAINING ANONYMOUS.
-ALBERT EINSTEIN

Rachel leaned against the door, looking tired. Paul watched as she continued to leaf through his journal like she was perusing a magazine in a waiting room. He knew he hadn't convinced her of anything, despite his best efforts. Regardless of the fact that Rachel had always struggled with faith, he continued to hold out hope that something he might say could awaken the dormant seed of hope he believed was in the heart of all people.

Even with her struggles, Rachel had usually been amiable and even affable when Paul had suggested they attend church services whenever his work schedule permitted. He knew her willingness to attend was more out of a desire to keep the family together on Sunday than it was out of any honest desire to find answers. Many times he'd tried to see things through her eyes. Her mother had taken her and her younger brother to church from time to time when they were little, but that had stopped shortly after her parents' divorce. Though he knew she tried her best to hide it, he observed in Rachel a rare reverence as she witnessed the rites and pageantry of the services. Once she had even admitted that attending church services was something akin to coming home.

Paul knew life's trials had served as a roadblock to Rachel's faith, even though what he knew about her challenges he had had to cobble together from the small details she'd left scattered across the years. Twice, she'd mentioned that if there were a God, she couldn't believe He answered prayers. This was due in large part to the trauma of her parents' divorce despite her sincere prayers for the opposite to happen. Many times he'd wanted to share with her what he knew about God's respect of man's free will, even when that free will violated the desires of others. But he knew the time had never been right that might allow her to hear it. He knew there had been many times that faith could have proven to be a wedge between them, but he loved her for the fact that she had never allowed it to become divisive, especially around Eve. She had always peacefully yielded to him when it came to matters of faith. When he shared with Eve what he knew, as her questions about God had become more frequent, he always hoped that Rachel was listening as well. He hoped that somehow the truths he held most dear would find a place in her heart also. Having come to the light of faith through his own dark and dreary wasteland, he tried hard to be patient and understanding as Rachel traveled her own road. Waiting with love at the crossroads, anxious to encourage, he hoped that one day they might share in the faith that had preserved and empowered him.

Staring out at the road ahead, he couldn't help but wonder how this journal, this relic of his past, had come to find him now. It had been more than twelve years since he'd last seen it, and he tried to imagine the details of where it had been and how it had been returned to him.

Max, the man he'd known by only one name had been the recipient of this gift. Filled with the fire he'd borrowed from a year's worth of funerals, Paul had passed on this gift to a man he hoped might benefit from it. Every year on Christmas, as he remembered the dream of the woman in the white dress and the second chance her Christmas visit had given him, he also remembered this journal and the man who'd received it. Wrapped humbly in a brown paper bag, Paul had carried the journal inside his jacket, protecting it from the falling snow. As they parted ways

COLLECT SOMETHING INTERESTING TO LEAVE TO THE KIDS.

that night, after a rather lonely dinner, he bid farewell to two friends, expecting to never see either the journal or the old man again.

But here it was. He turned to see his drowsy Rachel, reading quietly from the pages. There was part of him that wanted to grab the journal and hold it tight, closing out the light of day; hiding the weaknesses he knew would be exposed—without edits or elucidation. But he didn't. Though he knew he couldn't expect it, there was a part of him who secretly hoped that sharing this very vulnerable part of himself might inspire Rachel to do the same.

"Tell me about something," she said, sitting up in her seat.

"Sure, what's up?"

"I noticed that most of the people in this book are old. How come?"

"Uh, because old people die."

"Yeah, but so do young people and middle aged people. Why didn't you go to their funerals, too?"

"Remember the story I told Eve about the funeral for that guy who drowned when he was ice fishing?"

"Yeah."

"Well, I think he was the reason that most of the funerals that I went to were for older people."

"Why?"

"Because, as I observed, most of us have to live longer than thirty years before we figure out our story—before we have anything good to share. I'm sure I missed out on some good ones because of it, but I had to be pretty selective. If I'd had more time, I might have been more open to funerals for younger people, but I noticed something happens to most people between the ages of thirty and forty."

"We start getting fat and going gray?" Rachel mused.

Paul smiled, running his fingers through the hair behind his ears that had begun turning gray in the last couple of years to the point that he could no longer pluck them out. "That's part of it. But in addition to that, most of us start to realize that life isn't all about us; that we're part of a global village, and that we have some responsibility to be contributing members of society."

"You didn't feel that way before you were thirty?"

"Oh, I'm sure I did, to an extent. But something big changes in your life when you look at your kids and realize it's up to you to teach the next generation the most important truths you've learned—or should have learned when you were younger. It's like you move out of theory and into practice, and in the process your story develops. After that, most people start thinking about legacy and the stories they are going to leave behind. The longer you live, the more and better stories you tend to collect."

Rachel nodded, flipping through several pages she'd bookmarked with her fingers. "So far, I've seen about twenty funeral reports for people who were born between 1915 and 1925."

"That many? Are you sure?"

Rachel nodded, looking up from the pages. "Was there something in common with these people that inspired you?"

"Yes, but it wasn't just me they inspired. Tom Brokaw was inspired by them, too."

Rachel looked confused, but then her memory kicked in. "The Greatest Generation?"

"That's it."

"I remember seeing that book on your nightstand. It seems like you read it a few times, didn't you?"

"Probably four or five times over the years. It's one of my favorites."

"How come?"

"Because it's about the men and women who most impressed me; the veterans and those who worked hard to support the Second World War."

"That surprises me."

"Why?"

"Because you're such a pacifist."

"Now you know why. After visiting the funerals for veterans and hearing their stories, it made me appreciate their sacrifice, but also left me with a hope that war can be avoided in the future."

"But didn't those men and women become who they were because of those sacrifices?"

"Absolutely. I don't know if you can become the greatest anything without sacrifice. They had a reason to live. It seemed they were united in their belief that their efforts could change the world for the better. But more than four-hundred-thousand Americans didn't return and another six-hundred-thousand returned home wounded. After hearing some of their stories, I can't imagine anyone returned home without some mental and emotional damage. War is a terrible thing."

"So what was it specifically that impressed you about this generation?"

Keeping one eye on the road, he reached for the right-hand corner of the journal, flipping through the pages, searching for the picture of a man who could answer her question. When he found it, he opened the page and pointed to the photo.

"Robert Stuart Matthews," Rachel read aloud. "Why did you go to his funeral?"

"Because I hoped he would be like Dr. Dinglebottom."

"What made you think he would be?"

"That he went to medical school on the GI Bill and was a man of faith."

"Would you like me to read what you wrote?"

"Sure, but …"

"But what?"

"But don't be too surprised if parts of it sound familiar."

Rachel nodded, looking curious.

OH, BEAUTIFUL FOR HEROES PROVED IN LIBERATING STRIFE. WHO MORE THAN SELF THEIR COUNTRY LOVED AND MERCY MORE THAN LIFE. – "AMERICA THE BEAUTIFUL" KATHERINE LEE BATES

June 20, 1999

Robert Matthews, or Bob, as everyone called him, was an incredible man with an incredible story. Though he was obviously a man of faith, his funeral was held at the Dignity Memorial Funeral Home because his church is being renovated. I'm glad about that. I'm not sure how it would have been if the funeral had been held at the church, but this venue opened the possibility for each of his five children to share their thoughts about their dad.

Bob grew up in South Carolina, the son of a tobacco farmer. He was six months away from graduating from high school when the Japanese bombed Pearl Harbor, and like many of the kids his age, he couldn't wait to join the war effort. His older brother, Jim, joined the Navy that Christmas, but Bob didn't like the water so he set his sights on the Army Air Corps. He left for aerial gunner training the day after he graduated. A few weeks later he learned that the destroyer his brother was on was sunk at the battle at Midway and that he was presumed dead.

By 1943, after flying nearly 30 missions over Europe, Bob's plane was shot down over Germany. He and most of his friends were able to parachute safely to the ground, only to be captured the next day. He spent the next eighteen months as a prisoner of war, losing more than sixty pounds. But the misery he experienced there didn't keep him from making the most of his time. He taught himself German and French and planted a garden to help supplement their lack of rations. Then when he noticed that many of the men were losing hope, he started a Bible study and a Sunday School, inviting anyone who wanted to come.

When he returned home, his parents, who'd been mourning what they believed was the death of two sons, offered to let him take over the family farm. But prison camp had left Bob with the desire to help people, so he let his youngest brother have the farm. Instead, he headed out to take advantage of the opportunity to go to school and study medicine.

Each of his children spoke about some aspect of their father's profession, but all of them mentioned how he believed it was an honor to be a healer. They each accompanied him on house calls and loved spending time with their dad. One son said his father was the most honorable man he'd ever known. One of his daughters spoke of her father's generosity, providing free or discounted service to the poor and the widowed. When he found his children wasting time during the summer months, he purchased a garden plot and gave them chores to do, teaching them how to work and take pride in raising food and sharing the harvest with all their neighbors. He believed that we are all created for a unique purpose and that by learning hard work, service, kindness and love, anyone can discover that purpose. He taught his kids that if ever they were unhappy, all they needed to do to find happiness was do something for someone else. From the struggles for basic survival he'd known in the prison camp, he hated waste. While some of his peers set their sights on the accumulation of wealth, he gave his away, believing God would one day ask for an accounting of the blessings he'd received. He taught his children and his grandchildren that the three ingredients of greatness are fidelity, kindness, and generosity.

He also taught his family that every man, woman, and child on this earth receives the same 24 hours each day to perform their labors. He believed each of us should have something to show at the end of the day for the time God gives us. He taught his children that each of us is responsible for our lives and that we can change, with God's help, to become better, stronger, more compassionate, and happier.

Listening to them talk, his kids made it

Endure trials with dignity.

SOUND SO SIMPLE—LIKE LIFE CAN BE WHATEVER WE WANT IT TO BE IF WE'RE WILLING TO GET BUSY, AND REMEMBER GOD ALONG THE WAY. I WANT TO BELIEVE THAT WHAT THEY SAID IS TRUE, AND EVEN THOUGH THE WARMTH OF TRUTH WAS THERE, THE CYNIC WITHIN ME WANTED TO ARGUE. I WANTED TO BRING UP THE "IFS" AND "BUTS" THAT MIGHT NULLIFY THEIR STORIES. WHY DO I DO THAT? WHY, AFTER ALL I'VE EXPERIENCED, DO I STILL FIND MYSELF DOUBTING THAT I CAN DO IT; THAT I CAN BE BETTER AND MAKE A DIFFERENCE? WHY DO I STILL ENTERTAIN THE NEGATIVE THINKING THAT TOOK ME DOWN? IF IT'S TRUE THAT HAPPINESS COMES FROM DOING SOMETHING FOR SOMEONE ELSE, MAYBE I NEED TO FIND SOMETHING BETTER TO DO. MAYBE I NEED TO LOOK FOR SOMEONE WHO NEEDS MY HELP. MY LIFE IS ALREADY SO MUCH BETTER THAN IT WAS SIX MONTHS AGO, BUT I'VE LEARNED ENOUGH TO KNOW THAT I WANT MORE OUT OF THIS LIFE. I WANT TO BELIEVE THERE IS A BETTER WAY.

Rachel set the book down and looked up at Paul. "I know you've told me that there were times when your faith was weak, but there's something really nice about reading it; knowing you weren't just making up a line to make me feel better."

Paul nodded.

"I'm confused though about the timing of this one," she continued. "When did you decide to become a paramedic?"

"I think that accident I witnessed was just a couple of days after this funeral, so maybe a week later. Why do you ask?"

Rachel looked down at the book. She leafed quickly through the pages again, stopping at the poem, "Invictus," just a few pages before the entry she'd just read. "It almost seems like someone else was captaining your soul," she said softly.

"How do you mean?"

"I mean, here you talk about wanting to be the captain of your soul, about wanting to stop making pizzas and make a difference in the world …," She flipped over a couple of pages. "and here, you talk about finding something to do where you can help people, and then a few days later you witness that accident and make the decision to become a paramedic. It just seems fantastic, like one big, crazy coincidence."

Paul smiled slightly, but didn't respond otherwise, not sure if she wanted a response.

"I mean, look at this," she said, pointing to the journal. "It's like you decided it was time to make a change … and exactly six pages later, bam!— you've figured out what you're going to be when you grow up."

"I guess I like to think of it as more than a coincidence."

"What do you mean by that?"

"I … I don't know if you want to hear it."

She looked at him for moment. "You're talking about faith again, aren't you?"

"Yeah."

"Do you really think that's what it was? Do you really think God put you in those places?" she asked, pointing at the journal. "Why can't you accept that it's just a happy coincidence?"

"Why do you feel like it needs to be?"

"Pfff, I don't know, Paul. I guess it's just hard to believe that one day your life is so bad that you don't know which way is up, and six months later, you feel like God's directing your life, like you have all the answers. I guess it just seems … unbelievable—like "happy Christian fiction." You know, the kind of stuff that's so cheesy it makes you sick."

"Are you feeling sick?" Paul teased.

She shook her head, obviously trying not to smile. "Do you honestly

BE A GOOD TEACHER, EVEN WHEN YOU OPEN YOUR MOUTH.

believe that every coincidence is God's hand directing your life?"

"Of course not, but I …"

"What?"

"Forget it."

Rachel took a deep breath. She closed the journal and stowed it on the dashboard. "It always comes down to this, doesn't it?" She said after a long, awkward silence.

"What do you mean?"

She turned her body to face him. "It always comes down to my inability to hear what you have to say. I just apologized, and I've already done it again. I've been doing this since … since before we got married. Every time you want to talk about this; every time something comes up about faith … I get upset and shut off, and you—you big jerk—you don't even get mad. You just let me boil in my own juices. I wish sometimes—just once—that you'd get upset and tell me I was going to hell."

Paul bit the inside of his cheeks, trying not to smile.

"Stop that!" she said, louder than needed for a conversation between two people who love each other. "You're so infuriating! You think I'm kidding that I want you to be mad at me. I'm not. I want you to be so mad at me that you can't see straight! I want you to be furious. I want you to storm off and not talk to me for a couple of days. I want you to scream and yell every once in a while and tell me I suck at listening. For crying out loud, why can't you quit being so nice and get angry?"

Paul sat there for a moment, listening to the echoes of what she'd just said bounce off the windows. He didn't know what to say, and the inside of his cheeks were hurting. He'd never considered that his reactions to her inability to hear him could have inspired this outburst. He wanted to apologize, to comfort her, but considering what she'd just said, he didn't think that was a very good idea.

"Mommy?" a small voice said from the back seat. "Are we almost there?"

YOU LIVE AND LEARN. AT ANY RATE, YOU LIVE.
—DOUGLAS ADAMS

Max

Do something that helps other people.

-Chapter 19-

Max

I am ready to meet my Maker.
Whether my Maker is prepared for the
ordeal of meeting me is another matter.
-Winston Churchill

Paul and Rachel both turned to Eve.

"Did you have a nice nap, Baby?" Paul asked.

"Yeah, but I had a dream that people were yelling at me. We were at the museum and I wanted to get closer to the painting, so I went under the red ropes so I could see better. That's when the people started yelling, and I woke up."

Paul glanced at Rachel before turning back to the road. "Do you feel okay?" he asked, looking in the rearview mirror.

Eve nodded, looking tired, one pigtail gone askew. "How much longer till we get to the museum?"

Paul looked at the dashboard clock. "Less than an hour now."

"What are we going to do there?"

"Well, there are lots of nice paintings to look at, but I was thinking that maybe Mommy could distract the guards, and you and me could borrow the ones we want to hang in your room. I've got my eye on one in particular."

Eve smiled. "Which one?"

""American Gothic" by Grant Wood."

"Isn't that the one with the man and the woman and the pitchfork?" asked Rachel.

"That's the one. I took some measurements before we left, and I think it would be perfect over our mantel."

"Daddy, do you really think they'll let us borrow it?" Eve asked, magic dancing in her eyes.

"I don't know, but it wouldn't hurt to ask. The Art Institute has owned it since 1930 and I heard they've loaned it to lots of different places from time to time. I don't think it's ever been in Chagrin Falls. Maybe they would trade us for one of your drawings."

Eve looked serious. "Daddy, I was saving my pictures for Grandma."

"Well, we've got an hour. Maybe you could make another one for the nice people at the Art Institute."

Eve looked excited and began rifling through her stuff in search of the necessary implements. She set the pad of newsprint on her lap and opened her pencil box. "Daddy, your friend is in my box," she said as she pulled out the long strip of paper with Max's photo on the top.

"How did he get in there?" Paul asked. "Do you think he was looking for a quiet place to take a nap?"

Eve giggled, handing the strip of paper forward. Rachel took the paper from Eve and was about to slide it into the cover of Paul's journal when she paused, staring down at the grey-scaled image of the old man. Paul watched, wondering what she was thinking. Considering how their last

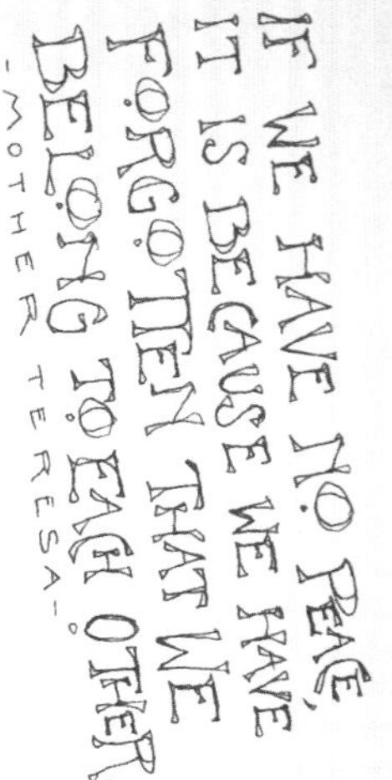

conversation had ended, he figured she was done for the day, if not the week. But he was surprised by what happened next.

"Eve, Daddy wants to go to a funeral tomorrow," Rachel said, craning her neck around her seat. "Is that something you would like to do?"

Eve looked confused. "I don't know. I don't think I've been to a funeral before, have I?"

"No," Rachel responded.

"Why not?"

"Uhh, well, we've never had anyone die who was close to us."

Eve nodded. "Do you think it will be fun?"

Rachel looked at Paul, deferring to him for the answer.

"Umm, I guess it depends," Paul stammered. "It's not the same kind of fun as playing at the park, but it probably will be interesting. I think there will be good stories and maybe fascinating people."

"The funeral is for your friend?" she asked, pointing to the strip of paper.

"Yes."

"Did you know him for a long time?"

"No, only about five or six months, but that was a long time ago. He was actually better friends with Wolf."

"How did Wolf know him?"

"He … he actually met him at a funeral."

Eve had a funny look on her face. "Was he alive or dead?"

"Why do you ask?"

"Because you said that most of Wolf's friends were dead."

"Well, that's true, but this friend was alive."

"Was he going to funerals to hear good stories, too?"

Paul couldn't help but smile. "No, he was going to funerals for different reasons than Wolf. Max was trying to figure out how to die."

"Why?" asked Eve, looking concerned.

"Max was tired of living, and tired of being lonely."

"But what about his kids and grandkids. Didn't they come to visit him?"

"No."

"Why not?"

"Because Max was a cranky, old man. He really wasn't very nice, not to anyone, and he liked to have arguments with anyone who was dumb enough to listen. I guess he was kind of like a spider who likes to spin big webs and wait for people to fall in so he can attack them."

"Did he try to drink their blood?" Eve asked with wide eyes.

Paul laughed. "No, he just liked to suck them into a conversation where he would try to convince them how smart he was by telling them about all the stuff he knew, trying to make them feel stupid. He was the kind of guy who liked to fight about everything from the color of the sky to who was the best baseball player ever, to who should be the president of the United States. He'd basically chased away all his friends and his family. He believed everyone except him was an ignoramus."

"What's an ignoramus."

"Uhh, it's like a nincompoop."

Eve started laughing. "You said poop!"

"No, I said nincompoop. There's a big difference," Paul responded, trying to keep himself from laughing. "A nincompoop is a fool—someone who doesn't think."

"Did he actually call people nincompoops?" Rachel asked.

"No, he usually called people much more colorful words than that. Wolf often wondered how someone who was so smart could have such a small vocabulary. On top of making everyone feel dumb, he cussed like a sailor, and liked to drink like one too."

"But he was Wolf's friend?"

"Yeah, well, Wolf tried to help him. He … he believed there was something good in every person, even if it was sometimes hard to find."

"He doesn't sound like a very nice person to hang around with."

"That's probably why he didn't have any friends."

"So, how does someone get like that?" asked Eve.

"Ya know, Max was really the only person I've ever met who was broken like that, at least to that extent. I think Max was so broken that he'd totally forgotten how to be happy. And when you're not happy, sometimes you trick yourself into believing that it's easier to make everyone else miserable than it is to change your own attitude."

"How did Wolf even stand being around him?"

"He probably couldn't have even imagined being friends with someone like Max if it weren't for the things he learned at a funeral, just a few weeks before he met the old man." Paul smiled shyly at Rachel. "He learned that if you want to be happy, the best way to do it is to be kind to other people and love them even if they have forgotten what love is."

"Even if they're cranky and call people nincompoops?"

"Yeah, well, it's not easy, but Wolf decided it would be kind of a fun project—to try to get to know someone who seemed so different than himself."

"Did it work?"

"I don't know. His obituary seems to suggest that he found something to be happy about. When Wolf knew him, he hadn't had any contact with anyone in his family for several years, and the idea of him ever being a crossing guard is laughable."

"Why?"

Paul smiled. "When you're a crossing guard, you kind of have to care if a kid gets run over by a school bus. The Max I knew probably would have figured one less kid wasn't such a bad thing."

"That's terrible," Rachel responded.

"Terrible, but true."

"How did you ever become his friend?"

"I guess Wolf must have introduced me," he said, winking at Rachel. "The old man left his car lights on at a funeral one afternoon and his battery went dead." Paul smiled to himself as the memory wafted through his mind. "Wolf had seen him at a couple of funerals. It was

GET AN EDUCATION.

hard to miss him with his big red bow tie and rainbow suspenders. On the day he finally met him, Wolf watched him sneak out of the back of the church when the congregation was singing the final hymn, but he didn't make it very far. By the time the rest of the congregation emptied out into the parking lot, Max had worked himself up into quite a lather. He was screaming at his car, kicking the tires, even cussing under the hood."

"What did Wolf do?" asked Eve.

"He sat in his car and waited to see what would happen, trying not to laugh. He'd never seen anybody act like that, and by the way the rest of the people responded, they hadn't either. One man tried to approach him, to see if he needed any help, but he ran away when Max yelled at him. The rest of the people tried to avoid him, taking broad detours to get to their cars as he continued to kick and cuss. By the time the parking lot was empty, Max had cooled down and was sitting on his bumper, pouting."

"Did Wolf help him?"

"He tried. He got out of his car and asked if he needed any help, but Max still had a lot of fight in him and pretty much chased him off. Wolf went back to his car and figured he'd tried. But as he pulled out of the parking lot, he felt like he hadn't tried hard enough."

"How can you help someone who doesn't want help?" asked Rachel.

"You can't. But there was something about that man that made Wolf think he needed to try again."

"You're kidding, right? Why would anyone go back to a hostile person who already tried to chase him away?"

"I suppose that question, or one real similar, was what Wolf asked himself, and as he passed a 7-11 on his way home, an idea for an experiment came to him. He turned around and picked up a couple of Slurpees and drove back to the church."

Eve smiled. "What flavor?"

"He couldn't decide, so he figured he'd put a little bit of every flavor in."

"A SORROW SHARED IS A SORROW LIGHTENED."

Eve's smile broadened. "Wolf knew how to make Wild Indians, too?"

"He sure did. Wolf is the one who taught me how to make 'em."

Rachel shook her head at the obviously politically incorrect term and probably would have protested if she thought it would have changed things.

"Anyway, when Wolf drove back into the parking lot, Max was in the driver seat of his big Oldsmobile. Wolf pulled up next to him and got out. Max was trying to ignore him, so Wolf opened the old man's passenger door and sat down on the seat next to him, handing him one of the Slurpees."

"What did he say?" asked Eve, bubbling over with enthusiasm.

"Who? Wolf or Max?"

"Max!"

"He took a big, long slurp of his Slurpee and then he said, "Ahhhhhhhh."

Eve laughed. "Daddy, what else did he say?"

"He said, "Who the heck are you?"—only he didn't say heck. Sailors don't say heck. But that's how they met, right there in the front seat of that giant Oldsmobile, and Wolf decided he'd found himself a project."

"Did Wolf help him get his car started?"

"Yep. He didn't have any jumper cables, so Wolf gave him a ride to Walmart so he could buy a new battery. Then he drove him back to the parking lot and helped him put the battery back in. By the time they finished, it was past dinner time, and Max surprised Wolf by inviting him to eat dinner with him. They went to Max's favorite diner where they spent the rest of the evening talking. Wolf told Max why he was going to funerals—that he was trying to figure out what life was all about, and Max asked him how many times he was dropped on his head as a child."

Rachel laughed out loud.

"He was pretty sarcastic, that old man, but he always made Wolf laugh, too—not that Max was really all that funny but because he was such a cynic. Wolf had never met anyone who was so sarcastic, and though some of the things he said were funny, most of it was pitiful. Wolf told him about Dr. Dinglebottom and some of the other cool people he'd met at their funerals, and Max told Wolf about cancer, heart disease and alcohol poisoning, the three most common causes of death in Wisconsin men. Max talked about his family and how each of his wives had died and left him lonely. As he spoke, Wolf recognized that deep, deep inside the cranky old man was a kind-hearted gentleman who'd probably eaten too much meatloaf and lima bean soup."

"That would make anybody mean," Eve said, a look of compassion on her face. "Did he ever turn nice?"

"No, not really, but it wasn't because of any lack of trying on Wolf's part. They usually met at funerals once a week after that first meeting. Max was retired, and he had a lot more time than Wolf, so he went to funerals every day, trying to figure out how the lucky people had died."

"Wait a minute. You weren't kidding about him wanting to die?" asked Rachel.

Paul shook his head. "No, his last wife had died several years earlier, and he couldn't think of any reason to keep living. Most days, he couldn't figure out if he was eating to live or living to eat."

"But what about his kids and his grandkids? Why didn't he want to play with them?" asked Eve. "I think old people like kids. Mr. Miller tells me that he likes it when I pretend he's my grandpa."

"Yeah, but Mr. Miller is nice. He still has a heart. Max … he really didn't have a heart anymore. I don't know if he'd thought about anyone besides himself since his last wife died. I'm sure there were times that he remembered he had kids, but he cut them all off. He told me they were all lazy, opinionated nincompoops. It was kind of a sore subject. He never had a nice thing to say about any of them, so Wolf always tried to change the subject, trying to find something positive to talk about."

"You make it sound like Wolf spent a lot of time with him," said Rachel.

"I guess he did."

"Why?"

"Because Wolf liked the challenge."

Rachel raised one eyebrow. "So, how many times *was* Wolf dropped on his head?"

Paul laughed. "I know it sounds crazy to want to hang around someone who is so cantankerous, but it kind of became a game for Wolf."

"What kind of game?" asked Eve.

"To see if being his friend could make the old man happy. But there were lots of times that made Wolf wonder if he was doing any good at all."

"Why didn't he just tell him to be nice?" asked Eve.

"I think Max had totally forgotten what it means to be nice—if he ever knew. There was some humor in it, at least at first, but when all you hear is the negative, its hard to look forward to the next time you get together. In the months that Wolf hung out with him, Max got kicked out of three diners because of the way he treated the waitresses."

BE A LOYAL FRIEND.

"Grandma's a waitress," Eve said, looking concerned. "Was he mean to her?"

"I don't know. Wolf was never with him when he got kicked out. There were lots of times that he felt like the reason he was with Max was just to smooth things over with the waitresses when things got ugly."

"Did he eat out often?" asked Rachel.

"At least once a day. When it's just you, it's kind of silly to cook, and I'm not even sure if he could cook if he'd wanted to."

"Mommy, remember, men need women to take care of them," Eve said, repeating once again the truth her mother had taught her.

Paul nodded. "You know, that's really true, especially for older men. Older women can function just fine without men, but men—they're a mess. Looking back on it now, I think Wolf might have had better luck reforming Max if he'd been a woman, but you put two men together—you might as well send them out on a fishing trip in a rowboat with only one oar. They just went around in circles and never got anywhere."

"Love people into change."

"So why did Wolf stick around for so long?" asked Rachel.

"Because he was a man, and he didn't want to admit defeat," he said, laughing. "Wolf had this crazy idea in his head that everyone could be saved from themselves. I think that's still the hardest game Wolf has ever played with anyone."

"Did he win?" asked Eve.

Paul shook his head, looking disappointed. "No. Wolf won a few minor battles, but he definitely lost the war."

"What does that mean—to lose the war?" asked Rachel.

Paul looked out at the road for a moment, looking thoughtful. "It was really hard for Wolf to admit it, but after five or six months of trying to soften the old guy up, he realized he wasn't making any progress. Max was just as smelly and hardhearted as he was the day Wolf met him. Wolf started getting tired of the way Max made him feel. He didn't think there was anything more he could do to help him change. For almost six months they'd been meeting at funerals and going to lunch or dinner afterwards. And while Wolf defended his reasons for wanting to live a long and happy life, Max tried to convince him that life was overrated and that happiness was for fools and nincompoops who didn't know any better."

"That's not true! It's good to be happy," Eve responded.

"I know it is, but some people forget that—they forget how—they forget that happiness is about having people to love and doing things for them. Of all the funerals Wolf went to, the really sad ones were always the same. Those funerals were for people who'd forgotten what life was all about and got caught up in believing it was about them. Wolf tried his best to keep the same thing from happening to Max, but Max refused any help."

"Did Wolf ever tell him about his dream about heaven?"

Paul shook his head. "He never got the chance. I guess … I guess sometimes we forget to share our best stories. Max had been so mean about all of Wolf's other stories that he didn't want to tell him about his dream and have him laugh at that, too."

"You don't think it would have helped?" Eve asked.

"I'm not sure. Wolf had started the experiment believing that anyone could change, but the more time he spent with Max, the more discouraged he became. It didn't seem as if there was anything he could do or say that could soften the old man's hard heart. He started coming home from his lunches with Max, believing he was wasting his time. Their discussions always came down to life and death. Wolf did his best to try to convince Max that life has a purpose and that making room in your life for God could help anyone understand that purpose better. But after all the sorrow Max had experienced, he had decided he was an atheist."

"What's an atheist again?" asked Eve.

"It's a person who denies the existence of God."

She looked confused. "You can do that?"

Paul looked at her wide eyes in the rearview mirror. "Some people do, yes."

"But how? Do they forget to go outside and look around and smell the flowers? How can people not believe in God when they see a sunset or watch bugs, or see birds fly?"

Paul thought of all the times he'd done these things with Eve and the lessons he'd taught her along the way about searching for God's fingerprints in the world outside. Everywhere they'd looked with a curious eye they had found those fingerprints on everything from a bird's feather to a pillbug's shell.

"I guess some people forget to look with wonder, and when you forget the wonder, it's impossible to find the wonderful. Wolf tried hard to help Max see those things, to open his eyes and ears and heart to the good and happy things in life. But he learned the hard way that you can't force anyone to see and feel anything. After hanging out with Max for several months, Wolf was tired of trying to help Max see. He became convinced that he was wasting his breath and that Max would never understand things the same way he did. He felt like he tried his best to bring a little bit of joy into the old man's life, but Max had taken it all and returned only cynicism, skepticism, and sarcasm. But as discouraged as

"DINNER IS NEVER COMPLETE WITHOUT DESSERT."

he was by the outcome of his project, Wolf still hoped something would reach Max."

"Did he bake him a magic happy pizza?" asked Eve.

Paul smiled. "No. If Wolf had any magic, that would have been a good idea. But since he didn't, and he knew Max wouldn't have any family who would invite him to hang out on Christmas, he decided to invite him to dinner at the only restaurant that would be open on Christmas night, The Star of India."

"Hey, we've been there, right? Where they have belly dancers, and the man at the front wears a towel on his head?"

Paul laughed. "Yes, honey, but it's called a turban, and I'm pretty sure it's not his towel."

"Yeah, and we had those yummy, thick tortillas."

"That would be naan," Rachel suggested.

"Yeah, that was good. We should go there again sometime."

"Sure," Paul responded, feeling a little distracted. "Anyway, so as Christmas got closer, Wolf spent some time thinking about a gift he could give Max, knowing that it would probably be the only gift he was going to receive. He thought about a new bow tie. He thought about a new pair of suspenders. He thought about a new pair of jumper cables. He even thought about a pair of fuzzy dice to hang from the rearview mirror of his Oldsmobile, but none of those things seemed like the right gift. So like men often do, Wolf put off buying a gift until it was too late. He went to bed on Christmas Eve feeling a little sad that Max wouldn't get a gift. But on Christmas morning, just before he woke up, Wolf had a dream."

"Did he dream about Santa Claus?"

Paul shook his head. "It was actually the same dream he'd dreamed exactly one year earlier."

"About the woman in the long, white dress?"

"Yes. He'd already had the same dream several times since then, but the timing of this one made him stop and think a little longer and harder than he had before. As he lay in bed, he picked us his journal, and he started reading about all the things he'd seen and the people he'd met in the last year. Just the day before he had filled up the last page, thinking about how his life had changed and become better in so many ways. He'd gone from a man who couldn't think of any reason to live, to a man who'd spent the last six months trying to convince a cranky old guy that life was beautiful. And the more he read, the more he knew he couldn't give that cranky old man a pair of fuzzy dice or a new bow tie. He knew he needed to give him the best thing he had."

NO MAN CAN JUSTLY CENSURE OR CONDEMN ANOTHER, BECAUSE INDEED NO MAN TRULY KNOWS ANOTHER.
—SIR THOMAS BROWNE

BE HAPPY WHILE Y'ER LEEVIN, FOR Y'ER LANG TIME DEID.
—SCOTTISH PROVERB

PLANT A GARDEN— SHARE THE FRUITS.

RECOGNIZE DEFINING MOMENTS AND MAKE THE BEST OF THEM.

"BE GRATEFUL FOR THE SHORT TIME WE HAVE ON EARTH."

-Chapter 20-
Old Men Don't Ride Ponies

The fear of death follows from the fear of life. A man who lives fully is prepared to die at any time. —Mark Twain

Paul paused and looked at Eve in the rearview mirror. Her eyes were wide in anticipation.

"I bet he gave Max a pony," she guessed, exuberantly.

Paul smiled, but shook his head. "That probably would have been easier, but he knew he couldn't."

"Why not?" she asked, looking disappointed.

"Well, for one thing, the pony stores were all closed on Christmas, and besides, old men don't ride ponies."

Rachel laughed.

"But there was an even bigger reason than that," Paul continued. "From all the things he read in his journal that day, and all the things he'd learned from borrowing fire from all the funerals he'd visited and people he'd met there, he knew that his gift had to be something that made Max think differently. The gift couldn't be a silly token. He knew

The only gift is a portion of thyself.

that fuzzy dice, as cool as they are, wouldn't help Max think about someone other than himself—they wouldn't help him think about love. But Wolf also knew the gift he needed to give him wasn't going to be easy to give away. He was stuck, knowing what he should do, but not knowing if his heart would let him."

"What was he supposed to do?" asked Eve.

"He felt like he needed to give Max his journal—this journal," he said, pointing to the book Rachel still held in her hands.

Eve reached for the book, taking it carefully in her hands and laying it in her lap on top of her coloring pad. "Wolf wanted to give this away?" she asked dubiously as she flipped through the book again.

"No, he definitely didn't *want* to give it away, but there was something inside him that told him that Max needed it. He fought with that feeling for several hours, trying to imagine what Max would do with it. He tried to figure out why he felt so strongly that he needed to give his journal away to a man who'd made fun of him for the things he'd learned and the things he'd tried to share with him. But every time he tried to find a way out of it, the feeling became stronger that he needed to give Max his journal. So Wolf wrapped the book up in a brown paper sack and decided to walk to the restaurant to give himself a chance to clear his mind."

"He gave away the treasure map?" asked Eve. "He couldn't think of anything else to give him?"

Paul smiled, but shook his head.

"He wasn't sad?"

"Ya know, that was one of the hardest things he'd ever had to do up to that point in his life, but as he walked to the restaurant, he thought about where the journal had come from. It had been a gift to him from Katie. It was a gift he knew that must have been difficult for her to give away, too, but she had given it to him in a spirit of love and friendship. That empty journal had changed his life as he filled it, one page at a time, with the things he was learning. He didn't know what, if anything, it could do for Max, but he decided it didn't matter. It was the best he had—the best gift he could think of, and though a part of him believed he was wasting it on a self-centered, cranky, old man, another part of him hoped that it might soften the man's hard heart; that he'd use the treasure map to find his own treasure."

"Did Max like his present?"

"I don't know."

"Wolf never found out?"

Paul shook his head. "Wolf waited to give Max the present until dinner was over, and they were walking out of the restaurant. That was the last time Wolf ever saw Max."

"How come?"

"That's something Wolf asked himself for many years. That night marked the ending of one year of his life and the beginning of the rest of it, and there was no going back. After he wished Max Merry Christmas and said goodbye, Wolf walked out into the snow and took the long way home."

"Where did he go?"

"He went back to the bench near the lake—the bench where the story began, but it was different this time. The year before, he had come to the bench hoping that the end would come quickly, but this time he came to the bench hoping the end wouldn't come for at least a hundred years. When he saw the place he'd almost died, he stopped for several minutes and watched the white snow falling, covering the mistakes he'd made like a fresh coat of paint. As he came closer to the bench, he noticed there was something there, shining, reflecting in the lamp light. Snow had piled up on either side of the bench, but this object, sitting in the middle—even though it was wet—no snow had stuck to it."

"What was it?" asked Eve.

"It was a rock—a heart rock."

Eve smiled. "You mean like the one the woman in the white dress gave him—like the ones we hunt for when we go to the beach?"

"Exactly, but this one was bigger than most, almost the size of my fist."

Eve's eyes widened. "Lucky! We never find any that big. Was it as big as the one on top of your dresser?"

Paul smiled. "Umm, yeah...in fact that's the rock Wolf found on the bench that night."

"How did it get there?"

"I don't know. Before that night, the only heart rock Wolf had ever seen before was the rock the woman gave him in his dream. Even though he'd had that dream several times since, the rock that she put in his hand was always gone when he woke up. When Wolf saw the rock on the bench, he sat down and cried like a baby. He just sat there, holding that rock, and even though the wind blew and the snow kept falling, Wolf had never felt warmer in his life. It was almost like there was a volcano in his chest.

"As he sat there, thinking about the way things had changed, he knew that life was so much better than it had been just a year before. After fifty-something funerals, he'd discovered the things and the truths that made life worth living. He was already five months into his EMT training, and for the first time in his life, he felt like he knew who he was; like he was on the right track. He leaned his head back and looked into the lamp that burned bright over the bench and cried again as he thanked the heavens for a chance to meet so many friends who taught him what life was all about by the way they lived and died. And when he ran out of tears, he stood up and put the rock in his pocket and walked home, dreaming about the treasure he knew was out there for him to find."

"Did he ever find it?"

"He sure did, and you know what? He's the richest man in the world."

Eve's eyes grew wide once again. "How much is that?"

Paul set his hand on Rachel's knee. "Exactly enough to give him everything he's ever needed."

"AN HOUR AT WORK WILL HAVE MUCH LESS OF AN IMPACT THAN AN HOUR SPENT WITH SOMEONE WE LOVE OR SOMEONE WHO NEEDS OUR LOVE."

"DEATH IS A TRAGEDY ONLY IF THE LIFE DID NOT SOMEHOW INSPIRE GREATNESS IN OTHERS."

"YOUR HUGS ARE THE FUEL THAT FILLS MY TANK AND KEEPS ME GOING."

"DO SOMETHING FOR SOMEONE BESIDES YOURSELF."

"I WAS SO WRAPPED UP IN MYSELF THAT I MISSED THE OPPORTUNITY TO BE WITH HER."

"CHOOSE ON YOUR OWN TO NURTURE RELATIONSHIPS AND VALUE LOVED ONES."

"SOMETIMES, PERHAPS MOST TIMES, YOU JUST HAVE TO DESIRE BEFORE BELIEF CAN COME."

"IT'S TIME TO FIX YOUR PROBLEMS."

"HIS HANDSHAKE WAS AS GOOD AS A SIGNED CONTRACT."

"COME HOME, COME HOME AND DWELL IN THE HOUSE OF GOD FOREVER."

-CHAPTER 21-
THE TRADE

FAITH IS THE BIRD THAT FEELS THE LIGHT AND SINGS WHEN THE DAWN IS STILL DARK.
—RABINDRANATH TAGOR

Eve had just completed her drawing by the time they entered the parking lot under Millennium Park. She tore the paper from the pad and rolled it up to keep it safe for the walk to the Art Institute. After making faces in the giant, mirrored ameba, "The Bean," they walked quickly to the beautiful pedestrian bridge that spanned Monroe Street and climbed sixty feet off the ground, linking the park to the Art Institute. A street musician was playing his guitar on the bridge, and Eve pulled on Paul's hand, halting their progression long enough for her to dance a jig and drop some of their fun money into his hat.

It was good they had come today, Thursday, the one day the Museum was open till eight o'clock. Paul had been here once before, but it had been years, and he'd been anxious to bring Eve here since she first began showing interest in art. Over his shoulder hung a backpack which held two sketchbooks and a small plastic bag filled with loose change. Rachel disappeared as they entered the security screening, and the alarms went wild as Paul walked through the arch carrying the bag. The screeners laughed as they searched the bag and found the change. "Admission fees," Paul offered as an explanation.

VARIETY IS THE SPICE OF LIFE.

"Are you a family of street performers?" asked the friendly black man with a grin that lit up his face.

"No, we're just artists," Eve said, as if no other explanation was needed.

"How many?" the woman behind the counter asked after they'd made their way to the front desk.

"Two adults and a seven-year-old."

"I'm actually seven and a half," Eve said, correcting her father.

"That will be fourteen dollars please."

While Paul pulled out the fun money, Eve caught the attention of the woman at the front desk again by unrolling her picture.

"What's this?" the woman asked, her previously stiff stance becoming more relaxed as she leaned over the picture.

"My dad said that sometimes you let other people borrow your paintings."

"That's right. We like to keep things fresh around here, so we often loan and borrow different works of art with other museums around the world."

Eve nodded. "I was wondering if maybe I could trade this picture for one of my dad's favorite paintings, so we could hang it on our fireplace?"

The woman raised her eyebrows and looked at Paul who glanced up from the change and winked at her.

She smiled warmly at Eve. "I suppose that would have to depend on which painting you were interested in?"

Eve stood up a little taller, impressed by the attention she was getting. Another woman dressed in the same official uniform stepped closer to examine Eve's picture.

"This is very good. How long have you been an artist?" she asked.

"Since I was a little kid. I was hoping you would trade me this picture for one of your paintings."

The second woman looked at Paul counting out his change on the counter. He looked up and winked again, trying to hide his smile.

ONE LEAK WILL SINK A SHIP, AND ONE SIN WILL DESTROY A SINNER. —JOHN BUNYAN

"Well, tell me which painting you like best, and I'll ask the director of the museum if she'll accept the trade."

"My dad said he wants to hang the "American Gothic" on top of our fireplace."

"I see," said the lady. She glanced at Paul again who smiled and nodded as if to encourage the play to continue. "Well, your father does have fine taste. That is one of our most popular paintings." She pulled a notepad and pen from under the counter. "Tell me how long you would like to borrow it?"

Eve turned to her father. "Maybe till Christmas? We could probably bring it back when we come to Grandma's next time."

Paul nodded.

The woman wrote down the title and dates. "Tell me your name," she said, smiling at Eve.

"My name is Eve Katherine Schafer. I'm from Chagrin Falls. That's in Ohio."

The woman smiled again. "Very good," she said, finishing her note. "If the director approves of your request, would you like to take it with you today?"

Eve looked at her father again and smiled. "Sure."

The woman ripped the note from the pad and paperclipped it to the corner of Eve's drawing. "I almost forgot to ask if your picture has a title."

"Yes, it's called "Milkshakes with a Boy Named Wolf.' "

"Oooh, I like the title. Should I page you when we hear from the director?"

"Sure. We'll probably be here till you close. Do you think he'll like it?"

"Absolutely, but the director is actually a woman. Her name is Sheron."

"Is everything okay?" Rachel asked, returning from the bathroom.

While Eve explained what had just happened, Paul slid the change across the black granite counter top and took the tickets, thanking the woman for entertaining his daughter. "It happens all the time," she spoke softly. "Listen for her name to be paged."

Paul nodded and smiled, unsure of what to expect, but happy someone was willing to play his games.

They looked at the map before climbing the marble staircase to the galleries. Paul tried to talk her into taking a guided tour, but Eve decided against it, her eyes dancing around like a kid in a candy shop. They made their way quickly through the Asian art, past the statues of Buddha and Shiva to a gallery filled with impressionist paintings beginning with Manet and Monet and continuing with Renoir and the huge painting, "A Sunday on La Grande Jatte" by Georges Seurat. But when they arrived at "The Bedroom" by Vincent van Gogh, Eve stopped and took a seat on the floor, staring up at the bold colors.

"Daddy, can I have my sketchbook, please?" Eve asked when Paul sat down next to her.

"Do you know who painted this?" Rachel asked, standing over her daughter.

"Of course. That's Vincent. Did you know that he cut off his ear because he was in love with a girl who told him to take a hike, and he sent it to her in the mail?"

"Yeah, I heard that. That's kind of creepy, don't you think?" asked Rachel.

Eve shrugged. "I thought that, too, but Daddy said boys do stupid stuff for girls all the time, trying to get their attention."

Rachel nodded, wandering off to another wall as her two artists sat shoulder to shoulder on the floor, drawing sketches of the whimsical painting before them.

An hour passed, then two, as they moved slowly from gallery to gallery, letting Eve take the lead. Paul watched her carefully as she soaked it all in. Just after seven-thirty, the speaker embedded in the ceiling above them squawked. The voice notified the patrons that the museum would be closing soon, but before signing off, Eve Katherine

MAKE LOVE YOUR GREATEST MOTIVATOR.

Schafer was invited to bring her parents and come to the front desk immediately.

Paul and Rachel hurried to keep up as Eve ran back the way they'd come.

"I'm Eve!" she said loudly from halfway up the marble stairs. The woman at the front desk who they'd met earlier turned to face her with a smile. Behind her stood a silver haired woman in a gray dress suit, a colorful scarf tied around her neck. Eve reached the counter, out of breath. "I'm Eve!" she managed. "Do you remember me?"

"Of course. We're glad you're still here. Director Martin has been looking forward to meeting you."

Sheron Martin walked out from behind the counter and stooped down to shake Eve's hand. "What a charming little girl," she said, grinning at her. "Are these your parents?" she asked, turning to Rachel and Paul who had finally caught up.

"Yes, we are. I am Paul, and this is Rachel."

"It's a pleasure to meet you. I assume at least one of you must be an artist."

Rachel shook her head.

"I'm a fireman," Paul said, "but I like to consider myself an artist."

"That's good. I'm glad you're encouraging your daughter. Has she taken any formal art classes?"

"Only from my dad," Eve said. "He taught me lots of stuff, but sometimes I teach him, too."

"That's excellent. You are a fortunate girl. I understand you are interested in a trade."

Eve looked at Paul then back at the director. "It's actually for my dad. He likes "American Gothic.""

"And how about you? What do you like?"

"I like Van Gogh."

Mrs. Martin nodded. "I've been watching you, Eve Schafer. You might not have noticed, but every room in this building has several cameras that help us protect our collection. I've watched you draw in your sketchbook. You have a wonderful talent. I hope you will use it to make this world a more colorful, happy place, like our friend, Vincent."

Eve smiled broadly and nodded.

"I don't normally do this, but I'm impressed with you. If you don't mind, I'd like to swap you that drawing of yours for a Van Gogh, actually two of them."

Eve looked at her, not sure if she should believe her.

Director Martin reached out her hand to the girl behind the desk who handed her a long white cylinder. "They are only giclee prints, but they're pretty darn good ones. One is of "The Bedroom" which you saw upstairs and the second is my favorite, "Starry Night," which you'll have to go to New York to see," she said, handing Eve the cardboard roll. "I was intrigued by the title of your drawing, "Milkshakes with a Boy Named Wolf." Where did that name come from?"

"From our trip. My dad likes to make up stories sometimes, but this one was different. He has a real friend named Wolf."

"Really?" Mrs. Martin asked, turning her attention to Paul. "Tell me about your friend."

Paul swallowed hard. "Umm, what would you like to know?"

"The story you told your daughter, I assume this boy, Wolf, is a real person?"

"Yes."

"And how do you know him?"

Paul looked at Rachel, then Eve, then back to Mrs. Martin. "I guess you could say we kind of grew up together."

"And where was that? Forgive my intrusion, but you don't often hear the name Wolf, at least not anymore. When I saw the title of Eve's drawing, I'm afraid it piqued my interest to the point that I, well, that I had my security team follow you around with the cameras."

"Security? I think you're probably thinking of a different Wolf. My friend, Wolf, and I grew up in a little town in Wisconsin."

"Which town."

"Oh, you wouldn't have heard of it. It's pretty remote."

Mrs. Martin smiled. "Try me."

"Have you ever heard of Adams-Friendship."

"As a matter of fact I have. I was there not so long ago." She looked at her watch, then back at Paul.

"Do you think I could buy you and your family dinner in exchange for some information?"

"Umm, what kind of information are you looking for?"

"I'll tell you over dinner."

"Aren't you closing in twenty minutes?" Rachel asked.

"The museum is closing, but as it turns out, I have a few connections and a key to the back door," she said with a wink. "Have you eaten? I don't mean to keep you if you have other plans, but our chef was recently recruited from Spiaggia, one of Chicago's best Italian restaurants. We're quite proud of him, and if you need to eat anyway, I would really appreciate any information you could share with me over one of the most scrumptious meals you'll ever eat. My treat."

Paul looked at Rachel, feeling sweat beading up on the back of his neck. "Uh, what time do we need to be at your mom's?"

Rachel shrugged. "She probably won't be home till ten-thirty. I think we're fine. You know how I love Italian."

"Can we have spaghetti?" asked Eve.

"Of course. When you eat spaghetti here you have four colors to choose from."

Eve's eyes danced with joy.

"Umm, I suppose a meal would be okay," Paul said, feeling nervous.

"Before we can see, we must first shed our tears and clear the way." —Indian Proverb

"Splendid, but I assure you it will be much better than okay." She turned to the girl at the desk. "Brenda, will you please ring up to the Piano and let them know I'm on my way with three guests."

Brenda nodded, picking up the phone.

"Please, follow me," she said, leading them to the elevator. "You won't regret this. There are two things no visitor to Chicago should ever miss—a day at the Art Institute and a meal at Terzo Piano."

THEY WHO HAVE NEVER LOVED HAVE NEVER LIVED.

AND YE SHALL SEEK ME AND FIND ME WHEN YOU SEARCH FOR ME WITH ALL YOUR HEART. —JEREMIAH 29: 13

SURELY HE HATH BORNE OUR GRIEFS, AND CARRIED OUR SORROWS ... HE WAS WOUNDED FOR OUR TRANSGRESSIONS, HE WAS BRUISED FOR OUR INIQUITIES: THE CHASTISEMENT OF OUR PEACE WAS UPON HIM: AND WITH HIS STRIPES WE ARE HEALED.
ISAIAH 53 : 2-5

A HEART THAT LOVES IS ALWAYS YOUNG
-GREEK PROVERB

GIVE ME CHASTITY AND CONTINENCE, BUT NOT YET.
–ST. AUGUSTINE

-CHAPTER 22-
THE LEGEND OF A BOY NAMED WOLF

THE TOTAL HISTORY OF ALMOST ANYONE WOULD SHOCK ALMOST EVERYONE.
—MIGNON MCLAUGHLIN

The glass doors of the elevator opened onto a white stone mezzanine. Huge windows to their right offered a stunning view of Lake Michigan from the Navy Pier to the north and the Shed Aquarium to the south. The lights of Dusable Harbor were just beginning to burn as they entered the restaurant. They were quickly seated at a table near the windows, and Eve's attention was immediately drawn to the sailboats returning to the harbor.

"Good evening, Mrs. Martin," said the waiter, pulling the visitors' attention back into the room. "Welcome to you and your guests." He handed each of them a tall, thin menu printed on thick, cotton-rich paper with the daily offerings printed on one side in dark, letterpressed relief.

While the waiter rattled off the daily specials, Paul perused the menu, feeling guilty at the price this stranger was willing to pay for his dinner.

"Can I start us off with a bottle of wine?" Mrs. Martin asked.

"Thank you, but no, I … I'm driving tonight."

"Of course you are. How about you, Rachel?"

"Uh," she paused looking at Paul. "Actually, I don't drink either."

"Splendid, neither do I. In that case, how about an Italian soda?"

They each ordered one and Mrs. Martin, after explaining that they were both small and delicious, told the waiter to keep them coming. She also insisted on appetizers, suggesting the cheese plate as well as the calamari.

"It's very kind of you to invite us to eat with you, Mrs. Martin," Rachel said. "We probably would have eaten at McDonald's."

"Please, call me Sheron," she responded. "It's my pleasure to host you tonight. It's not very often I get to eat dinner with live artists. Most of my artist friends are dead," she said, winking at Paul.

He smiled, but the wink made him nervous. Actually, there were lots of things about this woman that made him nervous and left him wondering what he'd gotten himself and his family into.

The waiter returned with the appetizers and sodas and took their orders, leaving them alone again in the nearly deserted restaurant.

"Tell me more about your friend, Wolf," Sheron said.

Paul shifted uncomfortably in his chair, unsure of what she wanted or even where to begin.

"Listen, I apologize for my nosiness—but I suppose I'm still in a bit of shock to have you show up today after painstakingly searching for information about Wolf. It's just … I find it interesting that you came here tonight and that our paths crossed." She paused to look at Rachel and Eve, returning to Paul with a warm smile that put him more at ease. "I've been looking for information about your friend,Wolf, for more than two years now. I even traveled to Adams-Friendship in April, hoping to find something, but I returned with only a file folder full of dead ends. I'm sure a professional could have done much better, but there has always been a missing link that I can't get past. It's almost like he doesn't want to be found."

Paul looked confused. "Tell me, how did you hear about Wolf?"

"A friend of mine told me about him a couple of years ago."

"Really?" he said, looking at Sheron more closely to see if he'd missed something.

"Yes. He must be quite a guy, but then you know him, don't you? Can you tell me why he wouldn't want anyone to find him?"

"Um, well, he's a pretty private guy. He's very shy. He really doesn't get out much. He's changed a lot over the years. He wanted a fresh start. He was tired of the baggage and the expectations, so he decided he needed to reinvent himself."

She looked thoughtful for a moment, then nodded. "Renatus," she said softly, her eyes losing focus.

"Excuse me?"

"Renatus," she said again, pulling her iPhone from her jacket pocket. "It's a Latin word and the title of one of my favorite pieces in our collection. It came to us in a rather round about way from a fourth-century monastery in Liguge, France." She turned the iPhone around for them to see. The gilded frame showcased a rather simple and crude rendering of two bearded men standing in a river, one with his hand raised above his head, and the other in a state of prayer. "It's one of the oldest Christian pieces in our collection. The word "renatus" means to be born again."

Eve reached for the phone, taking a closer look. "Did a kid draw this?" she asked.

Sheron laughed. "We don't know for sure. My guess is that he was probably a monk."

"Why did he draw the people with such big chests?"

"I'm not sure, but that's one of the reasons I like it. What's in our chest?" she asked, looking to Eve for an answer.

"Our hearts?" Eve said, unsure if that was the answer Sheron was looking for.

"That's exactly right, and I believe the artist who drew this understood the value of our hearts the same way we do today."

"GET OUT OF YOUR OWN WAY."

Eve nodded, handing the iPhone back to Sheron. “I like to draw big hearts, too.”

“That’s what makes you an artist. Before men and women learned how to communicate with written words, they drew pictures to express themselves and tell their stories. Artists have always had a special purpose, to tell the stories of their people. Caves and rock walls throughout the world record the stories of people who lived and died thousands of years before canvas and oil paint were even invented. They recorded what was important to them, telling their stories with pictures, so their children and their children’s children would remember them. Pictures like this,” she said, lifting her iPhone, “they inspire me, not just for the messages they evoke, but also for the passion of the artist that resonates through them. This artist, whoever he or she was, didn’t have the talent to be able to render things exactly as they were. But with the talent he did have, coupled with his imagination, he was able to share something with the world that we’re still enjoying almost seventeen-hundred years later. What I love about your drawing, Eve, is that you’re expressing your imagination and telling a story that is important for you and your family. I hope you’ll always do that. It’s those stories and our expressions of them that make life interesting and fill our homes and hearts with magic.” She nodded and winked at Eve.

Eve responded with a smile and a wink of her own.

“That’s a beautiful way to put it,” Rachel responded. “but I don’t have an artistic bone in my body.”

Sheron raised her eyebrows, looking surprised “Tell me what you do, Rachel.”

“I’m a writer.”

She took a sip of her soda. “What kind?”

“I work as a journalist part-time when Eve’s in school. But I’m working on a novel.”

“And you don’t believe your work is artistic?”

“Well, not in the same way. I’d never expect any of my articles to be framed and hung on a wall in a museum.”

DO THINGS WITH YOUR KIDS THAT THEY WANT TO DO.

"Perhaps not, but words can be a most beautiful art. The art on these walls can inspire, but words … words stitched together with passion and understanding have the ability to inspire people to paint and build and create new worlds. The human mind, when inspired by the imagination, is without limitations. You may not be able to draw a decent stick figure, but as a writer you don't have to. Your job is to inspire those who can, and for those who can't, your job is to inspire them to try. Your articles may never hang in a museum, but they can live in others' hearts and minds and inspire change. That, my dear, is one of the greatest arts there is."

Rachel nodded thoughtfully.

"And you," she said, with a wink, turning her attention back to Paul. "You are, to my knowledge, the only friend of a very elusive boy whose journal changed my life."

"You know about Wolf's journal, too?" asked Eve, looking quite excited.

Sheron's eyebrows shot up. "You know about the journal then?"

"Of course we do. It's in our car," Eve exclaimed before Paul could stop her.

"The original?" Sheron asked, looking very surprised.

"What do you mean, the original?" asked Paul.

"Well, I've only seen a photocopy. I actually was fortunate enough to acquire a copy that's fairly legible, but considering your association with Wolf, I'd be willing to bet yours is a much cleaner copy."

"Oh, our copy's great. It's leather and it smells like Mr. Miller," Eve blurted out.

"I'm afraid I don't understand. Who's Mr. Miller?"

"He's our neighbor," Eve continued. "He's an old man, but we adopted him into our family. He's a really nice guy, and he smells like Old Spice in the morning. I paint pictures for him because his grandkids live too far away to send him pictures, and he has a big lonely fridge that needs decorations."

Sheron nodded. "Please tell me the leather book you have is the original journal," she said, turning her attention back to Paul.

He glanced at Rachel, then back at Sheron. "There has to be a misunderstanding here. I'm not sure I know what you're talking about."

"Paul, please," she said, taking his hand in hers. "Two years ago, when my husband passed away, a friend of mine loaned me a photocopied manuscript of a journal that had been written by a young man named Wolf from Adams-Friendship, Wisconsin. I was devastated by the loss of my husband, but that journal—the stories I read about this crazy young man who was looking for understanding at the funerals of strangers—those stories healed my heart. They gave me hope." She reached into the top of her blouse and pulled out a silver cross that hung from her neck. "Those stories restored the faith I'd abandoned five decades earlier. I am here today because of those stories. After my husband died, I lost my will to continue, but those stories—that journal—I found myself again. I've read those stories at least a dozen times. The copy I have was made from my friend's copy, and hers was a copy of someone else's. I've shared several copies myself with people who needed the hope that flows out of that journal. Please, tell me you know what I'm talking about."

Paul nodded, taking a deep breath. He looked at Rachel who appeared to be at least as surprised as he was, then at Eve, whose smile filled her whole face. "I … I do know the Wolf you are talking about, and like my daughter said, we have his journal."

Sheron beamed. "Tell me about him. What has become of Wolf in the years since he wrote that journal? Has he written any more? Does he still go to funerals?"

Paul glanced at his family, wondering once again where he should begin and how much he should share, especially considering the questions that seemed to be without end. "He leads a very private life. I'm sure he'd be very surprised to hear that his journal has been photocopied and shared with others."

"Did he ever become an EMT? I noticed in his journal that that was his aspiration."

"He did become an EMT, and he works as an emergency responder."

"Can you tell me where he lives? I've been trying to track him down, just to thank him for saving my life."

Paul looked into her eyes, then looked away. "I'm sorry, but he's asked me to honor his privacy. If you'd like me to pass along a message, I'd be happy to do that. Then he could contact you if he wanted."

Sheron nodded, looking a little disappointed. "I understand. He'd probably be bombarded by people knocking on his door if anyone knew where he was. Apparently I wasn't the first person to go looking for him in Adams-Friendship. You'd think that the town would know a little bit more about one of their native sons."

"I'm a little confused, too," Rachel said. "I don't understand what the rave is all about."

Sheron sat back in her chair. "Have you read the journal?"

"Well, not really. A few things here and there. Paul told me about some of it. He's read it."

"Then you know," she said, turning back to Paul. "I tell you, there is a feeling of peace I get from reading that book that I believe the world needs. I have always been afraid of death, wondering what, if anything lies beyond. My husband was an atheist, and he never believed there was anything beyond this life. He was a fine man and lived a wonderful life, but he believed this was it—this was our one chance at glory. We did our best to make our days count, but something happened when he was diagnosed with a late-stage, rather rare form of cancer. Suddenly this life didn't seem to be enough for him—for either of us. We met when I was thirty-seven, and he was forty-three. By the time we finally sealed the deal a few years later, we felt as if we were too old and set in our ways to have children, finding purpose in our careers and our circle of friends. We had thirty-six glorious years together."

"I'm sorry," Paul said.

"Thank you, but there is nothing to be sorry about. We had a beautiful life together. That is more than most people get."

"Do you miss him?" asked Eve.

TRUTH SITS UPON THE LIPS OF DYING MEN. —MATTHEW ARNOLD

"Every minute of every day. Its amazing to me how we never fully appreciate the moments we have with the ones we love until those moments are gone forever."

"But you'll see him in heaven," Eve said, very matter-of-factly.

Sheron nodded. "I hope I will. It sounds as if your parents have raised you well, with hope and faith as your companions. My husband and I both were raised with religion in our homes, but both of us, in our own ways, set aside whatever faith we once had as we entered adulthood; believing faith was for the weak and the uneducated who didn't know any better."

The sound of the waiter distracted her, and they turned to see the man setting a tray down on the stand. After clearing the table of the appetizer plates and empty soda glasses, he removed the silver covers from each plate, setting one down in front of each of them. Eve squealed at the sight of her bright, yellow saffron spaghetti and dug in immediately.

"I'm interested by your choice," Sheron said, pointing at Paul's plate. "Salmon?"

"Yes. I don't know if you noticed but it's Alaskan salmon. Our selection of Inuit art here at the museum is quite small, but Alaska and the artists of the Northwest have always intrigued me. Did you know that some species of salmon migrate thousands of miles over the course of their lifespan, returning home to the same stretch of river where their parents spawned, and their story began?"

"Yeah, I've heard that."

"There is an old Yup'ik legend I heard once about a young man who fell into a river while he was fishing near his village in Alaska. Before his brothers could reach him, he was swept down the river and out to sea where his family believed he was lost forever. They cried and mourned his death, but the village elders promised his brothers that one day he'd return. Days passed, then months and years. The brothers grew old, but still they went to the river every day to fish. One day, their net was filled

"NOT EVERY MILE NEEDS TO BE RUN LIKE THE 50 YARD DASH."

with a haul of giant salmon and among them was their brother who'd come back to share the stories of his adventures with the people he loved the most."

Eve's eyes twinkled. She looked to her mother. "Is that true?" she whispered.

Rachel smiled.

"Every good story and legend has, at its root, some piece of truth. Sometimes, the more it is told, the truer it becomes. Since my husband's death, that story has taken on new meaning for me. It's stories like that that give me hope. Those stories make me want to believe that, like the salmon, there is something inside each of us that will one day awaken us to an inner longing for home, drawing us back to the celestial river that leads us to the headwaters where our story began."

THE OBJECT OF MOST PRAYERS IS TO WANGLE AN ADVANCE ON GOOD INTENTIONS.
-ROBERT BRAULT

DANCE FIRST THINK LATER

A FRIEND IS ONE WHO KNOWS YOU AND LOVES YOU JUST THE SAME
- ELBERT HUBBARD

THE SOUL HAS GREATER NEED OF THE IDEAL THAN THE REAL. IT IS BY THE REAL THE WE EXIST, IT IS BY THE IDEAL THAT WE LIVE.
-VICTOR HUGO

-Chapter 23-
Pumpkin Pie

Shared joy is a double joy;
shared sorrow is half a sorrow.
–Swedish Proverb

"I don't mean to pry," Rachel said, "but maybe you could help me understand something."

"Of course," Sheron responded. "And please, after all the questions I've asked your family tonight, you're welcome to pry all you like."

Rachel nodded and smiled. "I'm curious about what you said, or at least implied about your faith. You were an atheist, but you're not any more?"

"My husband was an atheist, at least until the day he died, but I was more of an agnostic—a skeptic."

"So, how do you go from that to someone who can profess their faith to strangers."

Sheron paused, wiping her mouth with her napkin. "I once read in a journal," she said with a wink, "a quote from an Irish poet, William Butler Yeats, who said, "There are no strangers, only friends you have not met yet." I couldn't have had this conversation with you two years ago. I would have had nothing to share. But life has a way of teaching you, of tenderizing you—whether you believe you need it or not. The day my husband died, I witnessed in him something I had never seen before. He'd been in and out of consciousness as we tried to manage his pain, but late in the evening, he woke up and looked at me. As I sat next to him, he raised his hand and pointed to the walls and the ceiling. His last whispered words were, "Oh wow! Oh wow! They're here to take me home."

"I can only imagine what that meant—he didn't stick around long enough for me ask, but even though I couldn't share his vision, I caught a glimpse of their reflection in his eyes, and the room was filled with a warmth I'd never known. I caught another glimpse of what that magic was as I read Wolf's journal. When you experience something like that, it's difficult to go on being a skeptic. I know there is something out there, and though I don't know for sure what it is, I have learned that true things have good feelings, and I am trying my best to surround myself with anything and anyone that vibrates with that goodness."

Rachel nodded. "I think I've always hoped that I could experience something like that."

Sheron reached out and took Rachel's hand. "Never give up that hope."

"Do you believe all people can have an experience like you've had?"

"No. I don't believe God forces anything upon us. I believe He waits patiently for us to be in a place where we want to know—where we're willing to listen. Sometimes we have to hit our head on the bottom of the deep end of the pool before we're able to look up and see that we've been swimming the wrong direction in our quest for a breath of fresh air."

Rachel looked at Paul and smiled. "That sound's familiar, doesn't it?"

"It should if you've read the journal. It's one of those truths that has always vibrated for me. But a truth I've discovered since I first discovered that one is that the surface of the pool, no matter how deep you are, is always much closer than we think it is. The Yup'iks have another legend, that the river of stars that flow across the sky—we call it the Milky Way—but they believe it is there as a gift from the gods of creation to remind us of where we came from, and like the salmon, where we will return one day. The Northern Lights, the Aurora Borealis, it is said, are the torches that are lit by the spirits above to guide the feet of new arrivals, while reminding the rest of us that the heavens are not nearly as far away as they may seem."

"How do you know so many stories?" asked Eve.

Sheron smiled warmly. "Because, since I was just a little girl, I have loved listening to stories. Stories have always made my life exciting. They inspire me and make me laugh and cry. Sometimes they reach into my heart and plant magic beans that grow and blossom, taking me to different worlds and faraway places. My friend, who gave me a copy of Wolf's book sent it to me a few weeks after my husband died. When I opened it, I was immediately intrigued. I felt like a peeping tom as I leafed through the pages, reading the stories about interesting people I'd never heard of before. She suggested I start with the story of a pumpkin pie. Do you know which story I'm talking about?"

Eve shook her head.

"Paul, you haven't told your daughter the story of "Don't Cry Pumpkin Pie?""

Eve laughed. "That sounds funny."

"No, we haven't gotten that far yet."

Sheron rested her hands flat on the table. "Never forget to tell your best stories to the people you love the most. That's the story that got me laughing again. I can't tell you how many times I've told it—so many times that it almost feels like it happened to me."

"Is it really about pie?" Eve asked, showing off her biggest eyes of the evening.

"Good guess," Sheron said cheerfully. "Do you mind if I tell it?"

"No, please, go ahead," Paul responded.

"Good." She looked at Eve and smiled broadly. "Have you ever heard of a parsnip?"

"Life is short. Drink chocolate milk with every meal."

Eve shook her head.

"They look a bit like carrots, but they're kind of a pale yellow, and even though they taste rather sweet, I don't think they were ever intended to be eaten for Thanksgiving Dinner, at least not all by themselves."

"No. You're supposed to have turkey and mashed potatoes," responded Eve.

"That's exactly right. But this story takes place during the Great Depression."

"What's that?"

"Well," she said, biting her lip as if she was trying to figure out how to explain it to a seven-year-old. "To be honest, there really wasn't anything that was great about it at all. It was a time when many people didn't have jobs, and almost everyone was poor. Many people worked all day just to earn enough to buy food for their families, and sometimes they couldn't even do that. But Jack and Margaret Mills had four young kids to feed who were under the age of ten. Even though they worked hard, money was always tight, and sometimes the parents went to bed hungry so their kids would have enough to eat.

"Jack was a carpenter and a handyman. Some days he would have lots of work, but other times he would go a whole week without a job. Two days before Thanksgiving, Jack came home with a ten-pound bag of parsnips that he'd traded for a half day's work. "This," he said, holding up the bag, "will be our Thanksgiving feast." Now, Margaret was a practical woman, and she knew how poor they were, but she also knew she didn't love parsnips, so you know what she did?"

Eve shook her head.

"Well, at first, she cried, but she knew how hard her husband had worked to get those parsnips, so she dried her tears and tried to be positive. That night, as she lay in bed, dreaming about sitting around the table eating turkey and mashed potatoes, and all the fixins, she had an idea pop into her head. She woke up determined that she was not going to eat parsnips for Thanksgiving dinner. So, when Jack left to look for work, she bundled up her oldest son and sent him out to see if he could sell the parsnips."

"Kind of like a lemonade stand?" asked Eve.

"A little bit like that, yeah. An hour later he came running home with a shiny silver quarter. She was very proud of him and sent him to the store to buy five cans of pumpkin pie filling. He ran all the way there and all the way back. Margaret put her boys to work and two hours later, she had five golden pumpkin pies cooling on the stovetop."

"They got to eat pumpkin pie for Thanksgiving?" Eve asked enthusiastically.

"Not so fast," Sheron said with a wink. "She sent her oldest son out to the street again, this time to sell pumpkin pies, and soon he returned with a dollar and twenty-five cents. That was more money than they'd seen in a week. But she sent her son to the store again to buy more cans of pumpkin pie filling, this time enough to make twenty-five pies. Her little oven wasn't big enough to keep up, so she talked to two of her neighbors and asked for help. As each pie came out of the oven, she sent her son out to the street to sell it, and before her husband came home, a line of people had formed outside their door. There were people who were waiting with money in their hands for the next pie to come out of the oven. By the time they went to bed, she had ten dollars, and with that, she sent her son and husband to the store to buy a turkey and all the fixins. The Mills family and their neighbors had a feast the next day; a feast that didn't include any parsnips. Every year after that, until the kids grew up and left, Margaret Mills baked hundreds of pumpkin pies to sell to her neighbors and the recipe was passed down the family line. She called it "'Don't Cry Pumpkin Pie.'"

Eve, who hadn't stopped smiling since the first mention of pie, began to laugh. "I like that story," she gushed.

"So do I. I think of it whenever I start feeling sorry for myself. It helps me change my tune and I find myself repeating, "I am the master of my fate …"

"… I am the captain of my soul," Paul said with her.

"You know "*Invictus*?"" she asked, looking a little surprised.

"Sure, I … it's something Wolf says all the time."

"I've imagined many times that he does. Tell me, Paul Schafer, do you know anything about the history of his journal?"

"A little."

"Towards the end of the book, there are several entries about an older man by the name of Max. The journal, as I understand it, was given to him as a Christmas present back in 1999."

"That's right."

"Do you know what ever happened to Max?"

"Yes. I just found out this morning that he passed away on Sunday. His funeral is tomorrow in Kenosha."

"Is that where you were heading before I derailed you?"

"Yes."

"Actually, our friend's wedding is on Saturday. That's the reason for the trip," Rachel said.

"Her name is Katie," Eve added. "She's kinda like my aunt. I get to be the flower girl."

"That sounds lovely. Her name isn't Katie Lewis, is it?"

Rachel looked surprised. "Do you know her?"

Sheron smiled. "Only by name. I believe it was she who gave Wolf the journal and started his adventure."

Paul nodded. She hadn't missed anything.

"Tell me, what she's like, this Katie Lewis."

"She's awesome. I'm actually named after her." Eve said proudly.

"Is that right?"

"Yep. We're going to visit Grandma, too. She has a museum, kinda like this one, only a little bit smaller, but it doesn't have a restaurant, and I've been making lots of pictures to hang all over it."

"Is your mother an artist?" Sheron asked, turning to Paul.

"It's actually my mother," Rachel said. "Apparently that gene skips every other generation. She took some pottery classes when she was in college, and she recently acquired a potter's wheel and a kiln. The museum Eve talks about is actually her garage, which doubles as the laundry."

"Marvelous! No space is too small to make art; I'm sure she'll be pleased to show off your work, Eve."

Eve smiled.

"And what about you, Paul? Is your family still in Adams-Friendship?"

"Uh, no, not anymore."

Sheron nodded.

"Daddy doesn't have a family anymore, except Aunt Jennie, who lives in Osh Kosh b'Gosh."

Sheron nodded again. She looked at Eve as if she were reviewing in her mind the information she'd just acquired. Then, without warning, she reached out and put her hand on top of Paul's hand, patting it softly. At that moment, he knew that whatever cover he might have had, had just been blown away by the wind of truth.

"Do something for someone else and it will all even out in the Universe's scheme of things."

Ye are better than all the ballads that ever were sung or said; for ye are living poems, and all the rest are dead.
– Goethe

Count your blessings not your troubles.
– Dale Carnegie

-CHAPTER 24-
THE REQUEST

THE PURPOSE OF LIFE IS NOT TO BE HAPPY. IT IS TO BE USEFUL, TO BE HONORABLE, TO BE COMPASSIONATE, TO HAVE IT MAKE SOME DIFFERENCE THAT YOU HAVE LIVED AND LIVED WELL. -RALPH WALDO EMERSON

"Eve, would you like to join me in the little girl's room?" Rachel asked after recognizing the sick look on her husband's face.

"Yes. I already drank three of those sodas." She stood up from her chair and Rachel took her hand.

"We'll be back in five minutes," Rachel said softly as they walked to the rest room.

"Why didn't you tell me who you were?" Sheron asked when the sounds of their footsteps had faded behind her.

"I'm sorry," Paul said. "I never intended to deceive you, but I've spent the last seven years trying to protect my daughter from the person I once was. She'd never heard of Wolf before today—before I began telling her the stories I wrote in that journal so many years ago. I've gone to great lengths to protect her from that person, even changing my name, hoping to bury the past in the past. She's never heard that I attempted to put an end to my life, and I hope she never does."

WORK FOR THINGS THAT HAVE ETERNAL VALUE.

"But Paul, don't you see that it's the fact that your life has been troubled that makes your story what it is and inspires everyone who reads it? Yours is a story of redemption, of forgiveness and grace. You have moved on, and I commend you for it, but I loved your story long before I knew what you became. Your story has inspired many to believe we can change—to believe we can be better—that life doesn't have to be defined by our past, or our family of origin, or the mistakes we've made. Even with the best laid plans, none of us get through this life without incurring a few wrinkles along the way. But it's those wrinkles that make us human, that make us believable, that enable us to empathize and understand the plight of others. I don't have children, but I was once a child, and though I had wonderful parents, I was keenly aware of their failings and imperfections. To be honest, those gritty truths enabled me to understand them and appreciate them in ways I probably couldn't have if I believed they were perfect."

"I don't think you understand how broken I was."

"Paul, I don't think you understand that we're all broken. Somewhere in that book of yours is a quote that I've written on at least a hundred notes I've sent to friends over the past two years: "We are each of us angels with only one wing, and we can only fly by embracing each other"[1]. You can never know how much your book has helped me. You laughed and cried at the funerals of strangers. I have laughed and cried reading about those strangers as I, like you, have been trying to figure out what I'm going to be when I grow up. When my husband died, a big part of me died with him. But when your journal came into my life, a new part of me was born—a kinder, gentler part that I never imagined could be part of me. As happy as I believed I was, looking back now, my life was very shallow. I was so wrapped up in myself and my small world that I'm afraid I missed out on understanding what happiness truly is.

"In my office, one corner of my desk is covered with Post-it notes that help me to remember Dr. Dinglebottom's recipe for happiness: someone to love, something to do and something to look forward to. If

1. Luciano De Crescenzo

ever I feel myself slipping, I take a look at those things and change what needs to be changed.

"As a childless woman, I never imagined the joy that can come from loving and encouraging a child. If it hadn't have been for your journal, I would have missed out on that. I would have missed discovering who I really am—who I can be. Nobody ever knows how many years they have left, but I hope the rest of my days will be my best. I hope that when I can finally see into the realm beyond, I won't be afraid of dying because I've learned how to live. Over the past two years, I have written and rewritten at least a dozen eulogies for myself, changing them as I grow and learn to embrace all that is good and true.

"Paul, like it or not, the Wolf inside of you has helped you to become who you are. I understand that he is dead to you, that you've done all that you can to kill him off. In the next twenty years or so, your daughter will likely make a few of her own mistakes. Your heart will ache as you watch her struggle, knowing the pain she will suffer and the damage to herself that those choices will cause. But the Wolf inside of you, the one you've tamed with the help of a loving God, will enable you to reach out with empathy and understanding. And if you'll embrace her with love and the one good wing you have, you'll be able to help her come home and to realize all that she is. We are by nature, a portion of the world's problems, but with understanding and love, we can each be part of the solution.

"It's obvious," Sharon continued, "that your daughter adores you, Paul, but I promise you that she has already recognized some of your weaknesses. And in the next ten years, she will know each of them and make you aware of many you didn't even know you had. I'm convinced that the only way to progress as a people from generation to generation is to humbly allow ourselves to examine our past and allow the next generation to recognize our faults. If we can't do that, we cannot be surprised when history repeats itself, as it so often does. I assure you Eve will make her own set of mistakes as she grows into adulthood, but with a little help—a little understanding—a little opening of the windows of the past—the mistakes she makes won't have to be the same mistakes you made." Sheron turned to face the window, then turned back.

"Imagine where the world would be today, if instead of burying our mistakes, trying to hide them from our prideful eyes, we could write them in an open book and invite anyone who cares to examine them and share them with those who need the understanding that comes from getting burned. How much better and kinder our world would be if we stopped believing we were individual islands, and instead, formed a continent where we could gather together? How much better would it be if we could borrow each other's fire, sharing warmth and light and understanding?

"We are each unique individuals, but I'm quite certain that we're not nearly as unique as we think we are. By opening our books and sharing our stories, our lives become richer, more compassionate, and filled with meaning.

How many lives could be saved from the perils of despair by the universal nuggets of truth and hope you found in a year's worth of funerals? Please, Paul, please don't hide the truth you know. My world would be much dimmer if I had not been able to borrow your fire."

Paul took a deep breath, shaking his head. "I'm glad my journal helped you, but I'm still trying to figure out how in the world you got a copy of it."

"I can't tell you for sure. As I said before, my friend loaned me her copy. I tried tracking you down through the friend she'd received hers from, but I became discouraged after I spoke to seven or eight people. No one seemed to have any answers other than pointing me to one more person down the line. I have no idea how many copies are out there, but if you saw mine, you'd know it's probably at least a tenth generation copy."

Paul shook his head again. "How in the world?"

"Paul, the world is hungry for truth and light. It's hungry for good news and hope. When people find something that brightens their way

A MAN MUST MAKE HIS OPPORTUNITY, AS OFT AS HE FIND IT. —FRANCIS BACON and gives them hope, they want to share it with everyone they know. That's the way it's been for me.

"There are so many things from your journal that I've shared with the people I love. Those things have become part of me, enhancing my story and making me feel like I have something to share that scatters sunbeams into sometimes gloomy places. People need light. We need hope. We want to believe there is meaning and purpose to our lives. Your journal—your experience—doesn't just glow with warmth and truth, it also allows us to see what can happen to a person who embraces those truths. We want to be like Dr. Dinglebottom. We want to have the unconquerable spirit of Margaret Mills. We want to embrace Bob Matthew's virtues of fidelity, kindness, and generosity. We want to believe our own lives can be transformed and improved the way Wolf's was. What you found, Paul, by attending all those funerals, are the secrets of life. You discovered that we all can be the masters of our fate and the captains of our souls. But you also discovered that an understanding of our spiritual roots can elevate and inspire us to know that the truths that matter most are those which are eternal.

"The wisdom you gathered and the words that came from your heart point us home. They bring us back to the rivers where we were spawned and point us upstream. They encourage us onward, giving us faith that our challenges can be met, and hope that the prize at the end of our journey will be worth it.

"And through it all, it is love, Paul. It's love that stitches us all together into a giant patchwork quilt. Love truly is what makes the world go round. It is both the fuel and the product of living right. I don't know if you noticed, but all of the stories in your journal, indeed all the stories that have ever resonated with the human spirt—they're all love stories. It is the greatest motivator the world has ever known. As light makes a quick end of darkness, love pushes out fear and distrust. It lifts us up with encouragement and fortitude. The world needs it. We all crave it, and you, my dear friend, have inspired me to believe in it once again."

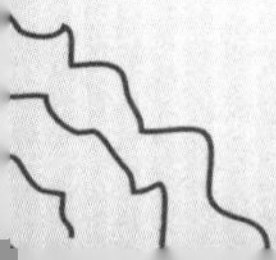

Footsteps behind them made Paul turn to Rachel and Eve. He nodded, encouraging Rachel to come.

"Eve, I have just been telling your father about how much his friend, Wolf, has helped me." She reached out her hand, encouraging her to come closer, until Eve stood by her side. Sheron put her arm around her shoulder. "I have one more story to share with you tonight, if that's okay with you?"

Eve nodded, smiling brightly.

"In the poster tube I gave you earlier, you will find copies of the paintings of one of the most beloved artists the world has ever known. Our friend, Vincent, was a genius. Those pictures I gave you are just two of the millions, probably billions of copies that have been made of his work. You can find his paintings on calendars and mugs and even mouse pads. He has inspired songs and poetry and innumerable books and stories. His paintings speak to us because they help us to see and discover the truth. When we look at the night sky, few of us see the stars the way he saw them, but we want to. And when we close our eyes, we imagine we can see stars that magically dance with creative energy and a moon that glows with beautiful boldness. And we see a celestial wind that rolls the clouds across the lapis sky. Each stroke of his brush tells a story; each one is filled with passion and love. When you stand in front of a Van Gogh, it pulls you in. It makes you want to stay and stare at the beauty he created. It makes your heart sing inside your chest, and it fills your mind with beautiful ideas. He has inspired millions of people around the world to stop and look and learn, and open their hearts to their imagination.

"But you know what? Our friend Vincent was broken. There was part of his head that didn't think the same way you and I think, and we're grateful that it didn't. If he'd been like you or me, we wouldn't have what he's given us. He had a gift to share with the world, but the world didn't always like what they saw. In the eight years he painted, he never sold even one painting. People couldn't understand him as he reached out for the love he needed. His brother, Theo, loved Vincent, but in the end, all the love Theo could give him wasn't enough to sustain him. He was only thirty-seven years old when he decided his life was no longer worth living."

"My daddy's thirty-seven," Eve said.

"And we're glad that he is," Sheron said, patting Paul's hand. "Can you imagine what Vincent could have done if he'd had just a little bit more hope and love? What could he have painted for us? Did you know that one of his paintings recently sold for a hundred and forty-six million dollars? Just one painting! We're grateful for the beauty he gave our world, but when I look out at the stars at night, I find myself wondering what he could have done with another forty or fifty years. I find myself daydreaming, wishing I could have met him. I wish I could have encouraged him to continue by purchasing one of his paintings. I wish I could reach into my pocket and pull out a piece of hope that he could set on his easel as he painted. I wish I could express to him the love and appreciation I have for him and tell him how his art has blessed my life. I want to believe that love and encouragement would have helped buy him another week, another year, maybe even another decade.

"We never know the impact our lives will have on the world we live in and eventually leave behind. Whether our lives last seven years or a hundred and seven years, we have something amazing to share with the world. Most of us will never have our life's work displayed on the walls of museums, but each one of us can hang our life's work on the hearts of those we love. It doesn't matter who we are, where we came from, or the family we're born into. If we can nurture the hope God has planted in our souls, beautiful things can blossom and grow and bless our broken world."

Sharen paused to smile at Eve. "You are a beautiful young lady and I hope you will think of me as a new friend."

Eve smiled and nodded.

"Can I make one request of you, my new friend?" Sheron queried.

"Sure?"

"When you look up into the night sky and see the stars, I hope you will remember this day when you traded your beautiful drawing for a Van Gogh and in the process brought joy into the heart of an old woman."

Eve nodded again and her smile filled her face.

Sheron returned the smile before pulling her close and giving her a warm hug. Then letting go, she spoke again. "One more thing," she said, wiping a tear from her eye "I hope you'll remember that I invited you to share a meal with me tonight because of the things I read in a journal written by a lost young man named Wolf, who spent a year of his life trying to find his way home by attending the funerals of common people who lived extraordinary lives and left magical stories to tell."

HE WHO IS NOT FORGOTTEN IS NOT DEAD.
- SAMUEL BUTLER

LIFE IS A BATTLE WORTH FIGHTING. BB

-CHAPTER 25-
FINDING A HOME

TO LIVE IN THE HEARTS
WE LEAVE BEHIND IS NOT TO DIE.
—THOMAS CAMPBELL

With the glow of the city lights behind them, they walked slowly down the bridge, back the way they had come. Paul held tight to one of each of his girls' hands. From here, Millennium Park sprawled out in front of them. The plaza where "The Bean" sat was still busy with people milling about, the joyful sounds of their laughter and revelry wafting towards them on breezes from the lake.

"Can we come here again tomorrow?" Eve asked.

Rachel laughed. "Did you like it?"

"This might be the best museum in the whole world!"

"I'll take that as a yes. What was your favorite part?"

Eve lifted the poster tube above her head. "Sheron! She was awesome. Can you believe she gave me two Van Goghs? I can't wait to show Aunt Katie and Grandma. I don't think they'll believe me."

"She was really nice; wasn't she?"

"Yeah. I was thinking that maybe we should introduce her to Mr. Miller, so they could get married, and then she could be our neighbor."

"That's a great idea," said Paul, deciding it wasn't necessary to explain the complexities of what she'd just imagined.

"I can't believe Sheron has heard of Wolf. When you told me his stories earlier today, I wasn't sure if he was a real person or not."

"Even after I showed you his journal?"

"Yeah, well, Daddy, you like to tell lots of stories."

"But you like 'em, right?"

"Of course. Do you have any more to tell about Wolf?"

"Are you kidding? We have a whole book of stories about him in the car."

"That's good. I like him. Do you think I could meet him someday?"

Paul glanced at Rachel. She smiled warmly.

"I don't know. Maybe, someday. He's kind of a private guy."

The traffic on Monroe Street distracted them, and they stopped to watch the cars rush by under their feet.

"Do you think all these people are going home?" asked Eve

"I don't know. It's late, and Chicago's pretty busy, even late at night. Some people are probably on their way home, and others might be going to parties or out to meet their friends," responded Rachel.

"And some of them are probably tourists like us who are driving around in circles, trying to figure out where they're going," Paul added.

"Is it easy to get lost?" asked Eve.

"What do you mean?"

She pointed to the traffic. "I've never driven a car before, but I don't think it would be very fun, especially in a big city. Sheron said Wolf was trying to find his way home by going to funerals. I was just wondering if he ever found his home."

"In some ways, yes."

"Did he go home to Adams-Friendship?"

"No. Sometimes, even when you've lived in a place all your life, it's not home because the people you love aren't there anymore. I think for most people, home is wherever you can surround yourself with love and the people who make you happy."

"Then what about Wolf? After his family broke—where is his home now?"

Paul took a deep breath, trying to think fast. An image came into his head, the image he'd imagined when Sheron talked about her copy of Wolf's journal. "I never thought about it until just now, but I suppose his home is in the hearts of the people who read his story, and the people who share his story with their friends and the people they love."

Eve looked up from the traffic. "So does he live in my heart?"

"Do you believe the stories that you've heard about him?"

"Yes."

"Then I suppose he does."

"Can I tell Grandma his stories?"

"Would you like to?"

"Yes. I think she'd like Wolf, too. Maybe I could even draw her some pictures of his stories."

"Why would you want to do that?"

"'Cause then he could have another house—in her heart. I think if he had lots of places to live, it would be like going on vacation. Then he could go and visit and feel at home. And people could tell him stories about themselves and help him know that even though his mommy died, he can still be happy."

"I like that. Where did you come up with that idea?" Paul smiled.

"From Sheron. She hasn't even met Wolf yet, but she has a copy of his journal, and she knows his stories, and she even tried to find him. It's like she kinda already made a house for him in her heart so he can visit if he wants. And she's already told her friends. Wolf probably doesn't even know that there are a whole bunch of houses in other people's hearts where he can come and visit and feel like he belongs. I think that would be good for him to know."

"How come?"

"Because it feels good to make other people happy, and if Wolf knew that his story made people happy, he would be happy, too. I think we should tell his story to lots of people."

"You really think so?"

NO MAN IS FREE WHO IS NOT THE MASTER OF HIMSELF. —EPICTETUS

"Of course. I think it would make lots of people happy. It's the best story you've told me so far. "

"Really?"

"Well, it would be better if you could put a pony in there somewhere. Maybe when I tell it to Grandma, I could change it a little bit and find a place for a pony."

"Ya know, maybe a pony isn't such a bad idea after all."

LIFE IS NOT A PATH OF COINCIDENCE, HAPPENSTANCE, AND LUCK, BUT RATHER AN UNEXPLAINABLE, METICULOUSLY CHARTED COURSE FOR ONE TO TOUCH THE LIVES OF OTHERS AND MAKE A DIFFERENCE IN THE WORLD.—BARBARA DILLINHAM

I HAVEN'T A CLUE HOW MY STORY WILL END. BUT THAT'S ALL RIGHT. WHEN YOU SET OUT ON A JOURNEY AND NIGHT COVERS THE ROAD, THAT'S WHEN YOU DISCOVER THE STARS. —NANCY WILLARD

WE ARE ALL IMPERFECT BEINGS TRYING TO MAKE SENSE OF OUR BROKENNESS.

-Chapter 26-
Surprises

One out of four people in this country is mentally unbalanced. Think of your three closest friends; if they seem okay, then you're the one. —Ann Landers

Eve was snoring softly in the back seat when they pulled into her grandmother's driveway. Only the porch light was still on, and Rachel wondered out loud if her mother had gone to bed early. Leaving Eve in the car, they both got out and went to the door, finding it locked. Not wanting to wake her mother, they kicked around in the dirt, looking for the hide-a-key rock they'd given her five years ago for Christmas. Finding it, they went inside and turned on the lights. It had been a whole year since their last visit, but after a quick inspection, they decided nothing had changed.

Rachel went to her bedroom, switching on more lights as she went. "Mom's not home," she said, returning to the kitchen where she found Paul with his head in the refrigerator.

"Are you sure she was expecting us?"

"Yeah, why?"

"There's nothing in the fridge except for a few carryout boxes and some ketchup."

"What? I wonder if she didn't get my message that we were coming today."

Paul turned to the phone and the answering machine. A red number 2 blinked on the screen and he pushed the button. "Mom, it's me. Hey, we're going to come a day early. I hope that's okay. We should be there around nine or ten. I love you … I love you, Grandma," a small voice chimed in the background. "See you soon."

"Well, that clears that up," Paul responded, pushing the stop button. "I'll go get Eve."

After tucking her into the hide-a-bed in the family room, they unpacked the rest of the car. They were both exhausted and didn't say much. Rachel offered to run to the grocery store to get some milk and bread, but Paul said he'd do it in the morning and she didn't argue. They tried to reach Rachel's mom on her cell phone, but there was no answer, so after another half hour, they decided not to wait up, figuring she was working late at the diner and would find them in the morning.

Paul's internal clock went off early Friday morning when the dream he was having ended. He'd been running down the beach when he tripped. He stuck out his arms to break his fall, but before he even reached the ground, his arms became wings, enabling him to glide over the uneven surface of the stones. Catching the wind, he soared upward, rising higher and higher until he was gliding effortlessly over the lake. He watched the boats bob in their slips at the dock and the fishermen lining up on the peer. Then he dove down to get a closer look, hovering over the bright-beaked gulls. He looked from side to side and saw Eve on the beach, waving to him. Without effort, he was there in the blink of an eye, hovering a few feet above her head.

"Daddy, come down. Look at the rocks."

He couldn't believe his eyes. Almost every rock was a heart rock.

"Let's take some to Mommy."

Paul nodded, forcing himself to land and as he did, Eve took hold of his fingers, smiling up into his face, the sun dancing in her green eyes.

He stared up at the ceiling, wondering where he was. The lamp. The clock. The bookshelf stuffed with silly teenage books and ceramic figurines. The wallpaper that ran around the perimeter of the room where the wall met the ceiling. Clouds—rather ugly clouds, splattered here and there with cheesy rainbows. He'd always hated that wallpaper. He took a deep breath and closed his eyes again, trying to go back to his dream, but it was no use. He was awake. He got up and slipped on his clothes quietly, sneaking out of the house without a sound. He was hungry.

He drove past one grocery store, then another, before he got to his favorite; the one store in town where he knew where everything was. The store had just opened for the day and the air inside was warm and moist and smelled of bread and cinnamon rolls. He followed his nose, picking up a tray of the fresh rolls. His mouth watered as he wandered the aisles, pushing his cart, adding chocolate milk, apples, bread, Cheerios, eggs, and bacon. He tried hard to resist the temptation of the cinnamon rolls. But by the time he pulled back into the driveway, three of them were lodged in his esophagus, and he was gleefully gasping for breath.

SOME PEOPLE NEVER GO CRAZY. WHAT TRULY HORRIBLE LIVES THEY MUST LEAD. —CHARLES BUKOWSKI

The house was still as he walked into the kitchen and unloaded the groceries. He looked at the clock on the wall. 6:53. He opened the cupboard where the glasses had traditionally been kept and was surprised to discover they'd all been replaced with handmade mugs of varying degrees of skill. He selected a large stein and poured himself a generous portion of chocolate milk before eating a fourth cinnamon roll. Leaning against the counter, he looked out the window above the sink and smiled to himself when he saw the picnic table covered with pottery vases and bowls. A squirrel ran across the patio, stopping only long enough to stash a nut in the mouth of a vase lying on the ground.

Several stones arranged across the windowsill caught his eye and drew him towards them. Heart rocks—seven of them, in various colors and shapes—all of them undeniably shaped like a heart. He smiled to himself, wondering if these had been there before. Had he missed them?

Surely, Eve would have noticed them. Since she'd found her first one on the beach a few summers earlier, she looked for them everywhere she went. Her small collection included only fifteen or sixteen, but each one had a story of a trip or an event where she'd found it. Picking up the middle one, Paul heard a humming sound coming from the far end of the house followed by muffled words.

He walked down the hallway, peeking into the rooms as he passed the doorways. Rachel was still in bed, but her mother's bed was empty. The humming led him forward to the garage door. He stopped at the door, listening.

"...and that's when Sheron gave me the pictures. I couldn't believe it! Daddy told me I should try to trade one of my drawings for a painting, but I kinda thought he was just kidding. I mean, I thought it was a good idea, but I'm just a kid; but Sheron traded me for a Van Gogh. Can you believe it?"

"You bet I can. You might have gotten cheated. I'd probably trade four or five Van Goghs for one of your paintings."

Eve laughed.

Paul opened the door just enough to peek in. Eve was sitting on top of a five-gallon bucket, situated right in front of her grandmother who was sitting behind a mustard-colored potter's wheel. He watched for a minute, amused by this picture of companionship shared between women of different generations.

"What are they doing?" Rachel asked from behind, startling him.

"Making memories, I think. When did your mom become a potter?"

"Oh, I think she's just playing around. I guess she got the wheel and stuff off of Craig's List. Does she look like she knows what she's doing?"

Paul turned around and handed her the oversized mug. "I'm not an expert, but I think she's doing okay."

"This is actually pretty good. I had no idea she could do this."

"Should we go out?"

"Yeah. I wanna try."

Paul opened the door. "Good morning."

"Hey, good morning. You guys surprised me. I wasn't expecting you until this evening."

"I'm sorry you missed my call. I would have let you know sooner, but it was kind of a last-minute decision. Where were you last night?"

"I worked until ten, and then I hurried off to my pottery class."

Rachel looked surprised. "What time does your pottery class start?"

"Whenever I get there. It's a private lesson."

"Really? When did you become a night owl?"

Marilyn looked up from her work and smiled deviantly. "Since Bud offered to teach me whenever I wanted. I've been taking classes from him since January. I've gotten pretty good, don't you think?" she asked, pointing to the mug in Paul's hand.

"Yeah, this is great. Can you make me a set?"

"Maybe for Christmas, if you're lucky, and if you don't ditch me like you did last Christmas."

Rachel looked around the garage that had been transformed from an overstuffed receptacle of all things useless into a functional work space. A shiny silver kiln sat in one corner, looking a bit like a formidable robot. A table ran along the wall, and several plastic buckets covered the surface. A stack of boxes labeled Continental Clay Company took up most of the space on the other wall. The whole garage, including the floor and ceiling, had been painted with high-gloss paint in a variety of psychedelic colors, as if a Jackson Pollock painting had exploded, embedding multi-colored shrapnel on every surface. The glass block window behind her mother cast a bright glow on everything.

"I like what you did to the place," Rachel said turning back to her mom and recognizing for the first time that she was wearing a tie-dyed T-shirt under her denim apron.

"Thanks. Eve's just been telling me about your trip. It sounds like you had a good time in Chicago."

"We did," responded Paul. "I guess Eve told you about the trade she made?"

"Are you kidding? I woke up with a poster tube about an inch away from my face. I thought I was about to be clobbered. She's just been giving me all the details. Sorry about breakfast, but it looks like you found something. I was planning on stocking the fridge this morning."

"No worries, thanks for putting us up," Paul responded.

"You're always welcome. I'm glad you finally came to check out my studio. I've been really excited about it, but it's even more fun when I can show it off."

"Yeah, Mom, I really can't believe you're doing this. I mean you mentioned it on the phone, but I had no idea you were into full production mode. What are you doing with all of your pots?"

"You mean these? This is just a handful of the stuff we've made. We've been selling at the farmer's markets on Saturdays at the park. We almost sold out our first week. I've been going crazy trying to keep up with the demand. It's a lot easier selling pottery now than it was back in the seventies when everyone thought they were a potter."

"Wait, you didn't tell me you're doing this for a business. I thought you were just making stuff for gifts."

"I was at first, but people started liking what we made, and we decided to go into business."

"You make it sound like you have minions working for you. Who's we?

"Oh, me and Bud. He has his studio and I have mine, but we do the shows together."

"Mom, I've never heard of Bud. Who is he?"

Marilyn smiled. "I've never told you about Bud? That can't be right. I'm sure I have. He's a great guy. I met him at the diner a while ago, and we hit it off."

Rachel smiled. She could hardly believe her ears. "Mom, are you dating someone?"

"Now, what kind of question is that? I'm a grown woman for crying out loud. It's been a long time since anyone has been interested in me."

"So you're dating then?"

"Sometimes the Lord chooses not to remove our disability, but changes our hearts instead."

"Oh, I don't know. When you get to be my age, you don't really date. We just kind of hang out and make pottery and listen to music. He's a great cook. In fact he wanted me to invite you all to come to dinner on Sunday. He's cooking. I thought it would be a good chance to get to know him."

"That sounds fun," Paul said.

"Wait a minute, Mom, what are you talking about? You make it sound like it's some kind of meet and greet, like we're meeting the future in-laws."

"Oh, Rachel, don't be so dramatic! Call it whatever you want, but it's dinner and a chance to meet one of the best potters this side of Kenosha. I'm going, and I'd love to have you come."

"Sure, count us in," said Paul. "I used to make a little pottery in high school. I'd like to meet him."

"You don't think it will be kind of weird? I mean, we don't even know the guy."

"Yeah, that's why we're going to dinner, honey. The whole time I've been part of this family, I've only met one guy that your mom dated—what was his name—Biff? Ben? …"

"Bob." Marilyn said.

"Thank you, Bob. He was a nice enough guy."

"Paul, he was a total loser. He stole my mom's car and ditched it at the liquor store."

"Well, okay, so he had a few issues, but over all …"

"Paul, are you even listening to yourself. Would you ever let Eve go out with a guy like Bob?"

"Of course not. Eve's only seven; that would be creepy, and we'd probably get arrested for child endangerment."

Rachel closed her eyes and ran her hand across her face, shaking her head. "Did I wake up in Jerry Springer Land?"

"Honey, what are you talking about? Your mom has a new friend who wants to meet us, and he's offered to cook us dinner. Your mom's a great waitress, I'm sure, but no offense Marilyn, I think I'd like to take my chances with Bud's cooking."

Marilyn laughed out loud.

"I don't see what the big deal is. Look at her," he said, turning to Marilyn. "Look how happy she is. She got up early, and she's out here because she has a passion. I've been in this family for ten years, and I didn't even know this garage had a window before today. Look at this—she's making stuff, and it's really good. Maybe you're missing it, but I haven't seen your mom this chipper in a long time. I don't know who this Bud guy is either. But if he's inspired this, if he's making her happy, if she's staying out late making pots with a guy she likes, I say good for her. What's wrong with that?"

"Paul, my mother is dating a potter. He could be an ax murderer who lures women to his home under the guise of teaching pottery classes!"

Paul tried hard not to laugh. "Baby, she's here today, isn't she? She came home from that pottery class last night, and from the looks of it, she's been coming home from all the other ones, too. I, for one, am happy for your mom. I'm glad she has a friend that she can share some common interests with."

"He sound's like a nice guy to me," said Eve. "And he's very handsome."

"How would you know that?" asked Rachel.

"Grams showed me his picture over there." Eve pointed to the glossy eight-by-ten hanging on the wall above the utility sink.

Rachel walked to the sink and stared at the photo of her mom in front of a table filled with pottery, standing next to a tall, muscly man with a Tom Selleck mustache and a shaved head. They were wearing matching tie-dyes and looking very happy together.

"Mom, when were you going to tell me about this?"

"At Christmas, but you didn't show up, remember?"

"Mom, we've gone over this! I'm sorry Christmas didn't work out for us last year, but you didn't need to cut me out of the will."

"Oh, Rachel, I was hoping you'd be happy for me."

"Mom, I'd like to be, but this is a shock. It would have been easier if you'd told me, that's all."

"Honey, I've been busy. I didn't know I needed to ask your permission to date a man I really like. He's a wonderful person. I know you'll like him. I appreciate your concern, but I'm a big girl. I think I know what I'm getting myself into."

"And what is that?"

Marilyn started laughing. "To be honest, it's none of your damn business."

Rachel folded her arms and walked back into the house.

"Where the hell did that come from?" Marilyn asked.

"I was just wondering the same thing."

"Mommy, must have woken up on the wrong side of the bed," suggested Eve.

The doorbell rang, and Paul looked to Marilyn. "Do you want me to get that?"

"Sure. Who'd be coming by at this hour?"

"I don't know. Maybe it's Katie."

Paul went inside and walked quickly to the front door, but Rachel was four steps ahead of him.

"It's probably Katie," she said as she turned the door knob. She pulled the front door open to reveal a mustachioed man, standing as tall as Paul, but much thicker.

"Ahh, you must be Rachel," he said, extending his hand warmly. "And that would make you Paul, right? My name is Bud Pace. Your mom left her cell phone over at my studio last night," he said shyly. "I thought she'd probably miss it."

"Come in," said Paul, gently nudging Rachel out of the doorway. "She's out in the studio already. I assume you know where it is."

He smiled and nodded. "And will I get to meet Eve?" he asked, taking a few steps inside.

"She's out there, too."

"Excellent. I've heard so much about you guys. I've been looking forward to meeting you. I hope you're planning on Sunday?"

Paul nodded. "Yeah, we just heard. We'll be there. What can we bring?"

"Just yourselves, and Eve, of course. It will be great. I hope you kids like ribs."

He walked down the hallway and entered the garage. Paul and Rachel didn't follow.

"He looks like a nice guy," Paul said. "I'm really happy for your mom."

Rachel shook her head, but smiled. "I don't know. He's a potter! Do you know any stable people who are potters?"

"No," he said, shaking his head. "but I don't know any real potters, and neither do you, so quit with the stereotypes. You make it sound like he's some kind of freak."

"I'm just worried about my mom getting hurt again."

"Hey, I love your mom, too, but come on. Don't you see how happy she is?'

Rachel smiled. "She's wearing a tie-dyed T-shirt."

Paul raised his eyebrows. "And …? Rachel, remember yesterday when I was telling you about the stories that get told about people at their funerals—how the kids and grandkids of the people who died often learn things they'd never heard before?"

"Yeah?"

"I know you think you know your mom, Rachel, but for the last ten years we've averaged seeing her twice, maybe three times a year. There are three states between us, and neither of you love talking on the phone. Things are bound to change over the course of a year. Let's just take the surprises as they come and be happy for them."

BE PASSIONATE ABOUT LIVING.

-Chapter 27- Plans

The grave is but a covered bridge leading
from light to light,
through a brief darkness!
—Henry Wadsworth Longfellow

"So, what are your plans today?" Marilyn asked as all five of them crowded around the kitchen table. Paul had made a bacon omelet, which he served with the rest of the cinnamon rolls and chocolate milk.

"We are going to hang out with Katie and Mike tonight, and Paul has a thing he wanted to go to at noon. Are you going to be around? I was thinking we could let Eve hang out here with you for a couple of hours." Rachel said.

Marilyn looked a little surprised before turning to Bud. "At noon, umm …"

"Is that a problem?" Rachel asked.

"Actually, yes. I'm sorry. I took the whole weekend off so I could spend it with you kids, but then something came up. We actually have a funeral to go to right at noon."

Rachel raised one eyebrow. "Who died?"

"Oh, just an old man from the diner, one of my regulars actually. But Bud's known him for about five years. He's actually the one who introduced us, so we really need to go."

"I'm not sure how much fun it would be for a kid," Bud interjected, "but we could take Eve with us if she'd like to go."

Rachel looked at Paul then back to her mother. "Don't tell me this guy's name is Max."

"You knew him?" Marilyn asked.

Rachel shook her head, laughing. "No, but Paul does."

"Really?" asked Bud.

"Yeah, that was actually what we were doing at noon. Katie called yesterday morning to tell us about the funeral. That's why we decided to come a day early," Paul explained.

"How did Katie know Max?" Marilyn asked.

"She was his doctor. I mean, not all the time, but she took care of him before he died."

"What a small world," responded Marilyn. "I never would have guessed you might have known Max. He was such a charming man, wasn't he?"

Paul smiled, wondering if they were talking about the same Max. "How long have you known him?"

"Oh, probably three years. He was always such a gentleman—and a great tipper. I saw him at least once a day, but there were some days that he'd come in for all three meals."

"Let me guess—meatloaf and lima bean soup?" Paul said.

"Wow! How'd you guess?"

"That's all he ever ate when I knew him."

"We actually named the soup after him. The cooks didn't make it before he started coming, so he brought them the recipe and even taught them how to make it. It must be a generational thing because a lot of ol' timers are coming in for it now. They say it's just like their mommas used to make it."

"I think I must have missed that generational thing by at least thirty years," Bud said. "I hate that soup. In my mind, there has never been a worse concoction created."

IN EACH OF US THERE IS A LITTLE OF ALL OF US. —LICHTENBERG

"I still get nauseous just thinking about it," Paul said, gritting his teeth.

"Oh, it's not that bad—with a lot of crackers," Marilyn mused.

"So I guess we're all going then," Rachel replied, looking at Eve. "Unless you want me to stay home with you."

"Will there be good stories there?"

"Oh, sure. That man was full of stories, and he knew just about everyone in town. There ought to be a lot of people there with some great stories to share," Bud said enthusiastically.

"How did you know him?" Paul asked.

"I met him at church. He was my AA sponsor."

"Really?" Paul looked shocked.

"Oh, I don't drink anymore. I've been sober for almost five years."

"That's great, but I really didn't mean it that way. I guess I'm just surprised to hear that he could be a sponsor. I thought you had to be sober yourself before you could help someone through that process."

"He'd been sober for almost six years when I met him. I think that's what made him such a great sponsor—he was so full of compassion."

"*Really*?" Paul continued, the look of shock remaining on his face.

Bud nodded heartily. "That was *my* introduction to lima bean soup. He tracked me down one night, shortly after we'd met. I'd fallen off the wagon, again, and wasn't answering his phone calls, so he came to my house. He peeled me off the floor and dragged me down to his favorite diner for a big bowl of lima bean soup. He made me eat every last bean, and then sat next to me on the curb as I puked up every one of those beans into the gutter. You only have to do that once," he said with as knowing smile. "That was the last time I drank, and the last time I ever ate lima bean soup. Like you, I feel like barfing every time I even get near it. How about you? How did you know him?"

"Uhh, a friend of mine introduced us," he said, glancing at Rachel, "but that was a long time ago."

Bud and Marilyn looked like they were waiting for more information, but Paul was quite sure he didn't want to go there.

"So, Marilyn tells us you've been teaching her how to make pottery and that you guys are selling your pots at the farmer's market. How'd you get started with that?" Paul asked, in an effort to change the subject.

Bud sat up a little straighter. "Oh, that's a long story. I guess you could say it's always been a dream of mine. I used to make pots in high school, but I got married young and had three kids pretty quick, and I chickened out. I got a real job to make sure the mortgage got paid. I worked for the City of Kenosha for thirty-five years managing the parks and public spaces."

"You got paid to play at the park?" asked Eve.

Bud smiled. "Sometimes, yes. Most days I was making sure the crews were taking care of the grass and flowers and trees, and keeping the sidewalks free of snow."

"That sounds kind of fun," Eve responded.

"There were days that it was," Bud admitted, turning his face to Eve. "But it's hard when you want to be creative, and you don't have an outlet to do it."

"What does outlet mean?"

Bud looked at Paul and Rachel for help.

"Umm, it's kind of like when you want to draw a picture, but you forgot to pack your crayons," Paul suggested.

"Do you use crayons to make pottery, too?" Eve asked after a moment's thought.

Bud shook his head. "It would be nice if you could, but pottery requires all sorts of tools and space to make it in. When you're busy working and raising kids, most folks don't have the time or space to follow their dreams."

"So did your kids finally grow up and move away so you could make pots in your garage like Grandma?"

"Well, not exactly. The kids are all grown up and married and I have five grandkids already. In fact, one of them, Maddie, is just about your age, and she's an artist, too. She likes to come to my studio and play whenever she's in town."

WHEREFORE, COMFORT YOURSELVES TOGETHER, AND EDIFY ONE ANOTHER... 1 THESSALONIANS 5:11

"Where's your studio?" Paul asked.

"In the old Woolworth's building on Main Street," Bud answered.

"Wow, that's a big space. How did you score that?"

"Patience. It was actually my wife's idea, but it wasn't available until just a few years ago."

"Is your wife a potter, too?" asked Eve.

Rachel looked uncomfortable at the bluntness of Eve's question, even though she was anxious to hear the rest of the story, too. "Sorry," she said, gesturing to Bud.

"No, no, that's quite all right. I'm sure you're all wondering what an old, grubby potter is doing hanging out with your mom and grandma. I should have mentioned it earlier. The truth is, my wife died nearly seven years ago."

"How?" Eve asked, her eyes wide with anticipation.

"She had a brain aneurism." He looked at Eve, recognizing the confused look on her face. "A blood vessel inside her brain broke and flooded her head with blood, cutting off oxygen to her body."

"How does that happen?"

"I'm sorry," Rachel said, putting her hand on Eve's shoulder.

Bud shook his head. "Don't be. There was nothing anyone could have done about it. It would have come up sooner or later—it might as well be now." He turned back to Eve. "No one knows for sure what happened. Sherry was on a walk with a friend when she fell to the ground and was unresponsive. By the time the ambulance showed up, she was brain-dead. They kept her alive long enough for two of my kids to get there, but there was no hope for her recovery. She was only fifty-four years old, and I was three weeks away from retirement." Bud set his hand on top of Marilyn's, squeezing it tightly.

"I'm sorry," Paul said, looking at the big man across the table who'd suddenly become much more human. "That must have been very hard."

"It almost killed me. I thought I'd experienced my share of disappointments in life, but I don't think you can ever be prepared for something like that. Susan had been a smoker most of her life, and her blood pressure was always on the high side, but there had never been any warning signs that something like that was coming. I don't remember even imagining the possibility of losing her. It really sent me into a tailspin. We'd been together since we were fifteen years old and always planned on growing old together. My life pretty much fell apart there for a couple of years. I'd always been a social drinker, but over the next few years, I'm sorry to admit, I became a drunk. I blew through a bunch of my retirement money and stopped caring about anyone or anything. I alienated my kids and grandkids and made an jerk of myself."

"So what got you back on track?" asked Paul.

"Whoever said I was?" he asked, his mustache curling up on the ends as he smiled.

"You know, it's an unfortunate truth, but some of us have to smack our heads against the bottom of the swimming pool before we can see that we've been swimming the wrong direction."

Rachel bumped Paul's leg under the table.

Ignoring Rachel, Paul nodded nonchalantly, encouraging Bud to continue.

"I guess things started changing when a friend of mine showed up at my house one Sunday morning and told me he was taking me to church. I hadn't been to church in forty years and I told him to go to … to take a hike," he said, winking at Eve. "But that son-of-a-gun wouldn't take no for an answer. I was so hungover I couldn't put up much of a fight, so he dragged me off to church with him. I'd always thought that Quakers were a bunch of weirdos and draft dodgers, so I was expecting it to be a little bit crazy. But it was different than any church I'd ever been to—not that I'd been to many. I was expecting a sermon or Sunday School, or something. Instead all they did was sit there in silence. So, I sat there too, trying to figure out what the heck was going on, wondering if the joke was on me." Bud laughed at his own memory.

"After about a half hour of nothing, just as I started drifting into dreamland, this white-haired man with a big nose stood up and talked about feeling the love of God by doing good things for other people. It was simple and short, and then he sat back down. The rest of the meeting was silence."

"Was that some kind of special meeting?" asked Rachel. "I've heard that Mormons have meetings like that, too, sometimes."

"No, that's the way all the Quaker meetings are, except for the business meetings," Marilyn responded. "It's a little different at first, but you get used to it. It gives you a chance to slow down and think."

Rachel stared at Marilyn. "Mom, have you been going to church?"

"Don't look so surprised." She laughed. "I've been going with Bud since March."

"So you became a Quaker then?" Rachel asked, turning back to Bud.

"Yes, about four years ago. That's actually where I met Max. He was the man who stood and spoke at that first meeting. I met him the next Sunday when my buddy dragged me to church again."

"So, Max really was a Quaker then?" Paul asked. " I saw his obituary—that his funeral was going to be held at the Quaker Church, but I guess I'm still surprised that someone like Max would choose to be a Quaker."

"What do you mean?" asked Marilyn.

"Well, the Max I knew wasn't really the Quaker type. My understanding of the Quaker church is pretty limited, but I can't imagine a guy like Max being a peaceable person, let alone getting up and talking about the good feelings that come from doing good things for other people."

Marilyn and Bud glanced back and forth at each other. "You must have known him before he … when was it that you said you knew him?" Bud asked.

Paul glanced at Rachel and Eve, then turned back to Bud. "I guess it must have been about twelve years ago."

Bud turned to Marilyn. "That must have been before his heart transplant," he suggested.

"What? Are we talking about the same Max? The Max I knew was probably eighty-five years old, and there is no way he would have been eligible for a transplant of any kind."

"No, we're talking about the same guy. He never really had a 'heart transplant,' Bud responded with hand gestures in the form of quotation marks. "I think it must have been about eleven or twelve years ago that he had a major change of heart. He always referred to it in our AA group as his heart transplant and suggested that maybe we all have to go through one of those before we can change our lives."

Paul shook his head. "Do you know what Max meant by that?"

"Sure. He talked about it all the time, especially when we had new people show up to group. He was never afraid of talking about where he'd come from and how he'd gotten to where he was—how he'd stepped out of the shadows and into the light and found a new heart and a new direction in life."

Paul shook his head again in disbelief. "I don't think the Max I knew ever could have done that. He was the most cantankerous person I've ever met."

"And you came out early to go to his funeral?" asked Marilyn.

Paul nodded after a moment's thought. "Yeah, weird, huh?"

"So, why did you come?"

Paul looked down at his plate, feeling a little embarrassed. "I suppose I've always wondered what happened to him. To be honest, I figured he must have died a lonely death a long time ago."

"Why?" asked Marilyn.

"Because when I knew him, he couldn't think of any reason to live. He was spending most of his time going to funerals just so he could find out how the lucky stiffs had died. I think he spent the rest of his time trying to get his picture in the dictionary next to the word "ornery."

"You know he lost three wives right?" asked Bud.

"Yeah, I do. That's probably why I put up with it for as long as I did. I knew he was broken, but I got to the point where I couldn't handle his negativity anymore. I spent a long time trying to figure him out—trying to soften him up. I tried to make him see that life is far better and more meaningful than just waiting to die. But you can only do so much for someone who doesn't want to change."

"You sound like you were disappointed," Marilyn responded.

"I was, but I think it was a good lesson for me to learn: that I can't change anyone but myself. I hoped I could help him. I hoped I could help him see that life is good and beautiful; that life is meant to be spent doing something more than thinking about yourself. But I never reached him. There were moments I thought I was making some progress, but the next time I'd see him he'd be even more wrapped up in himself and his own woes. After months of disappointment, I decided the torture wasn't worth it. I gave up," he said, shaking his head. "Part of me has always regretted it, but I couldn't think of any other way to maintain my sanity."

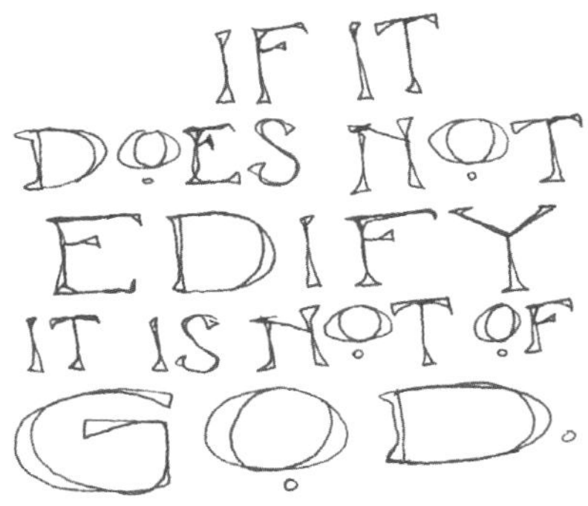

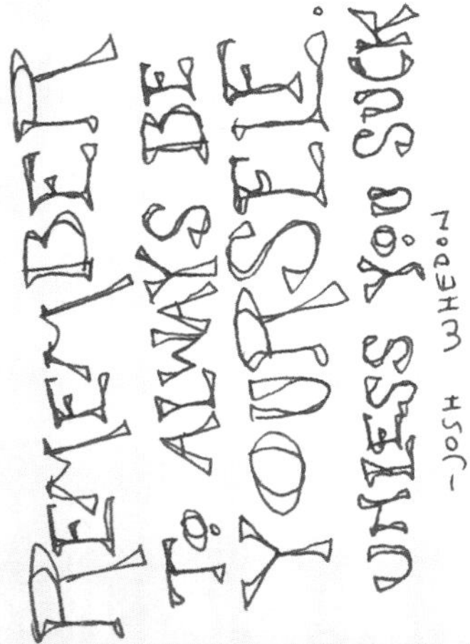

-Chapter 28- Changes

Whether you live to be 50 or 100 makes no difference, if you made no difference in the world. -Jarod Kintz

Bud and Marilyn looked at each other then turned back to Paul as if they were looking at a ghost.

"You didn't, by chance, write all of this stuff down in a journal, did you?" Bud asked, leaning forward against the table.

Paul took a deep breath, exhaling very slowly. He stared down at his plate knowing he'd blown his cover again.

"How do you know about the journal?" Rachel asked.

Bud sat back and shook his head, smiling. "That journal saved my life. I was a lost fool when Max gave me a copy. It gave me hope that I could change and become something more than a broken-hearted drunk."

"It's a beautiful story. I was a little suspicious when Max loaned me a copy. But after I read it, I was angry that he hadn't shared it with me earlier," Marilyn added.

"You've read it too, Mom?"

"Several times. I have a copy of it on my nightstand." She pushed back from the table and left the room before Rachel had time to respond.

She returned seconds later with the manuscript, sliding it across the table.

Rachel looked down at her husband's handwriting glaring back at her.

Paul was speechless.

"That looks kind of like Wolf's journal," Eve said, her words barely discernible through a mouth stuffed with cinnamon roll.

"Have you seen Wolf's journal?" Marilyn asked.

"Uh huh. Daddy got it in the mail from Auntie Katie, and he told me the stories about Wolf yesterday on our trip."

"You actually have the journal with you?" Bud asked, turning his attention from Eve back to Paul.

"Yeah, it's in Mommy's old bedroom," Eve announced.

Marilyn looked at Eve and nodded, reaching for the manuscript. She turned it towards her and pointed to the signature at the bottom of the page. "*Katie Lewis*." She shook her head. "I thought that sounded familiar, but I never made the connection. Why didn't you tell me about this earlier?" she asked, looking up at Rachel. "You could have saved me a lot of heartache."

Rachel shook her head, looking confused. "Mom, I'd never heard about any of this before yesterday. I should be asking you the same question. You usually tell me about the books you're reading."

Marilyn grimaced. "I'm sorry. I would have, I even considered it several times, but I … I didn't want to send you my copy because I wasn't sure if I'd get it back. This is already my second copy. I loaned the first out to Judy, one of the girls at work, and she loaned it to four or five other people before she lost track of it. I was really disappointed, but Max gave me another copy before … well, before he died."

Rachel flipped through the dog-eared pages. "This is starting to sound like the most read book never published."

"I think you may be right," Bud said. "I've shared it with everyone I know. I've probably made a hundred copies from the copy Max gave me, and I know for sure that many of the people I gave copies to have done the same. But that's nothing compared to Max. I'd be surprised if there isn't a huge bouquet of flowers from Kinko's at his funeral today. I think he single-handedly kept them in business. He was kind of the Johnny Appleseed for this journal; sharing it wherever he went."

"And you've really read it several times?" Rachel asked.

Marilyn nodded. "I'm sure there are parts of it I've read fifty times or more. Those are the things I dog-eared."

"Why?" Paul asked, looking at the manuscript and noting that the corners of nearly every page had been folded over.

"I'm surprised you'd ask. You know what's in that journal."

"Yeah, I do—the ramblings of a broken kid who was trying to find himself."

"Those ramblings are some of the most honest writings about life that I've ever read," Marilyn responded.

Paul shook his head. "They were little more than a stream of consciousness."

"And that's exactly what made them refreshing," Bud replied. "They weren't canned or sugar-coated. They're real and simple and understandable for everyone who reads them."

Paul shook his head again. "I don't understand. What is it that people are finding here that makes them want to share it with others?" He flipped open the copied manuscript to one of the dog-eared pages to find notes written in the margins and entire paragraphs underlined. He scanned the page stopping at a line that had been underlined, highlighted in yellow, and marked with stars.

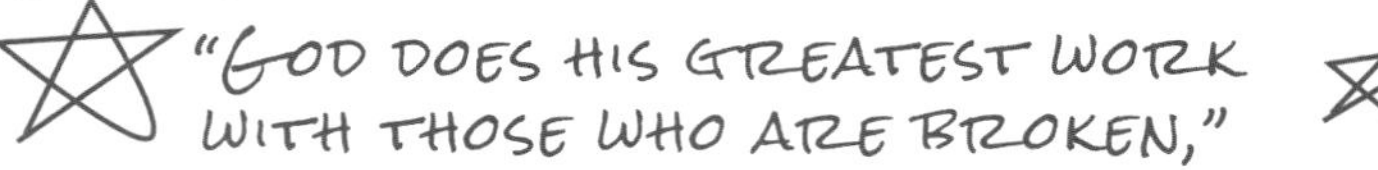

it read. He looked up to find Marilyn and Bud smiling at him.

"God does his greatest work with those who are broken," Bud said. "I think the thing that you're not understanding here is that this journal reaches each of us because it's not only the story of a boy named Wolf. It's our story, too."

"What do you mean?"

"Paul, this story—Wolf's story—it's not just the tale of a kid who's trying to find himself. This is the story," Bud said, pointing to the manuscript, "of the human experience. It's the story of discovering the reality of one's own nakedness in a world we all feel unprepared to face. It's the story we all share of wanting to find our way home to a place that's only a very distant memory. This journal helps everyone who reads it to recognize that we are not alone in our trials of life. We all share in a need for hope and nourishment to body and spirit. We are all sorting through struggles of faith. We are all trying to work through our weaknesses. The stories help us realize that we're not strangers in a strange world, but fellow travelers; brothers and sisters with common roots who share in all the realities of life from birth to death."

"When I first started reading," Marilyn added, "I thought it was crazy that anyone would want to spend so much time going to funerals for people whom they didn't even know. The more I read, the more interesting it became. It sucked me in. When I got to the part about Max, I actually had to ask him if he was really the same guy. Parts of it sounded like it could be him, but it was hard to believe that someone as kind and polished as he was ever could have been the rascal he was described to be. I think it was seeing for myself the changes that had happened in his life that kept me reading and that has kept me going back to it since."

"What kind of changes are you talking about?" asked Paul.

Marilyn looked thoughtful. "I guess it's the same kind of changes you must have made before we met you, Paul."

Like a blunt object, Marilyn's response hit Paul in the face with such force that he sat back in his chair, guilty of passing a judgment he himself had sought so desperately to avoid. He knew the changes he'd made in his own life were real and profound, but even though he'd read a little bit in the obituary about the changes Max had made during the last decade of his life, Paul had remained skeptical that a man with so many character flaws could change and become all he'd been reported

THE TRUTH IS MORE IMPORTANT THAN THE FACTS. —FRANK LLOYD WRIGHT to be—charitable, understanding, patient, kind, and *nonjudgmental*. It was that last one that most shamed Paul. He had judged the old man as one who was incapable of either compassion or change. Yet he had apparently progressed far beyond Paul's own puny accomplishments. He felt sick, ashamed, exposed. He humbly sat silent for what seemed to be several long minutes, struggling to know how to respond. But in that nurturing silence, the answer came in a flood of compassion that nearly overwhelmed his emotions.

"Can you tell me how he changed?" Paul asked softly, humbly.

TRY JESUS. IF YOU DON'T LIKE HIM, THE DEVIL WILL TAKE YOU BACK.

SIGN OUTSIDE CHURCH

"ALWAYS SAY YOU'RE SORRY WHEN YOU HURT YOUR CHILDREN'S FEELINGS."

-Chapter 29- The Gift of Nakedness

Faith is an oasis in the heart that can
never be reached
by the caravan of thinking.
—Khalil Gibran

"You know how he was better than we do," Marilyn responded. "The Max described in the journal is much different than the Max we knew."

"But I don't think we'd fully understand the miracle of Max if we didn't know what he'd started with," Bud interjected.

Marilyn nodded.

"So, what happened? I mean, I know how he was, but the man you both have learned to know and love seems to be a different man completely. How did that happen? How did he change?" asked Paul

Bud looked at Marilyn then back to Paul. "He received a very unusual book as a gift for Christmas."

Paul looked down at the manuscript and shook his head. "I don't understand."

"No change ever comes without sacrifice, and in order to have a new life, we have to be willing to give away the old. That journal was filled with truth, Paul—truth Max needed to hear; truth that no one had been able to tell him; truth that ultimately set him free from the shackles of his own making."

"What does that mean?" asked Rachel.

"It means that book—this book," Bud said, pointing at the journal, "this was the beginning of change. It was a gift given from one man to another that has now changed the course of countless lives. I've had dozens of talks with Max over the past five years about those truths that slapped him in the face and left him with the undeniable reality that his life was a mess. Before he got this journal, he told me he'd deceived himself into believing that life was all about him. He'd been so caught up in his own woes and sorrows that everyone else disappeared."

"I don't think they really disappeared. I think he chased them away," Paul added.

"That's true. The same way I chased my own kids away, not believing I could be comforted," Bud responded.

"Why do we do that?" asked Paul. "Why, when life is the darkest, do we turn our backs to the sun?"

"You know the answer to that," Bud said. "Marilyn and I both learned it from this journal. You discovered a truth that cold night by the lake. It has blessed our lives and so many others who have lived lives of quiet desperation."

"Are you talking about pride?" Paul asked.

"Yes, in part, but I was really thinking about fear."

"Fear?" Rachel asked, looking very confused. "Fear of what?"

"Fear of being loved," Marilyn responded.

"Fear of being loved? Isn't that what we all want?" asked Rachel.

"Yes, of course, but love is dangerous. It opens us up and makes us vulnerable to disappointment and pain. Fear is safer. It sews us up into an iron-clad cocoon and makes us believe we have to protect ourselves by pushing others away. And the more isolated we become, the more the darkness gathers around us. It's all a trick, a dark and cruel lie."

"Just as it says there—that God does his best work with those who

HUG MORE OFTEN.

are broken, I've learned that God can't help us in our fears. We have to step away from our fears and be willing to expose our own vulnerability before we can experience love," Bud said.

"I don't think I get it," Rachel responded.

Marilyn nodded. "I didn't either, at first. It sounded like a bunch of esoteric mumbo jumbo. But Max encouraged me to take a closer look at my heart and try to understand the reasons for the choices I'd made in my life. I was really surprised to see how many decisions I'd made based on fear. And as I took a closer look at those choices, I recognized that the areas of my life that contained the greatest regrets and sorrows were those that still weighed me down with the darkness of fear."

"Like what?" asked Rachel.

"Rachel, after your father left and life went to hell, I'm afraid I spent far too many years simply trying to survive. I know firsthand what it is to live a life of quiet desperation; to feel like you're drowning, but you can't open your mouth to scream for help because water always rushes in to silence your voice. The journal has given me a new perspective. It's made me believe I could change my life. It's made me believe in myself again."

"I didn't know there was ever a time you didn't believe in yourself, Mom."

"Rachel, I put on a pretty good show, but I don't know if I've ever really believed in myself, at least not since your dad left. I was so busy trying to make ends meet and care for you and your brother that I forgot who I was. And when your brother died, a big part of me turned off after that. I feel like I lost two decades of my life, living each day in some sort of fog."

"Why didn't you ever tell me about this?" Rachel asked, emotion hanging from her words.

Marilyn shook her head. "I didn't have the words to express what I was feeling. I just kept telling myself that things would be better next week. But the next week always had at least as many problems as the week before. I was surviving, but there were lots of years that I felt like I was barely breathing."

"Mom, why didn't you ever talk to me about this?"

"Because I was supposed to be the mother. I'm supposed to be the one who had the answers. You were busy with your own life, and then your own family, and I didn't want to rain on your parade."

"I'm sorry you felt that way. I wish you could have talked to me about this," Rachel responded. "I wish there was something I could have done."

"There was lots you did do, honey. You and Paul are raising a beautiful daughter, and you're not allowing your past to determine your future. That's a big thing. It's made me think I didn't screw up as bad I always felt I did."

"Mom, you did the best you could with what you had."

"Maybe, but I was always less than I wanted to be. I recognize now that I've spent a lot of years feeling unworthy of happiness. It wasn't until I read this journal that I began to believe I could do more than survive," she said, reaching her hands across the table to take one of Paul's and one of Rachel's hands. She squeezed their hands tightly until they both looked her into her eyes. "I want you to know that I've never been happier in my life. I feel like the fog I lived under for so many years has all been burned off by the light of hope." She turned her full attention to Paul. "You need to know that this journal has given me hope for the first time in more than twenty years. It's made me want to live a long, long life, so I can make up for the years I lost believing I could save myself."

"What do you mean?" Rachel asked.

"Rachel, I've made a lot of mistakes in my life, but I think my biggest mistake of all has been ignoring the quiet voice of my conscience, believing instead that I could make things better by myself. That kind of thinking has caused me to waste far more time than I'd like to admit. You know faith has been a hard thing for me, but I think I'm beginning to understand why. I've been too concerned about protecting myself and

"MOM MADE IT EASY TO BELIEVE IN THE LOVE OF GOD."

have not been open enough to love. I now understand that love and faith are far more simple than we make them.

"If we can just get our heads out of the way and push out fear, love and faith fall from heaven like a gentle, nourishing rain. A part of me has been broken for a long time and unfortunately, it's the part that once allowed me to listen to my heart. I've missed out on a lot of things because of that, and I'm afraid I've probably influenced you as well," she said, nodding to Rachel.

Rachel looked surprised, then turned away.

"What are you thinking?" Marilyn asked.

"I guess I'm wondering if I should be offended."

"Please don't be. We all have influence on the people around us. That's one of the great things I've recognized from this journal. Reading how the stories of people's lives influenced Wolf and then Max, has made me wonder what pain and sorrow could be avoided if I could just share a few of my stories with the people I love. I wish I could go back and do so many things differently."

"What would you do differently?"

Marilyn waited until her daughter looked into her eyes. "I'd try to forget about my own pain and fear and love you and your brother more. I think maybe every story could be better with a big dose of love. I've blamed myself for your brother's death. I've blamed myself for choices you've made. I'm really sorry that I haven't always been the mother and friend you needed me to be. I know I've told you these things before, but until I started reading this journal, I didn't believe it could get any better. I believed I'd go to my grave with the burden of all those things on my head and shoulders, but I'm beginning to believe I don't have to."

"Mom, are you getting religious on me? I thought you told me our family didn't get that gene."

"I'm sorry that I did. I was foolish and faithless to ever suggest that. I've learned from this journal that all the denial in the world can't put out the light of truth. I've looked for relief from every other source, and I've learned that the burden I've been carrying around for years can only be lifted by God's grace. I've realized that the little voice in my head and heart has been whispering all along that the road to happiness is far shorter than I ever imagined. The miracle of it all is that change begins the moment we sincerely desire it."

"Why haven't you spoken to me about this before, Mom?"

"I wanted to. I was hoping to have this conversation with you at Christmastime, but then you didn't come. It's not really a conversation you can have over the phone, and to be honest, I wasn't sure if you wanted to hear it."

Rachel nodded.

Marilyn turned to Eve. "You helped me see some of this."

"Me?" Eve asked, sitting up a little straighter, excited to be included in the conversation.

"Yes. There's something beautiful and miraculous about a young person's heart that loves without complications. I learned that again in the story of Dr. Dinglebottom and his son. It seems like something changes between the ages of eight and twelve when we lose a connection to our hearts. We start thinking too much, complicating the rest of our lives with fear. For the last several months I've tried to remember my seven year old self. You've been my inspiration," she said, winking at Eve. "It's made me more believing, more trusting, more creative. I've thought of you each time I've put my pottery out in front of people at the farmer's market. You don't worry about what other people think of you or your art. You're far braver than I am, but I'm learning."

Eve smiled from ear to ear. "I just remembered that I brought you some more pictures for your museum."

"Wonderful. I can't wait to see them."

Eve nodded and excused herself from the table, running to her mother's old bedroom where her sketchpad had been stowed. She returned a moment later with both the sketchpad and Wolf's journal. She handed the sketchpad to her grandmother and the journal to her father.

"That's really the journal?" Marilyn asked, looking up over the top of the sketchpad.

"Yes."

"I only saw it once," Bud said. "Max kept it under lock and key. He offered a copy of it to anyone who wanted one, but very few of us ever got to see the original. Do you mind if I take a look?"

"No, sure," Paul said, handing the journal across the table.

"These are beautiful," Marilyn said to Eve as she turned through the pages of her sketchpad. "This one must have taken a long time."

"That one's my favorite. Maybe I could trade it for one of the pretty heart rocks in the window."

Marilyn looked up. "Umm," she said, biting her lip. "Those are Gram's special rocks, but maybe Bud could help us find some for you. He's really good at finding them."

Bud looked up from the journal. "Sure, we could go this afternoon if you want."

"Daddy told me he'd help me, too. I didn't know you collected heart rocks, Grandma."

"Uh, I didn't until a few months ago. Bud has given me one of those for each of the months we've been dating."

Rachel turned to the window to see the seven rocks on the windowsill. She wondered what else her mother had failed to mention.

Bud responded by blushing, leaving his bald head covered in red splotches.

Paul watched the interaction with intrigue, and as Bud unwrapped the long leather strap from around the journal, a thought came to him. Before he could stop himself, he opened his mouth. "How do you know about heart rocks?" he asked Bud.

Bud looked up from the journal. He stared at Paul for a moment as if he were searching for the right words. "You don't know, do you?"

"Don't know what? I was just wondering, with your connection to the parks in Kenosha, if you go hunting for heart rocks at Eichelman Park, too."

Bud smiled. "Absolutely. Max introduced me to heart rocks. The beaches at Eichelman Park were the first place I'd ever noticed them, but now I look for them wherever I go."

"Max introduced you to heart rocks.?" Paul asked, looking both surprised and confused.

"Yeah, we spent a lot of time down on the beach. I've since met a lot of people who have heart-rock collections, but he had more than anyone I ever met. His last wife used to collect them, and after she died, he kept adding to her collection right up until the end. He was actually down at the park looking for rocks when he fell."

"When he fell?"

"Yeah, that's why he went to the hospital. That's when they found his brain tumor. He'd been dizzy for a few weeks, but he insisted on spending time down at the park every day, looking for rocks and making friends. His daughter told me that his pockets were filled with rocks, and spilled out all over the floor when he arrived at the hospital. I thought it was poetic for a man who was filled with so much love."

Paul smiled, but his smile faded as he thought about the first real heart rock he'd ever seen—the rock he'd taken from the bench where he'd almost died. That rock had remained an important reminder. For more than a decade, it had sat on top of his dresser, reminding him daily of a cold winter's night and the joyful warmth he'd felt as he remembered the beautiful things he'd learned from a year's worth of funerals.

"You don't know, do you?" Bud repeated.

"What do you mean? What don't I know."

Bud glanced at Marilyn before setting down the journal. "Paul, I spent many afternoons with Max down at the park. He always told me he was looking for rocks, but I knew what he was really looking for. He was really looking for a boy named Wolf."

"Why?"

"Because he wanted to thank you for giving him ten of the happiest years of his life."

"Why did he think he'd find me at the park?"

"99 yards does not a touchdown make."

"He didn't know where to find you. He didn't even know your last name. Before his driver's license was taken away, he drove all the way to Adams-Friendship looking for you, but he returned home disappointed. He went back to the park because that was the first place he'd ever met you."

Paul looked at Bud, wondering what he was talking about. "I met Max after a funeral."

Bud smiled. "That was the first time you ever met him officially, that you ever shook his hand, but I know that one dark and snowy Christmas night, Max Green pulled a half-frozen young man off the ground near a rather special bench and hauled him off to the hospital, saving his life."

Paul's eyes swelled with tears. "How do you know that?" he spoke softly.

"Max told me all about it. Your journal filled in the rest."

"Why didn't he tell me?" Paul managed to say, choking on his emotions.

"He didn't remember you any more than you remembered him. He didn't know who you were until he read about it in your journal. He went to the lake every day looking for you, Paul, hoping you'd come back so he could return your journal. He wanted to tell you he was sorry for the way he had treated you. He wanted to show you what he'd done with the time your influence had given him. Your journal is a wonderful story of redemption, but you and most of those who read the story only know the half of it. I used to think that only those who knew Max would ever know the whole story. But the story of redemption continues in the hearts and lives of all who are touched by your words. If Max hadn't been there for you, your story would be much different. It would have ended years ago and life for all of us in this room would have been very different. But by saving you, Paul, Max has indirectly saved hundreds, if not thousands, of lives by sharing your journal and giving us hope. You'll probably never know the numbers of people who have been touched by your journal. Marilyn and I are only two people who have been blessed by your words and the truths those words speak to our souls. I'm sure you had no idea, as you went to a year's worth of funerals, that by doing so, life would have greater meaning and understanding for all who would read about it. One of the greatest lessons I've learned from all of this is that we need each other, strangers and friends alike. I'm convinced that we're limited only by our own fears. If we can set the fears aside and love without reservation or judgment, this world can be a better place for all of us.

"Max often spoke of a recurring dream he began having shortly after you gave him your journal. In his dream, he saw a weaver's loom with thousands of threads forming a colorful pattern. As he examined the cloth he became alarmed by holes that broke up the pattern, leaving unsightly blemishes in the cloth. He interpreted the cause of those blemishes as the results of the people he'd neglected and cut out of his life. The truth, Paul, is that we're all connected. We're all threads in each other's tapestries, and each of us is necessary to the creation of the whole. Life, for many of us, would have been very different if any of the events associated with this journal had been different, and the ripples you started when you shared your journal with Max continue to spread. It seems there are no coincidences, only spiritual designs we don't understand."

THERE IS NOTHING WE CAN'T LIVE DOWN, RISE ABOVE OR OVERCOME.
-ELLA WHEELER WILCOX

THANKS BE UNTO GOD FOR HIS UNSPEAKABLE GIFT.
2 CORINTHIANS 9:15

RISE AND SHINE

-CHAPTER 30- THE SONGS OF REDEEMING LOVE

YOU CAN CUT ALL THE FLOWERS BUT YOU CANNOT KEEP SPRING FROM COMING.
-PABLO NERUDA

The phone rang, and Marilyn excused herself to get it.

"Oh, hey, Katie. Good morning to you, too. Yeah, they got in last night. Yes. No. We're just finishing breakfast. No, no. I think everybody's done. Would you like to talk to Rachel? Of course, here she is." Marilyn handed the phone across the table, and the breakfast conversation died as everyone eavesdropped.

Bud looked up at the clock on the wall. It was 8:45. "I think I better go," he said turning to Marilyn. "I've got a bunch of bowls to trim before the funeral."

"Do you need any help?"

"No, stay here with the kids. I'll be fine. Do you want to just meet me at the funeral?"

Marilyn looked at Paul. "Do you mind if I ride with you?"

"No, of course not."

"You probably ought to get there early. I took the canoes over yesterday so we wouldn't have to worry about them." Bud stood up from his chair. "You might ask if the kids want to float the river with us, too." He leaned down and kissed Marilyn quickly before blushing again. "I'll see you guys later," he said, making his way quickly to the door.

Paul watched him go, and as the door closed, he turned back to find Marilyn blushing also. Rachel's lively conversation with Katie had ended abruptly, at least on their end, as Rachel stared at her mother, a slight smile on her lips.

Eve giggled. "Grandma, you have a boyfriend!"

Marilyn smiled and nodded. "Are you okay with that?"

Eve nodded. "He's handsome."

"I really like him," Paul offered. "He seems like a really down-to-earth guy."

"Would you expect anything different from a potter?"

"Katie, did you know my mom has a boyfriend?" Rachel asked into the phone.

A squeal erupted out of the receiver.

"Yeah, I'll tell you about him later."

Marilyn rolled her eyes.

"Yeah, why?" Rachel continued. "You're going, too? Do you have time, I mean with all your wedding stuff? Oh. Sure, we'll save you a seat. Yeah, sure. We can't wait to see you either. Yeah, we'll see you in a couple of hours." She hung up the phone and turned and smiled at her mom. "I'm sorry about earlier. I think Bud's a really nice guy."

"Thanks, honey. He's really good to me," Marilyn responded with a smile.

"How did you say you met him?"

"Max introduced us last October. I started taking pottery classes from him a couple of weeks later. We've spent a ton of time together since then. I was worried about getting my own wheel and kiln at first, wondering if I'd see him as often, but I've seen him even more than before. He's really a wonderful guy. I'm kind of mad that Max didn't introduce me to him sooner."

"Do you think you would have been ready to date him any sooner?" Paul asked.

Marilyn smiled but shook her head. "No, I think Max must have known that. There were lots of things that had to line up just right in order for all of this to work. I don't know where it's going, but I'm having a really wonderful time experiencing love again."

Rachel smiled at her mom whose smile hadn't faded since she started talking about Bud.

"What's this about the canoes?" Paul asked.

"Oh, that, yeah, um, a few of us are planning on riding the canoes down the river with Max's ashes," Marilyn said.

"He was cremated then?" asked Paul

"Yeah, about five or six years ago, from what I understand, Max decided to become an organ donor."

"Wasn't he like ninety-something years old?" asked Rachel.

"Yes. Ninety-two, I think."

"And they still wanted his organs?"

"I thought that was interesting, too, but apparently they've been able to use organs from people that were even older. He was in surprisingly good shape for his age. He hadn't smoked in sixty-something years, and he gave up drinking more than ten years ago. He hoped they'd be able to use whatever still worked and wanted whatever was left of him to be cremated. His ashes are going to be scattered from the bridge behind the church right after the funeral."

"That's an interesting way to wrap up the end of your life," said Rachel.

"Yeah, I thought so too, but he was pretty open and vocal about what he wanted. When he heard that his body could help as many as fifty people, he had Kinko's print off fifty copies of the journal so everyone who received a piece of him would also get a piece of his story. I was inspired by his thoughtfulness. I actually registered to be an organ donor, too, when I renewed my driver's license."

ONE CANNOT BE BOTH FAITH FILLED AND STRESS FREE. —NEAL MAXWELL

"I can understand being an organ donor, but I don't know about being cremated. Why did he want that?" asked Rachel.

"I wondered the same thing, but his reasons made me think about our cultural traditions. He told me that he'd always been both claustrophobic and frugal and couldn't imagine spending ten thousand dollars on a casket and embalming services just to make him look like a piece of wax for a couple of hours before they would lower it all into a grave and cover him with dirt. He said he figured that since we all turned back into dust anyway, it just made sense to speed up the process."

Rachel squirmed. "I don't think I could do that. I can't imagine burning up and turning to ash."

"I don't think you'd feel anything, honey," Marilyn teased. "I always thought the same way, but maybe I'd prefer that over having my body be eaten by worms."

Rachel pulled a disgusted face and turned away. "Mom, yuck!"

"I know, I'm sorry. But Max's death has made me think a lot about it. Did you know that in Europe and many other parts of the world, farmland is so important that you can't buy a plot in a cemetery? You can only rent it for twenty to thirty years. Then they dig up whatever's left and cremate the remains to make room for the next person who dies. They even resurface the headstones."

"Are you kidding?"

"No. At least that's what Max told me. I don't have a funeral plan, but if I had to decide today, I think I'd rather be cremated. I'd rather have you kids get some inheritance than spend all that money to make me look good for the worms."

"Where would we put your ashes?" asked Rachel.

"I don't know. I'll get back to you on that. Maybe I'll make an urn for myself. Bud wants his ashes to be turned into a glaze and fired on the last of his pots that can be given to his family and friends. That's not a bad idea either."

"That's kind of gross," Rachel responded, pulling a face.

"Maybe, but we forget sometimes that our world is made up of exactly

"THE GOSPEL OF CHRIST IS FOUNDED ON LOVE AND SUSTAINED BY IT."

the same elements today as it was whenever it was created. When we die, our bodies eventually turn back into those same basic elements and get recycled to nourish future generations."

ELEMENTS OF THE HUMAN BODY

OXYGEN 65%
CARBON 18%
HYDROGEN 10%
NITROGEN 3%
CALCIUM 1.5%
PHOSPHORUS 1.0%
POTASSIUM .35%
SULPHUR .25%
SODIUM .15%
MAGNESIUM .05%

*ACCORDING TO WWW.ABOUT.COM

"It sounds like you've been thinking a lot about this, Mom."

Marilyn nodded. "I suppose I have. I'm almost sixty, and even though I don't think I'm old, my body is starting to remind me that I'm not eighteen any more. I've been thinking a lot about my story; about the kind of stuff that might be said at my funeral. I've got a lot to learn and a lot of things to figure out. I think I know what I want to be when I grow up, but until recently, I didn't feel like there was a bridge that spanned the canyon between where I am and where I want to be. I think I probably knew all along where I needed to look, but I was unwilling to look for it there."

"Are you talking about God?" Paul asked.

Marilyn nodded. "It's such a silly thing really—to think that I spent so much time denying myself the help and power of God because I didn't want to complicate my life. My life has been so much easier since I came back to faith. I still have lot of questions—maybe I always will. But I realize I've spent the last twenty years trying to hide from God." She smiled and shook her head. "But He knew where I was all along. I feel as though He's been waiting for me to open my heart again, because when I finally did, He flooded it with twenty year's worth of love."

"Mom, why didn't we ever talk about this?"

"What would it have helped, Rachel? Did you have any answers for me? I know I didn't have any answers for you. It would have been a case of the blind leading the blind. I don't believe answers can be found through commiseration. Believe me, I spent more than twenty years trying. I think we're all looking for unmovable truths that can give us an anchor in our shifting world, but I never found any that worked for me until … until I read a journal by a boy named Wolf."

Rachel turned to look at Paul. "What is it about this journal?" she asked as she reached for the original. She opened the soft leather cover and began flipping through the pages. She noted several words that were written in bold script, scattered from page to page in the margins. They watched as she stopped at these words and phrases and the pixilated, yellowing photos of the people who had inspired Wolf to record them.

"It's a love story, honey," Marilyn said.

"What do you mean?"

"I don't know where it is exactly, but somewhere in there Wolf came to the same conclusion—that the only way to real, enduring happiness was through discovering the truth of God's love for each of us. That was the missing link for me; recognizing that God is more anxious to love me than he is to judge me or condemn me. That journal is filled with the songs of redeeming love.

"I'm sorry I didn't understand these things earlier, Rachel. There are so many sorrows I believe we all could have avoided if we'd understood the reality of God's love. I hope to spend the rest of my life helping other people recognize it. I know our world is filled with people leading lives of quiet desperation. If they could only know that God loves them, I believe they would feel much less desperate and actually begin to live.

"If we could see all the ways we're connected to each other, I think we'd probably do a lot of things differently. If you hadn't shared your journal with Max, I wouldn't have met Bud. Bud would probably still be an alcoholic, and Max would have died a lonely death. Things happen the way they do for a reason. We each play a part in each other's lives."

"I'm confused," Eve responded, looking up at her father.

"About what, baby?" asked Rachel.

"About Wolf."

Rachel and Marilyn turned to Paul. He shifted uncomfortably in his chair. "What would you like to know, baby?"

"Are you Wolf?"

Paul stared at his daughter for a moment thinking about the things Sheron had told him the day before, that knowing the truth about his past might help his daughter avoid life's troubles. He knew he couldn't lie to her. "Yes, I am."

Eve's face lit up with a smile. "Why didn't you tell me?"

Paul bit his lip, fighting his emotions. "Because I was afraid."

"Of what?" she asked innocently.

"I was afraid of what you'd think of me after you knew the truth of who I am."

Eve blinked, looking confused, then she smiled again. "You're my Daddy."

IF I COULD SAVE TIME IN A BOTTLE
THE FIRST THING THAT I'D LIKE TO
DO IS TO SAVE EVERY DAY TILL
ETERNITY PASSES AWAY
JUST TO SPEND THEM WITH YOU.
"TIME IN A BOTTLE"
—JIM CROCE

IT IS UP
TO YOU TO
ILLUMINATE
THE WORLD.
—PHILLIPPE VENIER

"IF EVER YOU ARE
SAD, LOOK UP AT THE
CEILING AND SMILE
AND COUNT TO TEN
AND YOU'LL LOOK SO
SILLY THAT YOU'LL
START TO LAUGH AND
SOON YOU WON'T FEEL
SAD."

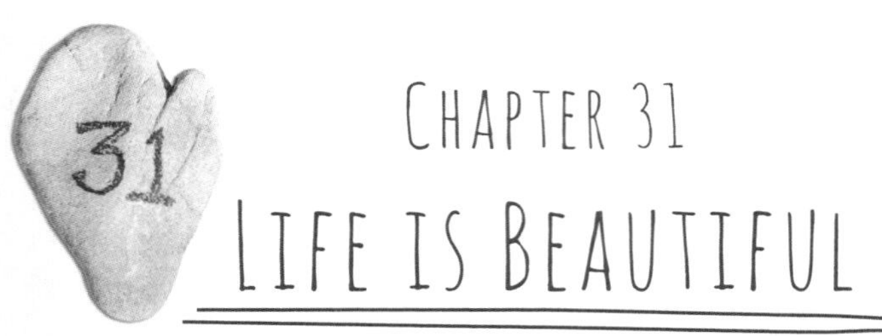

CHAPTER 31
LIFE IS BEAUTIFUL

LOVE CANNOT SAVE LIFE FROM DEATH, BUT IT CAN FULFILL LIFE'S PURPOSE.
– ARNOLD TOYNBEE

"We'd better get moving if we're going to make it to the funeral on time," Marilyn said, glancing up at the clock.

"I'll do the dishes if you girls want to get ready," Paul responded.

"That hardly seems fair. You made breakfast."

"I insist," he said with a smile. "I know how long it takes girls to get ready for the day, especially if they're going out in public."

Rachel turned to her mom. "What do people wear to a Quaker funeral?"

"This is the first Quaker funeral I've ever been to, but I think you'd feel most comfortable in a skirt, if you brought one. That's what I'll be wearing."

Rachel looked at Eve. "Neither of us brought anything black."

"I don't think it's that kind of funeral," Marilyn suggested, turning to Paul for help.

"I think I only went to two Quaker funerals, and if I remember right, both of them were fairly informal. I'm sure some people will be wearing jeans, but I planned on wearing my khakis and a white button-down shirt."

"What are you going to wear to the wedding tomorrow?" asked Rachel.

"Umm, probably my khakis and a white button-down shirt," Paul replied.

Rachel laughed. "You men don't know how good you've got it. I brought three outfits for Eve and four for myself, so I can change my mind if I want."

"I'm sure any of those would be fine, but you might want to consider what would be comfortable in a canoe," Paul responded.

"Do you want to do that?" asked Rachel, looking at Paul.

"Yeah, if it's okay with you."

"I haven't been in a canoe since Camp Pochalahookee when I was twelve. I seem to remember it being pretty tippy. Were you thinking of taking Eve, too?"

"That sounds fun," Eve said, making the decision for them.

While the women hurried off to the showers, Paul cleared the table and washed the dishes. Standing at the sink in front of the windowsill, his attention was once again drawn to the heart rocks that Bud had given Marilyn. He picked up the largest one, a nice mottled tan stone with chocolate colored stripes. He turned it over in his hand, examining the back side which was even prettier, and was just returning it to it's place on the windowsill when a mark at the tip of the heart caught his attention. He held the stone closer to his eyes, trying to figure out what the mark was.

To his surprise, Paul discovered a small spiral that looked like it had been made with a tiny snail shell. He knew that the beaches of Lake Michigan were littered with tiny snail shells, but he'd never seen one make an impression in stone like this. He wondered if it might be part of a fossil. He set the rock down and picked up the one next to it and was surprised to find a similar marking on the underside of that one, too. He picked up the next one and the next. Of the seven rocks in the windowsill, he discovered the same mark on five of them.

The squirrel in the yard drew his attention once again, beckoning him to come outdoors. He returned the rocks to the windowsill and quickly wiped off the table before grabbing his journal and heading out the backdoor. After wiping dried needles off the Adirondack chair, he took a seat under the shade of an overgrown pine. Already, the day was warm and humid and Paul leaned forward to stretch his back, feeling lazy and road-worn. The squirrel stopped to chirp at him until it realized Paul was no threat. Then it continued its work of carrying the acorns from the oak tree in the corner of the yard to its hiding place. Paul watched several of these trips until he began to daydream, thinking about the events of the last twenty-four hours. So many things had changed in that short period of time.

The journey home to Kenosha had been a journey to the center of his core, to the roots of who he was and had been. For more than twelve years, he'd kept these roots private in an effort to protect himself from the judgment of others. But now that the truth was out, he wondered what he'd been afraid of. He'd been most concerned about Eve—how she might respond to the truth of who her father was and the mistakes he'd made along the way. But her response in the face of that truth was anything but judgmental. As he pondered that reality, he became emotionally overwhelmed with the recognition that the light of love had overpowered the darkness of the fear he'd carried with him for far too many years.

Opening his journal, Paul flipped through the pages, stopping at the photos of these near-strangers who had left him inspired, teaching him lessons that had changed his life, offering wisdom, experience, and perspective. With only a few minor exceptions, these men and women had lived their lives without position, authority, or celebrity. If they'd enjoyed the spotlight at all, it was a short-lived fifteen seconds of fame. To an untrained eye, each of them had led common lives, but nearly all of them had given Paul at least one piece of a complicated puzzle. They had enabled him to discover who he was by trying on the truths he'd learned from them, figuring out which ones fit. Page after page, the pictures he'd attached and the quotes he'd written years before triggered

"TRUE LOVE ALWAYS BREAKS THROUGH THE HARDEST TRIALS."

memories. He recognized that many of his best ideas had been directly inspired and influenced by these people. Some, like Dr. Dinglebottom, had had a profound effect on his life, but all of them had been helpful, even the few painful ones that had left him feeling empty. Page after page, he looked into the faces of these men and women who had become his friends, his heroes, his inspiration. Once again, he laughed and cried at the notes he'd taken at their funerals.

Solemnly, he read through several of his own eulogies that grew as the journal progressed like a snowball gathering mass and strength with each revolution. He smiled to himself as he read through portions of those eulogies that he'd already accomplished—becoming a husband and a father and securing a brighter future for himself by obtaining an education. But he was also humbled by the reality of all he still lacked and hoped to accomplish. His extended lease on life had offered him so many opportunities for obtaining joy. And though he'd tried hard to take advantage of those opportunities, he felt a renewed sense of responsibility to make whatever time he had left count for something good.

He was distracted from his thoughts by Rachel's hand on his shoulder, and he turned to see her smiling.

"It's your turn for the shower," she said. "Mom says we need to leave in about twenty minutes."

Paul nodded, wiping the tears from his eyes. He stood quickly and kissed her, handing her the journal as he rushed off to the shower. But as he passed through the kitchen, he stopped at the window once again. Rachel was sitting on the edge of the chair he'd just vacated, his open journal, resting on her knee.

"You'd better get moving," Marilyn said from behind him.

Paul nodded, but didn't turn.

Marilyn came closer and stood beside him. "Is that your journal?"

"Yeah."

She nodded. "I've wanted to share it with her for months."

"Why didn't you?" he asked.

"Because I worried that she wasn't ready. I didn't want to turn her off from it before she gave it a chance. You know how she is about spiritual things," Marilyn responded.

"Yeah. What happened to her?"

"What do you mean?"

"I mean, how did she become so cynical about … that kind of stuff?" asked Paul.

Marilyn pressed her lips together. "We're all the products of our environment, aren't we? I'm sure I wasn't any help, Paul. I was one of the biggest cynics I ever knew."

Paul looked at Marilyn and nodded. "So what changed?"

"An old man took the time to convince me that I was worth loving."

"Max?"

Marilyn nodded. "I learned that from Max, but I was just realizing I've learned the same lessons from you as I've watched you love Rachel."

Paul looked sideways, ignoring the time. "What are you talking about?"

"Paul, I've meant to tell you this a hundred times before, and I'm sorry I've been stingy with my compliments. I've always been very grateful for the way you've loved my daughter. You've inspired me many times over the years to be a little kinder and more patient to those around me. I realized this morning that I listened to Max because there was something about him that reminded me of you."

"Me? What?"

"I know you didn't know this side of Max, but the Max I knew was a peacemaker, a big man with a gentle heart and a soft touch who loved the people around him with patience and empathy. You're *that* kind of man, Paul. You're *that* kind of husband and father. I'm sure there have been many times that Rachel has tried that patience. I know; I lived with her for the first eighteen years of her life. I used to think she was more like her father, but I'm beginning to realize how my cynicism undoubtedly influenced hers," Marilyn lamented.

Paul stared out the window at Rachel, not knowing how to respond.

"I'm sorry for the sorrows and pain you experienced before we met you," Marilyn continued. "But you need to know that those trials and the perspective you gained along the way, and the record you kept of it all have been the balm so many of us have needed."

Paul shook his head. "I still don't understand that. I was only trying to wake up a grumpy old man and help him see that life can be beautiful."

"And in the process, you've woken us all up, Paul. Life *is* beautiful if we can open our hearts to the love God intends us to have."

Paul pressed his lips together as he continued to watch Rachel through the window. "Do you think she'll ever see it?"

Marilyn nodded and smiled. "It looks to me like she already is."

I LIKE THE SILENT CHURCH BEFORE THE SERVICE BEGINS, BETTER THAN ANY PREACHING. —RALPH WALDO EMERSON

LIVE SO EVERYONE THINKS YOU ARE THEIR BEST FRIEND.

THERE IS NOT ROYAL ROAD TO ANYTHING. ONE THING AT A TIME, AND ALL THINGS IN SUCCESSION. THAT WHICH GROWS SLOWLY ENDURES. —JOSIAH HOLLAND

-CHAPTER 32- RAISING EBENEZER

LET US BE SILENT,
THAT WE MAY HEAR THE WHISPER OF GOD.
-RALPH WALDO EMERSON

"I think we might have underestimated the turnout," Marilyn said from the backseat as they neared the Quaker Church on Green Bay Road. Cars were parked on both sides of the road, narrowing the passage as Paul approached the driveway and small parking lot that were already filled beyond capacity a half-hour before the funeral was slated to begin. He continued driving past the turnout, finally finding parking a hundred yards down the road in the thick grass.

"He sure knew a lot of people," Eve said as they entered the church's humble drive. People of all ages were milling about, visiting in clusters in the shade of the large cottonwood trees. Several men scurried about, carrying wooden planks and logs from the beds of two pickup trucks that were double-parked in the small parking lot.

"That's Bud's truck," Marilyn said, pointing to the license plate that read POTRMAN.

"You made it," Bud said, rushing past them with several other men. He looked haggard and sweaty. "The AC's out of commission and too many people have come anyway. We're setting up benches down by the river."

"Do you need any help?" Paul asked.

"Sure! Grab an end."

Paul let go of Eve's hand and took one end of the stack of boards that had been resting on the tailgate. Another man, about sixty-five years old, grabbed the other end. They carried the boards quickly and awkwardly to the far side of the church then down the gentle slope to a flat area not far from the river's edge. Several other men were busy setting up makeshift benches in concentric circles using the logs and boards that the men and a few women continued to feed them. Paul noticed with each trip to the parking lot that the crowd continued to grow. On his final trip, he smiled to himself when he saw Katie wrapping her arms around Rachel and Eve.

People began occupying the benches before the last of them were even set up. Ushers encouraged the visitors to squeeze in tightly, despite the heat, to make room for everyone who wanted to sit. When it became clear that there would still not be enough seats, the ushers invited the men under fifty to give up their seats to the women and move to the sloping grassy banks that formed a natural amphitheater around the gathering. Rachel, Marilyn, Katie and Eve were some of the last to arrive, and they found space on a bench on the outermost row, just a few feet from where Bud and Paul had claimed a shaded patch of crabgrass.

Just moments after they'd taken a seat, an older man about seventy years old walked to the center of the large circle and cleared his throat. The people stopped talking and turned their attention to him until the gentle babbling of the river could be heard.

"Friends, I welcome you here today to help us celebrate the life of John Maximilian Green, probably known to most of us as Max. We're sorry the air-conditioning in the church house is out of commission, but I'm convinced that it wouldn't have done any good anyway if we'd have tried to cram all four hundred of us into a space designed for eighty. I hope you'll excuse the potentially slivery nature of our improvisations and make the most of this short time we have to share together."

A hushed bit of laughter rolled through the audience as people adjusted to their slivery seats.

"Somehow, I think Max would have wanted it this way," the man continued. "All of us sitting shoulder to shoulder, keeping each other warm." He smiled a friendly smile as the crowd stirred again with light-hearted laughter that immediately seemed to cool things off by at least ten degrees.

"Our small congregation has only about sixty people in attendance most Sundays, so I am going to make the assumption, if I may be so bold, that many of you here today are not Quakers and therefore may be unfamiliar with our religious traditions an practices."

Many in the gathering nodded.

The man in the center of the circle smiled. "Quakers are also known as the Religious Society of Friends, but today we welcome you all as friends and as friends of Max. Our religious practices are different from what you may be accustomed to, and I have been asked to offer a brief explanation of these customs. We believe that no man is above any other, and for this reason, we have no clergy. Silence is our sacrament, and we believe, as the Good Book says, that where two or more are gathered together desiring to feel of God's love, that love will be made manifest through his Holy Spirit[1]. We gather in silence, waiting expectantly for that spirit to light upon us. Our services are traditionally much … how shall I say this … quieter than anything you have probably experienced in such services before, but not necessarily so.

As part of this funeral service, each of you is invited to participate, to stand, or sit where you are, as the spirit enters your heart, and to share what you will as a tribute to Max or to the God of heaven and earth. Traditionally, funeral services such as these last about an hour and end when two members of the Society of Friends shake hands. We have asked Johanna Pratt and Darby Mulligan," he said, gesturing to the women seated next to each other on the front row, "to give us that signal when they feel the

"LOVE THEM IF YOU EVER HOPE TO CHANGE THEM."

1. Matthew 18:20

meeting should come to a close. At which time, we invite you to shake hands with your neighbors. You are welcome to leave afterwards, or to stay and linger with us as Max's ashes are scattered.

"In the interest of reverence, I invite you all to turn off your cell phones now, so the spirit of peace and love can be with each of us without interruption." He waited as most of the people contorted their bodies to reach their phones in the crowded space. When silence fell again, the man in the center lifted up a beautiful black urn from a small table next to him and held it high enough for the people on the back row to see it.

"In keeping with the virtue of simplicity, many Quakers choose cremation over burial. You may or may not be aware that Max was an organ donor. His daughter, Stephanie, has informed us today that even at his advanced age, doctors were able to give nearly thirty people a new lease on life from organs donated by Max. The rest of his mortal body has been cremated, and his ashes have been placed within this beautiful urn. We reverence these remains as we would any other human remains as the tabernacle of clay that once housed Max's eternal spirit. As we gather here together in his honor, we invite that eternal spirit, as well as the spirit of God to be with us, to comfort and sustain us in our sorrows and loss. We will miss him. We will miss him for the man he was, the friend he was to each of us, and the love and light he gave to this world."

The man carefully set the urn back on the table and nodded to the women on the front row before humbly excusing himself, taking a seat on the last row of benches. With that, silence fell across the congregation. The sound of the river babble grew louder, as did the rustle of the giant Cottonwood leaves high above their heads, but these sounds were calming and peaceful. The songs of birds echoed around them, and many heads were turned to the patchwork of sunlight and sky that filtered in through the overhead branches.

Paul closed his eyes, trying to focus his attention. Silence was not new for him. He often sought it out, especially after long, noisy shifts at the station. And many times, following those shifts, before opening the door to his home, he'd climbed the ladder to Eve's treehouse in search

Marry a truly quality person— One who makes you work hard to be worthy of them.

of the silence that nurtured a spiritual connection with the unseen world. "Be still, and know that I am God," he'd often repeated to himself, almost as a mantra, when he found himself in noisy or chaotic surroundings. And most times it had worked, bringing him the inner peace he craved.

But as he found himself silently repeating those words in his mind now, with nothing but the gentle sounds of nature humming in the background, a different kind of peace filled his heart and mind. He closed his eyes tighter, trying to discern exactly what that peace was. As he did so, he opened his mind to a gentle breeze as it wove its way through his memories. Paul was surprised where it stopped, focusing on the face of Dr. Dinglebottom and the vision of him asking the nurses if his young roommate could stay—despite the fact that the end was near. "Why had this permission been granted?" Paul asked himself. The question was immediately answered by another vision of a nearly incoherent Dr. Dinglebottom holding the hand of his daughter and asking that the boy in the next bed be allowed to stay in his room until he passed.

The vision startled Paul. Where had it come from? He couldn't think of a time he'd seen this memory before. He wasn't even sure it was *his* memory to begin with. And yet here it was, leaving him filled with the spirit of mercy. He felt a tear trickle down his cheek, as he considered how that selfless act of love and concern from a near-stranger had started big changes in his heart.

In quick succession, the events that had followed played out again in his mind. The funeral. The feeling of warmth he felt there. The other funerals he'd attended in his search for meaning and understanding. The people he'd met along the way. The eulogies he'd written for himself. The decision to become a paramedic. To go back to school. To become a fireman. And then there was Max. The Slurpee that had opened the door. The lunches and dinners that were often painful and long. The determination he'd had to change him. And finally, the last time he saw him, Christmas night, 1999—the night he gave him his journal.

He'd been hesitant to give the old man this gift despite the undeniable, unrelenting promptings to do so. He slipped the gift into his hands, shook the old man's hand and walked out into the cold night, confused by the warmth he felt in his heart, somehow knowing he'd done the right thing.

And then there was the rock. Paul knew better than to seek for signs, but that rock, waiting for him on the bench where he'd tried to put an end to his life the year before was the sign he didn't know he needed. It had served since that night as reminder of the love of God. He'd never talked about it with anyone, but he'd wondered from time to time if the woman in the long, white dress might have put that token there for him to find.

The silence was broken by the voice of a woman. Paul opened his eyes to see a gray-haired woman near the center of the circle.

"I'm not a Quaker," she said, nodding to the women on the front row, "but I was Max's friend, and I'm grateful today to be your friend. I had a lot of things I thought I wanted to say when I came here, but in this silence, I've changed my mind. I want to sing you a song instead. This was one of Max's favorites. But before I do that, I'd like to say thank you, Max. Thank you for being my friend."

She closed her eyes and opened her mouth, and the voice that came out of her was much different than the voice that had just spoken. It was strong and rich and filled with conviction.

Come, thou Fount of every blessing,
tune my heart to sing thy grace;
streams of mercy, never ceasing,
call for songs of loudest praise.
Teach me some melodious sonnet,
sung by flaming tongues above.
Praise the mount! I'm fixed upon it,
mount of thy redeeming love.
Here I raise mine Ebenezer;
hither by thy help I'm come;

and I hope, by thy good pleasure,
safely to arrive at home.
Jesus sought me when a stranger,
wandering from the fold of God;
He, to rescue me from danger,
interposed his precious blood.

As she began the third verse, she was joined in singing by one, then three, then dozens of people, mostly older folks, who lifted their voices in a joyful noise.

O to grace how great a debtor
daily I'm constrained to be!
Let thy goodness, like a fetter,
bind my wandering heart to thee.
Prone to wander, Lord, I feel it,
prone to leave the God I love;
here's my heart, O take and seal it,
seal it for thy courts above.

By the time the hymn ended, there was hardly a dry eye to be found. The spirit of love and peace had entered in through the doorway of music, bringing with it the glory of God's grace. Paul was grateful for it. The silence before it had been nurturing, but the sharing of this beautiful hymn was even more so. He remembered one Quaker funeral he'd attended where it had been suggested that during their services, Quakers would speak only when they believed that what they had to say could improve on the silence. And as silence fell again like a shroud over the huddled congregants, the spirit of peace intensified.

Paul looked to his right to see Bud smiling through his tears. This big, teddy bear of a man was not afraid to wear his emotions on his sleeve. He turned to his left at the sound of sniffles and saw two other men sitting on a neighboring patch of crabgrass who had also become emotional. There was no shame in grown men crying here. Paul remembered that he'd once heard this outpouring of emotion referred to as "liquid happiness," and he smiled to himself when he noticed tears on Rachel's cheeks as well. He knew she'd felt something. Eve turned around to look at him, her face filled with a smile.

Near the center of the circle, another woman stood. "I didn't think I'd be able to share anything today, but after that beautiful song, I can't help myself." She reached into the pocket of her skirt and pulled out a fistful of something, cradling the small object in her hands like a delicate bird. "The words of this hymn reminded me that I hold in my hands an "Ebenezer" that Max gave me several years ago. I've carried it with me ever since to help me remember. I don't know many of the stories from the Bible, but Max, when he gave me this stone, told me the story of the prophet Samuel, who celebrated the victory of the children of Israel over their enemies by setting up a stone marker. He called the place Ebenezer, which, if I remember correctly means 'stone of help.' It was to serve as a reminder of the love and mercy and divine help God offered them."[1]

She held up the stone in her hand for everyone to see, and even from where Paul sat, more than forty feet away, he could clearly see that it was a heart rock.

"Max gave me this stone on the day I met him at the park. That must have been eight years ago." The woman's eyes filled with tears, and she looked down for a moment before lifting her head again. "I had just taken my husband to a rest home. After taking care of him by myself for five years, his Alzheimer's had become more than I could handle. I had watched him suffer and decline, but I knew I couldn't do it any more. I felt like a traitor, like I'd abandoned him, and I was hopelessly in need of comfort. Max found me crying on a bench near the lake and invited me to dinner. That night and many times over these last few years, he has reminded me again and again what it is to be a Christian. To offer comfort to those who need comforting, and to mourn with those who mourn. I've heard that he has shared dozens of these Ebenezers with people he's met along the way, but I believe mine is special. It reminds

1. Samuel 7:12

me that God has not forsaken me; that He cares. I believe He's watching over me and placing angels, like Max, in my path to help me remember His mercy. My life has been blessed by knowing Max and by the love he gave me." She nodded solemnly and sat down.

Silence fell again over the congregation but didn't last long before a man stood from the crabgrass on the outskirts of the congregation. Paul recognized him as one of the men who had helped set up the makeshift chapel. His rainbow-colored suspenders helped hide a smudge of dirt on the side of his ample belly.

"My name is Peter Caldwell, and I am proud to say that I am a stepson of Max Green." Many heads turned to look at him. "He met my mother, Millie, at a bowling alley a few years after my father died. We were all suspicious of him at first, but my sisters and I learned to love him, as did our children and their children. He took care of my mother and loved her with a gentle kindness." The big man took a white handkerchief from his pocket and wiped his eyes before he continued. "When my mother died, we lost track of Max for a while. We were all grieving her loss, but I don't think any of us realized how much Max missed her. It seems like his buggy hit a patch of rough road there for a while. He cut the ties we had, and my sisters and I didn't see him for over a decade. We became reacquainted almost ten years ago when he became the crossing guard for my youngest grandchildren's school. I think that saved him. Many of us here today remember the recipe for a happy life that he shared with us, someone to love, something to do and something to look forward to. He taught me those things by watching him care for the children at the school as he got up every morning in the sun, rain, and snow to help them cross the street. Those kids were the medicine he needed to heal his heart and come back to life.

"Over the last ten years or so, he's become a friend to all of us once again. I never imagined I could use a male role model at my age, but I learned to love that old man like he was my own father. He helped me to remember that the greatest joys in life come from giving and loving the people around us, and connecting regularly with a higher power. He invited all of us to be his friends and his family. I'll always remember his advice to enlarge the circle and invite others in. He was my stepfather for only a few years, but he'll always be my friend. I love him, and I am grateful that he shared his life with me and my family. He often talked about heaven, how he imagined it would be. And somehow in my mind, I imagined something like this gathering here today—people united in love and the grace of God. I hope to live my life in a way that I can see him again. Thank you, Max, for all you've taught us. "

Peter Caldwell sat back down on the grass. The sharing of experiences that had started out slowly began picking up speed. One woman stood to say she had come because she'd recognized Max's picture in the obituaries as the man who'd bought her groceries a few years earlier when she was down on her luck and without a friend or a hope in the world. A silver-haired man wearing a bow tie spoke of his experiences as Max's barber and the stories they'd swapped about the war. A young girl stood briefly and said how much she was going to miss his happy face. His pockets were always full of bubble gum that he shared with the kids as he helped them cross the street.

Another woman stood and wept, unable to speak for nearly a minute before she began to recall her story of finding hope in a book Max had shared with her. She thanked him for the faith the book had renewed in her. She reported that she'd waited for years for her daughters to apologize to her for a small, unfortunate incident that had hurt her feelings. The hurt had festered until it became a monster. After reading the journal, she'd gone to her daughters and apologized to them, rekindling the fires of love where there had been only apathy and bitterness.

Bud nodded to Paul, placing his large hand on his shoulder for support as he stood. He recounted a shorter version of the story he'd shared at breakfast and thanked Max for his service to so many whom he'd mentored and helped to free from addictions. He, too, mentioned the journal as well as the time he'd spent collecting Ebenezers on the beach with Max. Paul was happy that Bud returned to his place on the grass without mentioning that he knew Wolf's true identity.

After Bud, several people stood in quick succession to share thoughts centered around the themes of hope and the love of God they'd experienced both at the funeral and through interactions with Max. Silence came again and lingered for several minutes. Paul found himself wondering if everyone had spoken who wanted to. But just as these thoughts crossed his mind, a beautiful, silver-haired woman stood in the center of the circle. She wore a cream-colored dress with a scooped neckline that outlined her brilliant strand of turquoise beads. Her eyes were wet, but still they were bright and cheerful.

"My name is Elizabeth Green Jackson, and Max was my father." The call of a raven distracted her, and she turned heavenward to the branches that crisscrossed the sky. When she looked back at the congregation, she wore a broad smile across her face. "In the Bible, the Holy Spirit is symbolized by a gentle dove. My father could perhaps be best symbolized by a squawking raven." Many laughed while others looked surprised.

"I've only attended a few funerals in my life, and this is my first experience with a Quaker funeral. I would like to thank you for allowing me to share this time to remember my dad. I am grateful for the sense of family I have felt here today. I may not know you, but as was said earlier, today we are all friends. We all share in the loss of my father. We all share in the blessing of having known him. I feel the love you brought with you for my father, and I thank each of you for sharing it with me and my family. There are nine of us here today who claim Max as either their father or stepfather, but there are many more who claim a familial tie. Many of us over the years have chosen to ignore these ties. Believe it or not, dad was not always an easy person to love. There were times when he was downright rotten. I don't want to dwell on those dark years because time, and especially love, have healed our wounds.

"As I look out at you today, and as I have listened to the words and thoughts of love you have shared with us, I recognize that I am a witness to a miracle of epic proportion. I dare say that if this funeral had been held fifteen years ago, none of us would have attended. Many of you who have read the journal he shared with everyone know that my father was a broken man. We watched my father's fall from happiness with the death of each of his wives, beginning with my mother when we were still children. My father became an emotional man, and with each disappointment and tragedy, his emotions became increasingly raw. Before his last wife, Millie, died, we all saw moments of gentleness that occasionally escaped his rugged exterior. But when she died, something inside my father snapped. Over the course of the next few years, he alienated all of his friends and family. He became a drunk, medicating himself to the point that he wouldn't have to feel anything. But each new day brought new sorrows and new levels of loneliness as he chased away the light of love with his indulgences and rude behavior."

She paused to look around before speaking again. "I recognize in many of your faces a look of surprise. I know that funerals are usually a time of praise, but my father asked me before he died to tell the truth about his story; not to defame him, but to remind us all that life isn't over till it's over. We all have the potential, until our last breath, to change the course of our lives and how we'll be remembered. In the last twelve years, legacy—his legacy— has played into every decision, every interaction, every thought he's had and made.

"The Max Green you know is different from the Max Green I grew up with. I'm grateful for that. I'm grateful for the changes he's made. Despite all the good he's done in his life—particularly these last twelve years, his soul was troubled by the knowledge that he'd never be able to repair all the damage he'd done—the people he'd hurt—the pain he'd caused. He was blessed in his desires to fix many of the relationships he'd neglected and ruined. But even after all the work he did to try and rectify his wrongs, my father was convinced that only through the grace of Jesus could he ever have hope of satisfying the claims of justice.

DO YOU SEE HOW NECESSARY A WORLD OF PAINS AND TROUBLES IS TO SCHOOL AN INTELLIGENCE AND MAKE IT A SOUL?
—JOHN KEATS

"You see, the truth is, my father spent at least a decade being a rotten, selfish son-of-a-gun who was difficult to tolerate, let alone welcome into home and heart. Many of us in the family chose to create boundaries, a force field of sorts, to protect ourselves from his acidic nature. My brothers tried to get him some professional help, but he refused to listen and sent them and every other do-gooder packing, until there was no one left to be his friend. He wanted to die, and I'm ashamed to admit there were many of us who weren't at all opposed to that idea. For almost a decade, none of us knew where he was or what he was doing. It wasn't until later that we learned that he spent these years fishing, drinking and reading the works of French and German philosophers. As he used to say, he was 'on a fast train to nowhere.' He gave up on life and God, and with that, he gave up on hope itself.

"This was also the time he began going to funerals. In the beginning, many of these were for his friends and fellow members of the Greatest Generation; soldiers, sailors and airmen who shared a portion of his history. But he told me once that he'd missed the point of most of these by being less interested in the stories of their lives and more interested in discovering how they died. I once asked him, a few years ago, what had kept him, during those years of despair, from putting an end to his own life. His answer surprised me. He told me he'd gotten close many times, but each time, he remembered an experience from the war where one of his friends had sacrificed his own life by throwing himself on top of a live grenade that had been lobbed into their shelter. My father rarely spoke of the war, but that single event reminded him again and again of the value of life and the pact he and his comrades had made that day to honor the sacrifice their friend had made for them by making their lives count for something. My father outlived all of those men, and though he has struggled to find his way from time to time, each of us, in the end, has been a witness to the infinite power of redeeming love and forgiveness. Hope truly does spring eternal[1]. It changes men from the father I knew and was often ashamed of, into the man you knew and loved.

1. Alexander Pope

"I have learned some incredible lessons from watching my father change over these last years. I'm embarrassed to admit that I used to believe that I was better than him; that my choices and lifestyle would lead me to a much better place than he would inherit. I misunderstood the concepts of heaven and hell, believing I was on track for glory, despite the knapsack full of favorite sins that I carried on my back. I tricked myself into believing that God grades on a curve and that as long as I was better than my father, I'd be fine. I judged my father, and in the process, I built a dam between myself and the truth.

"I might have been happy in my ignorance if it weren't for the changes my father made. I didn't believe the stories I heard at first that Dad had changed and become soft and kind and pleasant to be around. Unfortunately, I was the last of my siblings to recognize those changes. I was the last one to read the journal. I was the last one to believe in the truths it contained. But I've learned something important from these last few years. If we can put away our tendencies to judge, if we'll open our hearts to each other, if we'll practice kindness, recognizing that we're all broken souls, life can be magical and meaningful and miraculous. My father taught me those things, not only by what he said, but by the way he lived.

"When we get into our sixties, I think most of us tend to think we have life figured out, that there aren't many more surprises around the corner. We like things to make sense, to be categorized and alphabetized. We like things to fit into nice manageable packages that we can shuffle around and convince ourselves of the illusion that we're actually doing something to improve our world. We don't like messes, and we don't like change, at least not when it involves getting our hands dirty. We've been there and done that and are ready to leave the messes for younger generations. In short, we believe we have life figured out, that we're as good as we're gonna get, that we can kick back with our life on cruise control as we ride off into the sunset. We buy a condo, a membership to the country club, and life finally becomes comfortable and predictable and …"

OPEN YOUR EYES.

The silence that followed was deafening as all eyes turned to her, waiting for her to complete her thought. Tears fell from her chin and left damp marks on her dress. "And then a friend hands you a journal about a kid who likes to go to funerals in a quest to figure out the secrets of life, and suddenly your afternoon at the country club seems less exciting. And it just gets worse the more you read because you start to realize that even though you've tried hard to find meaning and provide a comfortable life for yourself, you might have missed out on the things that really matter. You begin to recognize that the comfort you've surrounded yourself with has retarded your growth and progression and then you wake up one day and realize you're sitting in a velvet-lined rut that leads to nowhere.

"That's bad enough, but when you get to the end of that book and recognize aspects of yourself in the character who is your father, that pretty much ruins your whole day."

Her comment drew subtle laughter from people throughout the congregation.

"I had written my father off for good. But after reading that journal and then hearing that he'd been spending a couple of hours everyday as a crossing guard, my world, as I'd rather selfishly defined it, started feeling very small, even claustrophobic. My father, the man I'd used as my touchstone for years, had become a saint overnight, completely throwing off the curve I'd been grading myself against.

"I'd considered myself a Christian my whole life, but faith had always been an enigma for me. I like to believe I tried, but in truth, I tended to only believe what I could perceive through my five senses. I avoided the hard questions and tended to look at the world through customized rose-colored glasses that had been built with blinders on the sides. It's not a very pleasant thing to wake up one morning and discover you've become a Pharisee who said the right things and looked the right way but didn't have the conviction to live without hypocrisy. I was faced with a big dilemma, to embrace the new truths the journal had exposed me to and follow them wherever they might lead, or to remain comfortable in my clean, simple, uncomplicated world.

"IT WAS WORTH IT."

"Well, against my better judgement, I chose comfort. I chose to stick my head in the sand and ignore my conscience. For two years, I continued on my merry way doing all I could to avoid changing the course of my pleasure cruise. My husband and I were happy and content, and life was simpler that way.

"But ya know, some of us spend far too much time in deep end of the swimming pool before we recognize that we're out of air."

Paul watched as dozens of heads in the congregation nodded in agreement.

"Had I changed my course earlier, I know life would have been better for me. I likely would have landed on my feet, but instead, I belly-flopped. In a matter of a week, my sandcastle came tumbling down. My kids turned against me. My husband of more than forty years moved out, and my credit cards were deactivated. The condo on the golf course was sold out from underneath me, and I fell into a deep depression. It was only then that I learned that God does his best work with those that are broken.

"As I packed up my things and prepared to move into a hotel room, I stumbled upon the journal I'd tried to ignore two years earlier. This time, I was humble enough to listen. I was looking for a savior to get me out of my mess. I pored over that journal, and like my father, and perhaps many of you here today, it made me want to change. It gave me hope and that hope only intensified as I began hearing more stories about my father. Dad had tried to reach out to me several times, but I had rejected him repeatedly out of pride and fear. My oldest brother, Clarence, had reconnected with our father a few years earlier, and as I listened to the stories and heard about the changes he'd made, I decided it was time to set aside that pride and fear and see these fruits of change for myself.

"My brother drove me to the school where dad worked as a crossing guard. We sat in the car and watched him interact with the kids. I remember his big ears poking out the side of his hat as he leaned over to hug his young friends. I was surprised at how natural his kindness appeared to be. By then, it had been well over ten years since I'd seen him. Time and choices had aged him, but I wept as I watched my father and remembered the tenderness he'd once expressed to me and my siblings in our younger years. Somewhere inside that old man was my father, the man I loved and respected as a child, the man who'd had great capacity for love and tenderness before time and tragedy wore him down.

"I was the last child he helped cross the street that day," she said, wiping a tear from her cheek. "He took my hand and held it in his as we crossed over into a world of understanding and forgiveness. Over a bowl of my mother's famous bean soup, we cried about the years we'd wasted and things we'd missed out on. These last six years have been some of the best years of my life. I have been blessed by getting to know my father again, to know the love and kindness he's capable of. I am grateful for the fruits of love and forgiveness he has shared with me and our family. And I am grateful for the love of a young man named Wolf who helped my father believe he could change."

Elizabeth paused and turned around slowly, taking in the faces of all the people who had come to honor her father. "Love changes everything, doesn't it? Love is the miracle. It wakes us up and opens our eyes and hearts and souls to truth. It strips us down and leaves us exposed where we can recognize our brokenness and our need for a God who knows who we are and what we can become. You all know that dad was a believer, and as I look into your faces, I see that his life and love have made believers out of all of us. I don't know what heaven looks like, but I pray, if I get there, that my father will be there to meet me with one of his hugs, and help me cross the street to the pearly gates. I love my father. I am grateful for his love and patience. I am grateful he didn't give up on me. I am grateful for you, his friends, who have become an extension of our family as we share an appreciation for his life and the love he shared with each of us. Thank you for loving him. I believe he is with us here today, and I believe he will continue to live in our hearts as we share the love he gave us.

"As I have grown older and have begun to recognize that my years are numbered, I am grateful for the example my father has given me to follow. Life, he taught me, is meant to be much more than a period of time to be endured in quiet desperation. Nor was it meant to be spent dreaming of mansions in the world to come. Each of us has a song to sing, and dad was convinced that if we could forget ourselves and sing our song with courage and conviction, life could be beautiful. My father proved that. He taught his song to each of us and I hope, with whatever time I have left, I can share my own song of redeeming love with the world." She pressed her lips together and nodded graciously several times as she slowly turned around the circle.

"Before you leave today, my father asked that I give each of you a gift. As one of you mentioned earlier, Dad had a fondness for heart-shaped rocks. This began when he married his last wife, Millie, who shared her hobby and collection with him. Many of you have already been a recipient of one of these rocks. Over the past couple of years, as he's grown increasingly aware that the end of his life was coming, he's been collecting heart rocks to share with those who might come to his funeral. It was his hope that these *Ebenezers*, as he liked to call them, will remind you of the love of a merciful God. Let them be your *stone of help*, to remind you that all pain is temporary, all sorrow is fleeting, but love … love is eternal and will last forever."

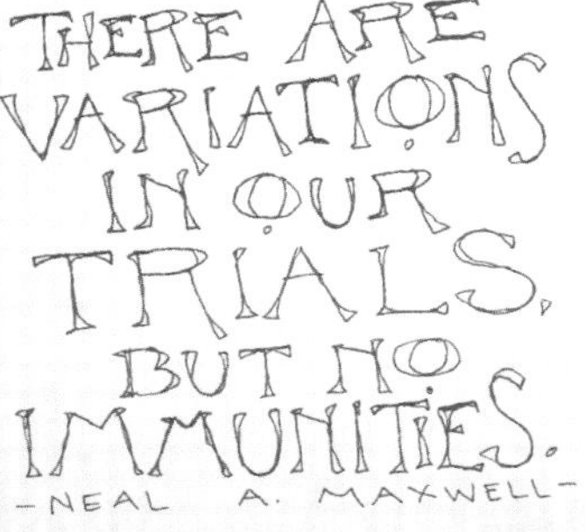

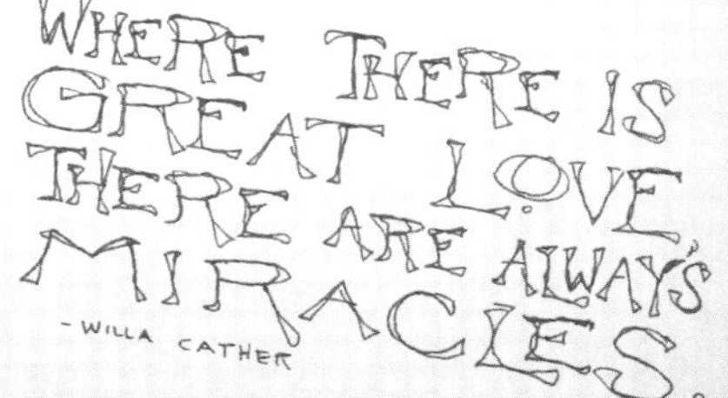

---CHAPTER 33--- OF LIGHT AND FIRE

SEEK TO DO GOOD, AND YOU WILL FIND THAT HAPPINESS WILL RUN AFTER YOU.
—JAMES FREEMAN CLARKE

A reverent hush washed over the congregation after Elizabeth sat down, interrupted only by the occasional sniffle. Paul looked at Eve, wondering what she was thinking about the funeral and noticed her head was tilted back as she stared up at the canopy of branches above them. He followed her line of sight and was surprised to see the raven still perched on a high branch, silently observing the proceedings of the gathering. In the placid stillness, he watched as Eve sketched the ebony bird on a small sketchpad she pulled from her pocket. It looked like she was nearly done when the women who'd been appointed to end the meeting, stood and shook hands.

The silence was broken as the congregants stood and stretched, shaking hands with their neighbors.

Paul joined in, shaking hands with the men who'd shared his patch of grass. He watched as Rachel and Katie resumed their conversation, hanging back to give them space. But it wasn't long before Katie noticed him and ran to him, wrapping her arms around his neck in a friendly embrace. She held on tight, and when she pulled back, she had tears in her eyes. "Why didn't you tell me more about that journal of yours?" she said, punching him softly in the chest. "Elizabeth brought me a copy yesterday afternoon and told me her dad would've wanted me to have one."

"Sorry, I …"

"I feel like I'm always the last to hear about the good stuff. I remembered you telling me about your project all those years ago, but I had no idea it would turn into this," she said, gesturing to the crowd.

"Believe me, neither did I," he responded humbly.

"I started reading yesterday, Paul. It's given me a lot to think about, both personally and as a doctor. I think a lot of people, like me, who see death and suffering every day, can become jaded if we're not careful. Your journal, and what I've seen here today have given me a different perspective."

"Then I've finally been able to return the favor."

"What are you talking about?"

"You started this. Your name is on the front page of that journal. It was once yours, remember?"

Katie nodded as a tear rolled down her cheek. "And you did exactly what I hoped you'd do with it—you filled it with magic." She held onto Paul's arm as she turned her body to stand in between him and Rachel, looking out at the crowd. "I asked for magic, but this is a miracle. I remember sitting across from you at the diner—that night you took me to dinner to tell me how you were spending your spare time—making friends with dead people. I remember leaving that night thinking you were quirkier than ever! But look at this, Paul. Look at what's become of your project!"

Paul nodded somberly.

"I don't think he gets it, Rachel," she said, shaking her head.

"What is it I'm supposed to get?" Paul asked, taking a closer look.

"Paul, from what's been said here today, I think most, if not all of these people have read your journal. And those who haven't have been touched by Max. From what I understand, he became the man he was because of the things you wrote in that journal. These people have been touched and changed to the point that they'd come to a funeral on a hot, humid Friday afternoon to sit on hard benches and scattered patches of grass so they could honor the man who shared your magic with them. They're here for the same reason you went to Dr. Dinglebottom's funeral—they're hoping to fill their canteens at that same magic fountain you described before it runs dry. Look at them," she said pointing, "drinking it in as they embrace each other, as they share stories, as they reach into those baskets full of rocks and choose one that will help them remember the love and the magic Max shared with them. This is more than a funeral; this is a celebration of love and miracles."

She let go of his arm and turned to stand in front of him. "The world needs hope like this. Look at them. They're here because they're hoping they can take a piece of hope home with them to share with family and friends. I'm sure they're hoping, like I am, that the hope they feel will be as tangible tomorrow as it is today. They're filling their lungs and pockets with the stuff as if it were manna which might disappear in the heat of the day."

Paul put his arm around Rachel and squeezed her shoulder as he scanned the crowd, feeling overwhelmed and humbled.

"Rachel, Paul," Marilyn called from behind them. "There's someone we'd like you to meet."

They turned around to see Marilyn and Bud on either side of Elizabeth, the woman who'd just spoken. She reached out her hand to take Rachel's. "Your mom has told me a lot about you two." She reached into her pocket and withdrew a small sketch that had been torn from a spiral notebook. "And I'm happy to meet the parents of this talented artist."

"You already met Eve?" Rachel asked, quickly looking around for their daughter.

"Yes, she's helping hand out the rocks," she said, pointing over their shoulders to the center of the circle where Eve stood next to three large baskets full of rocks. "She's a beautiful little girl." She looked to their right and saw Katie. "Oh, Dr. Lewis, I'm sorry I didn't recognize you. You look different outside of the hospital."

"Oh, thank you. I sure hope so."

"You all know each other?" asked Elizabeth.

They all nodded.

"Thank you again for taking care of my father. We all appreciated your kindness to him. It was very nice of you to come today," Elizabeth continued, addressing Katie.

Katie smiled and nodded. "I wish I would have known your father better. He sounds as though he was an incredible person."

"Thank you, he was, but he's carved out a wide path for us to follow." She pressed her lips together and nodded. "Say, I forgot to ask you yesterday if you were able to get that package back into the right hands."

Katie glanced sideways at Paul. "As a matter of fact, I did. Would you be interested in meeting him?"

"You mean you could arrange that? I know many people in my family have been looking for him. I might have told you that my father went all the way to Adams-Friendship to see if he could track him down."

"No, I don't remember your saying that."

"Yeah, Wolf just seemed to have disappeared without a trace. I honestly couldn't believe it at first, that you're the same Katie Lewis who gave him the journal. It's such a small world, isn't it?"

Katie nodded again as she put her hand around Paul's arm. "I don't think we ever fully recognize how small it really is. Elizabeth, I'd like to you to meet one of my oldest friends. We grew up together in Adams-Friendship. This is Wolfgang Paulus Schafer, but when I was young, we used to call him Wolf."

Elizabeth looked at Katie incredulously as if she were waiting for the punchline, but when it didn't come, she looked up into Paul's eyes. "You're really Wolf?"

Paul pressed his lips together then nodded. He extended his hand, but Elizabeth brushed past it, wrapping her arms around his chest. He looked at Rachel, then Marilyn and Bud, then Katie before putting his arms around her awkwardly.

"I'm sorry," she said after a moment, pulling back. "I've been doing a lot of hugging lately. I can't believe it's you, and that you're here. I'm sorry to gush all over you. I just … I hope I didn't scare you."

Paul shook his head, but he wasn't very convincing.

She turned to Marilyn. "Why didn't you tell me that your son-in-law was Wolf?"

Marilyn smiled. "I just found out myself earlier this morning."

"How do you guys know each other?" asked Rachel, looking at her mom and Elizabeth.

"Oh, from pottery class, at Bud's," Marilyn responded.

"And from the diner, too," Elizabeth added.

"Yeah, of course. Max used to bring Elizabeth with him all the time. That must have been where we first met."

Elizabeth nodded, but she was staring at Paul. "You're a lot taller than I imagined."

"Yeah?" Paul responded, feeling self-conscious.

"I guess I just imagined someone smaller—someone my father could pick up and drag to the hospital from Eichleman Park. That must have been quite a struggle."

"I was a lot skinnier back then," Paul offered. "I was living on leftover pizza and Poptarts, and that was long before my metabolism slowed down."

Elizabeth smiled warmly. "Tell me what you're doing with your life. Did you become a fireman like you wanted?"

"Yes, I did, about ten years ago."

"Where do you kids live?"

"In Ohio," Rachel answered. "Just outside of Cleveland."

"I guess that's why my father never found you. I don't think he ever looked as far as Ohio; but then it's hard looking for a boy named Wolf without the advantage of knowing his last name. Next time you write a journal, do us all a favor and write your telephone number in it, would ya?"

Paul cracked a smile. "I never expected anyone but your father would ever read it. I didn't know about any of this," he said, gesturing to the crowd.

"No, we didn't think you would. That's why dad wanted to find you, to tell you what had become of his life and your journal, and to thank you for helping him wake up. I think all of us have wondered about you; wondered who you became and where you landed. I've often imagined you as a fireman, saving people's lives, being a hero."

Paul shook his head. "I'm sorry to disappoint you, but I'm just an ordinary guy."

"There's no such thing as ordinary, Paul—not if we learn to sing the song God puts in our hearts. I've discovered over the last few years that most of the real heroes in life are the ones who don't know their own strengths. They just keep moving forward, silently inspiring others to do the same. I've always imagined you as a humble man, and I'm grateful to see that you are, but look what you've done," she said, turning her head from side to side. "Look at what your humility and your search for answers has done for all of us."

Paul turned again to look at the crowd, but his eyes fell quickly to the ground.

"Dad never wanted the attention either," she said, putting her arm around him. "That's one reason why he gave away copies of your journal—so people would realize he was no guru; that the happiness he found in his life came from God through an indirect source. He always gave you a lot of the credit for the changes he made in his life."

"I'm sorry, but I'm definitely not a guru either," Paul responded, feeling overwhelmed by expectations.

"And that's exactly what makes your story compelling and believable—that you were as broken as the rest of us. But the inspiring thing about you, Paul, is that you weren't afraid to stop and ask for directions when you realized you were lost. That's a hard thing to do sometimes. You found your way out of the hell you were in by asking questions, searching for answers and sincerely listening to the answers that came to you."

"Isn't that what we all do?"

"Yes and no. I think we all want to do that. Some of us even give it a try, but I think most of us stop asking if we don't get an answer right away, or if the answer comes, and we don't like it. Truth is sometimes a hard pill to swallow, especially if the way you're living is contrary to that truth."

Paul nodded knowingly.

"The great thing about your journal is that it showed us all how good life can be if you open your mind and heart to truth and love. She smiled warmly. "I've imagined meeting you many times, but never like this. I want to tell you that for the last six years, as I've tried hard to exercise more gratitude for the good things in my life, nearly every day I have thanked God for a boy named Wolf who had the guts to share his light and his song with my father."

Paul exhaled as if he'd been holding his breath all day. "Tell me how this happened," he said, turning to look at the crowd that still lingered. "Until yesterday, I always imagined that Max had died years ago and that my journal had been lost or sent to Goodwill. I never imagined I would see it again. Never, in a million years, could I have imagined this."

"You cannot hide light in darkness," she responded. "I learned that from reading your journal. Light begets light and fire kindles more fire until it consumes all darkness with the brightness of hope. Your journal melted a hole in the ice surrounding my father's cold heart. That really started when he discovered who you were; that it was you who he'd dragged to the hospital—half dead—you, the same kid who'd bent over backwards to try and reach out to him with charity and patience. That lit a fire inside him. He realized he had to do something more than sit around like a stick in the mud, feeling sorry for himself while he waited to die. All of this happened because of the love and light you gave him,

Paul. Your journal woke him up from a deep sleep, like it has so many of us, by opening our eyes to our own potential. It has enabled us to believe we can change our future."

"I was only trying to help a grumpy old man see that life isn't as bad as he believed it was," Paul replied.

Elizabeth nodded. "I don't think any of us will ever know the extent of how our actions affect the world around us. I try to remember that everyday. It's crazy how a small tremor on one side of the ocean can create a tsunami on the other side of the world; destroying countries and killing thousands. But the opposite is also true—that an act of love or kindness can sweep through a family and a community, and the entire world if we'll keep it going. Your journal, started a tremor that has become a tsunami of hope. It has swept us all up in its wake, gaining momentum as we have learned about love and perpetuated that kindness, bringing all of us back to hope."

Paul took a deep breath and smiled at Elizabeth.

"You wrote something in your journal that has meant a lot to me as I've faced the challenges of the past few years."

"What was that?"

"Be of good cheer!"

Paul nodded. "That's a good thing to do, but I don't remember writing it."

"Do you know where it comes from?"

"It sounds familiar. It probably came from one of the funerals I went to."

Elizabeth nodded. "I didn't look it up until just a couple of years ago. It comes from a verse of scripture in John where Jesus is explaining to his disciples that his life and their lives would soon be changing as He'd be killed and return to his Father. Despite the hardships those things would bring into their lives, he promised them they'd see him again and said, 'These things I have spoken unto you, that in me ye might have peace. In the world ye shall have tribulation: but be of good cheer; I have overcome the world.'"[1]

1. John 16:33

Paul nodded thoughtfully. "That's what hope is, isn't it?"

"Yes, it always comes back to that. Every fragment of hope in this world somehow points us to that redeeming love and sacrifice. God's love is the miracle that can bring us all home. Most of us don't find it until we're broken, but if we let it in, it changes everything."

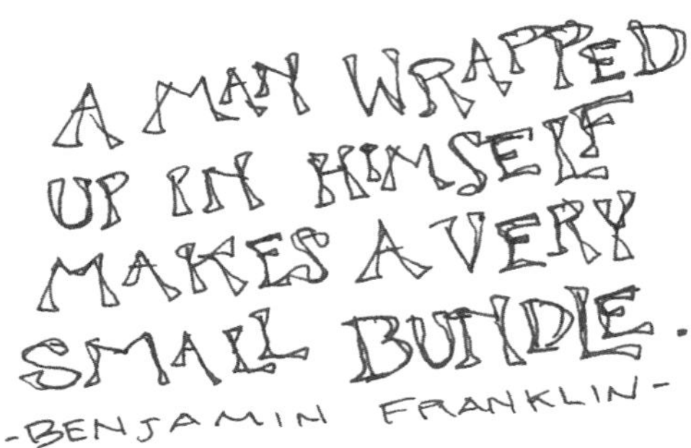

THERE IS NO KNOWLEDGE THAT IS NOT POWER.
-RALPH WALDO EMERSON

I HAVE FOUGHT A GOOD FIGHT, I HAVE FINISHED MY COURSE, I HAVE KEPT THE FAITH.
-2 TIMOTHY 4:7-

NO PANG THAT IS SUFFERED BY MAN OR WOMAN UPON THE EARTH WILL BE WITHOUT ITS COMPENSATING EFFECT IF IS BE MET WITH PATIENCE.
-JAMES TALMAGE

CHAPTER 34

REFLECTING LIGHT

YOU CANNOT DO A KINDNESS TOO SOON, FOR YOU NEVER KNOW HOW SOON IT WILL BE TOO LATE.
-RALPH WALDO EMERSON

After reluctantly agreeing to allow the whereabouts of the boy named Wolf to remain a mystery, Elizabeth thanked Paul and Rachel for coming and gave them both hugs before excusing herself to greet the other funeral guests. Katie stayed and chatted for a little longer, but excused herself to check on the wedding cake and other last-minute details. She explained that her parents had announced they'd be arriving earlier than expected to take her and Mike to dinner, and asked for a rain check on their double date. She suggested that they might all meet for dessert instead. Rachel was obviously disappointed, but she and Paul both understood and agreed to meet at 9:00 at The Twisted Cow for frozen yogurt. After embracing each of them and thanking them for going out of their way to come to her wedding, Katie stopped at the baskets to pick out a heart rock and give Eve a hug.

As the crowd began to thin, Paul helped Bud move the canoes from the trailer to the river, lining them up on the bank. While Bud made arrangements for his truck and trailer to be dropped off at the park where the river met Lake Michigan, Paul went looking for Eve. She'd made friends with another little girl, and the two of them had taken it

"Death is premature only for those unprepared to meet God."

upon themselves to make sure each of the guests had received one of Max's special rocks.

"Is it okay if Eve comes with us?" Marilyn asked as she handed Paul two life jackets.

"Uh, sure, that's fine with me, if it's okay with Rachel."

"She told me to check with you. I think it might help. Rachel's a little nervous about this, and I thought it might give you two a chance to talk.'

"Do you have room?"

"All of Bud's canoes only have two seats, but he brought a cooler that Eve can sit on. He does this a lot, and I was thinking Eve might actually be safer with us."

Paul nodded, trying not to laugh. "You didn't tell Rachel that, did you? She might want to jump in with you, too."

Marilyn smiled and dropped a smaller life jacket over Eve's head. As Eve explained to her new friend that she was going on a big adventure, Paul turned around to look for Rachel. After a minute, he found her standing alone on the bridge. He watched her for a moment, wondering what she was thinking, wondering what she'd thought of the funeral, hoping she was okay with all of this. He thought about joining her but stopped himself, noticing the look of serenity on her face. He decided to keep his distance and allow her to enjoy the time alone. He helped move the boards and logs back to the higher ground where other men loaded them back into the trucks and stacked them in piles. When they were done, he was surprised to find Rachel, still standing on the bridge, watching the mirrored, rippled surface of the dark water.

"Did you see Max's urn?" Marilyn asked, as she walked up beside him.

He looked down at her, distracted. "What?"

"Bud made it for him. Isn't it beautiful? I was afraid it was going to be a little dark, but I think it really turned out nice, don't you?"

Paul nodded, walking a few steps closer to the table where the urn had been sitting. He stooped down to take a closer look and noticed a familiar mark near the bottom—a swirl imprint that looked like it had been made by stamping it with the top of a small snail shell.

"That's Bud's chop," Marilyn offered. "Pretty cool, huh?"

"He makes that mark when the clay is wet?"

"Yeah, he puts it on all his stuff. I told him I thought his chop should have his name on it, or at least the name of his shop, but he likes that one."

"Does it have a special meaning?"

"Yeah, it does," Bud answered from behind them.

Paul stood and turned around.

"I'm just gonna go check with Elizabeth to see if she's ready," Marilyn said, leaving the men to talk.

Bud stood next to Paul and lifted the urn from the table; he ran his thumb over the mark, looking thoughtful. "I started using this mark about four years ago, but it has ties to something much older. When my last son graduated from high school, my wife surprised me with a trip to a little town in Pennsylvania called Niederbipp. Have you ever heard of it? It can't be too far from where you live."

Paul shook his head.

"You'd like it. It's a quaint little town on the banks of the Allegheny River. I think the whole town is on the historic register, and in the center of it all, there's a pottery shop. I'd wanted to go there for years, ever since I'd stumbled upon a travel brochure and saw the picture of this old potter out in front of his shop. We bought a couple of mugs from him, and every day as I drank my coffee, I'd dream about being a potter. Those dreams kept me going on hard days." He smiled and his mustache curled up on the ends.

"It's kind of a quirky town, and on the outskirts, there's this crazy farm for abused and neglected snails."

"Snails? Seriously?" Paul responded.

"That's exactly what I said. I couldn't believe it myself at first, but we stayed right across the street from it in this awesome bed and breakfast, and the morning we left, we walked by that snail farm and found some old shells out near the road. My wife picked up a few of them, and on the way home, she suggested that I call my future pottery shop, Snail's Pace Pottery, since my last name is Pace and she knew it would be another ten years or more before I'd finally be able to live my dream."

Paul grinned. "So is that what you called it?"

"No, I never really liked the name—I didn't want to be reminded of how long it took me to do what I always wanted to do. I called the shop Muddy Fingers, but I decided to keep the snail idea because of my wife … and because of Max."

"Why Max?"

"I was with him down at the lake one evening, looking for rocks for his collection, telling him about my crazy dream of opening a pottery shop, and he was the first of my friends to encourage me since my wife had died. Everyone else thought I was crazy." Bud smiled at the memory. "I needed someone to believe in me, and Max became that person. That was all I needed to take the leap of faith. Among the rocks we found that night, I found an unusually white snail shell, and I … I took it for a sign that my wife was looking out for me, and that I was on the right track. I'd moved at a snail's pace to get to my dreams, but I was ready to live them. I opened my shop two months later, and I've used that stamp ever since."

Paul nodded. "That's a great story. I'm curious about something though."

"Shoot."

"I was noticing this morning, as I was washing dishes, that those rocks in the windowsill—the ones you gave Marilyn—most of them have a little mark on them, that mark," he said, pointing to the swirl at the bottom of the urn.

"Really?" Bud asked, sounding surprised but looking like a child who'd just been caught with his hand in the cookie jar.

"Yeah, it was just like that," Paul continued. "The mark was quite a bit smaller, but it was right at the bottom of five of those hearts."

Bud looked over his shoulders before lowering his head and his voice. "Don't tell anyone, but those aren't real rocks."

"What do you mean? They look like rocks to me."

Bud smiled. "Thanks. I've been working on them for a few years. Sometimes I can't even tell the difference myself. They're actually made out of my clay scraps."

Paul laughed. "Are you serious?"

Bud pursed his lips and nodded.

"But, why?"

"Do you have any idea how hard it is to find heart rocks in Kenosha these days?"

"Uh, I guess not. It's been a year since we last went looking for them."

"And how many did you find then?"

"Five or six, maybe."

"Then you should consider yourself lucky. Thanks to Max, all sorts of people have started their own collections, and it's tough to find one anymore."

"It looked like Max was able to find a bunch of them to give away. There must have been four or five hundred heart rocks in those baskets."

Bud smiled and looked at his shoes. "I think maybe only ten of those were real," he said under his breath.

"What?" Paul said, laughing. "Are you serious?"

Bud nodded again.

"DON'T PUT A QUESTION MARK WHERE GOD PUT A PERIOD." -REV. TERRY SEMONS

"Did Max know they were all fakes?"

"I don't think he had any idea. I'm really pretty good at it. They don't look exactly like the same kind of rocks we have around here, but they definitely look like rocks."

"Why did you do that? I mean, it's been twenty years since I worked with clay, but I know that must have taken a long time."

"I don't even want to know how many hours. It was ridiculous."

"So why did you do it?"

"Because it bought me time with Max."

"Huh?"

"I often went collecting with him, but when they started getting scarce, he got a little discouraged. Those hours I spent making rocks was a small price to pay for the smile on his face when we'd come back from an evening together with a bucket full of rocks. It kind of became our tradition every Wednesday night to get together and go down to the lake for a couple of hours and talk about life while we hunted for heart rocks."

"I imagine that must have been entertaining," Paul said, genuinely intrigued.

"Yeah, it was fun. It was kind of like an Easter egg hunt. I'd stop by the beach on my way to pick him up and hide all the rocks, and then we'd come back and find them. Occasionally we'd find some real ones, too, and lots of times we'd go home with fewer hand-made rocks than I'd deposited. I'm sure there are lots of people out there who were stoked to find the ones we left behind."

"I'm sure lots of those people are wondering, like I did, what the little spiral came from."

"Oh, I just started doing that recently. The first two I gave Marilyn didn't have my mark on them. I decided it was a good way to keep track of them, and who knows, maybe my heart rocks will end up on "The Antiques Roadshow" someday. All the old pottery they have on that show is more valuable if it has the potter's chop."

Paul looked at the baskets. Most of the rocks were gone, but a few stones remained in each one. "That was very kind of you," Paul said, turning back to Bud, "taking Max to the beach with you. I bet he enjoyed that."

Bud pressed his lips together like he was fighting back emotions, and when he spoke, his voice was soft. "I loved every minute of it," he said, his voice breaking. "I'm sure it sounds like a silly thing—a couple of grown men combing the beach for heart rocks that aren't even real—

but that time we spent together—the things we shared—I'm really going to miss that."

"Then maybe there's nothing fake about these at all," Paul suggested after a moment's thought.

"Pardon?" Bud responded, wiping his eyes.

"Maybe they are counterfeits of a sort, but you made them out of kindness and love. The other rocks, the ones we all look for on the beach, those are just rocks, but these," he said scooping up several from the basket, "these are special. Does Marilyn know?"

Bud shook his head. "I've thought about telling her, but I figure it's not doing any harm. I'm sure she'll find out sooner or later, and I'll have some explaining to do, but it's been fun making a new rock for her each month since we've been dating."

"Are you going to keep making 'em?"

"I think I will. I've wondered if making those rocks isn't part of the song I'm supposed to sing." He stopped and smiled. "People will be disappointed if they stop finding them. Each of my grandkids has started a collection. That's the first thing they want to do every time they come to visit me—grab a bucket and head for the beach. It was always fun to see Max's smile whenever we found one, but it's even more fun to see the smile on my grandkids' faces when they find one. I had a wonderful time being a father, and despite the challenges we went through in raising our kids, I like to think I did a pretty good job of it. But that's nothing compared to the joy I've found in being a grandfather. I almost missed out on that, Paul. If it hadn't been for Max—and your journal, life would be very different for me right now."

Bud bent over and picked up a couple of his rocks out of the basket. "Ya know, there were several times after my wife died that I didn't believe I could go on. I felt like life had lost all of its meaning. There were many times that I lost all desire to live. I thank God everyday that Max wandered into my life and helped me find purpose in living again. Every day around the world, people make the decision to end their own life. Others make the decision to give up on hope. I've learned through my own experiences that we can never judge those who make those decisions. Every time I hear about another person who has given up hope and chosen to walk into the darkness, I find myself wondering what our world has missed by the loss of that person."

He turned to face Paul, handing him one of his rocks. "Paul, have you ever thought about the life you would have missed if you'd died that night on the beach?"

"Are you kidding? There hasn't been a day since that awful night that I haven't thought about how grateful I am for another chance to figure this out."

"But you never talked about it with Rachel?"

Paul shook his head. "I tried in the beginning—I didn't want her to feel like I was trying to hide anything, but I never really got the chance."

"Why not?"

"Because she … she didn't want to hear it. She wanted to let the past stay in the past."

"And?"

Paul shrugged. "I don't know. I was a little frustrated at first, but I understood. Who wants to dig up the past when you're trying to make a future together? I felt like it was important for her to know I'd … you know, dealt with depression, but was doing better—that I'd been able to make sense of my struggles and find direction in life. But the past always seemed like a black hole she wanted to avoid."

"Interesting."

"What?"

"I've noticed that Marilyn is the same way."

"Aren't we all protective of at least some of the details of our past?"

"Yeah, we are, but do you think we need to be?"

"I don't know. Have you told your children all of your darkest secrets?"

"No, not all of them. But I learned from that journal of yours that sometimes we forget to share our best stories with those we love the most. Sometimes our best stories are the ones where we were able to learn from the mistakes we've made. I've been thinking lately, that if we could share our song a little louder, and love each other a little more, and be a little better at not judging other people, life would be better for all of us. That's the magic I've learned from all of this, Paul. I've spent enough of my life being afraid of what other people think. I've decided I'm done with that kind of thinking. Can you imagine how great life could be if we didn't allow fear to cripple us and hold us back?"

Paul nodded. "I remember a quote from that year of funerals, and I think about it all the time when I feel fear making decisions for me. 'When all that you retain is lovable …"

"… there is no reason for fear to remain with you[1]," Bud said, finishing his sentence. "I've thought about that a million times over the years. Max used to always say that the opposite of fear wasn't faith, but love. That's why he asked Elizabeth to be sure to share the gritty truth at his funeral. He didn't want anyone to be unaware of his past and miss out on knowing the miracle of redemption that your journal inspired."

Paul shook his head. "Bud, I gave up on him. I walked away. I have a really hard time accepting any credit for whatever Max became. Yeah, I put up with a lot of his crap, but I walked away."

Bud sat silent for a moment. "Sometimes, in the expression of love, that's the only option we have left."

"What do you mean?"

"Paul, I don't think things could have changed if you'd stuck around."

"Why not?"

"Because, in the end, it wasn't you who changed him, was it?"

Paul thought for a moment, trying to understand what Bud was saying, but then he shook his head as the meaning of his words sank in.

"You gave him the tools he needed—you gave him the truth he needed to hear, but God had to work the miracle in Max's life. Sometimes, despite our best intentions, we stand in the way of the miracles by giving someone a crutch to lean on."

"Isn't that what being a Christian is all about?" asked Paul.

"In part, yes. Our role as Christians is to reflect light into dark places,

1. A Course in Miracles

but we have to be careful not to claim that light as our own. Light is and always has been a gift from the heavens. I believe each of us has a role to play in the salvation of the world, but only as supporting actors who know when to exit the stage, so we don't detract from the Star. Our role, as I understand it, is to invite people to look to God and live. That's what you did, Paul. You invited Max to take a step out of the darkness and open his heart to God's love and light. Then you got out of the way, and let God work His miracles. It's an interesting paradox that we have to die before we can live again, but I'm certain God never intended that we all had to literally die before we could experience a new and better life in this one. Change in the right direction enlarges our future, regardless of our past, and opens the way for a new life."

WISDOM IS ONLY FOUND IN TRUTH.

- JOHANN WOLFGANG VON GOETHE -

"WE ALL KNEW A GREAT MAN LIKE MY DAD MUST BE SHARED."

"A MAN'S STATURE IN NOT MEASURED BY HOW TALL HE IS BUT BY HOW OFTEN HE BENDS TO LOVE AND TEACH."

-Chapter 35-
Walking on Water

Our birth is but a sleep and a forgetting:
The Soul that rises with us, our life's Star,
Hath had elsewhere its setting,
And cometh from afar:
Not in entire forgetfulness,
And not in utter nakedness,
But trailing clouds of glory do we come
From God, who is our home:
—William Wordsworth

"Are you boys ready?" Marilyn asked.

Paul and Bud turned to see Marilyn and Elizabeth walking down the sloped embankment.

"Ready when you are," Bud responded.

Most of the guests had left, leaving only about twenty people near the canoes waiting to ride down the river with Max, with a few dozen family members who'd been waiting to see the scattering of his ashes.

"You know I've never done this before, right?" Elizabeth said, looking down at the urn. "Is there anything I need to know?"

Bud smiled and shrugged. "Uh, try to get the ashes in the river, and if the wind picks up, hold your breath?" he said, his answer sounding more like a question.

"You've never done this either?"

Bud shook his head. "I've seen it done a couple of times, but no … I don't think it's rocket science. If you just hold onto the handles on the side of the urn there, you'll be able to shake them out slowly into the river."

Elizabeth looked nervous.

"We'll help," her brother, Clarence, said, stepping forward. Their brother Joseph also stepped forward to support them.

While the canoes were moved into the water and lined up against the bank, many other family members came forward to lend a hand, steadying the canoes and escorting Elizabeth and her brothers, along with their father's ashes onto the bridge over the river.

After making sure that Eve's life jacket was secure and that she was comfortable riding with Marilyn and Bud, Paul and Rachel made their way upriver to their assigned canoe, the second to last one in the line. They had just taken their seats when the haunting sound of bagpipe drones cried out from the embankment. The sound echoed through the hollow as the kilted piper played "*Amazing Grace,*" signaling to the family to begin the scattering of the ashes.

Elizabeth was sandwiched between her two brothers who each held onto one of the urn's handles. She reached for the bottom of the urn and tilted it away from them; and together, they slowly sifted the ivory colored ashes into the river. Paul and Rachel were over a hundred feet upriver from the bridge, but the sight of the ashes coupled, with the cry of the bagpipes was no less compelling and electrifying. When the urn had been emptied, the canoes in the front of the line pushed off from the bank; and like a long, multicolored serpent, the other canoes followed the lead, becoming one with the gentle current.

Paul smiled and waved to the family members as they approached the wooden bridge. Elizabeth winked at him, tossing him a small heart rock which he caught carefully without rocking the boat. He smiled and nodded in return as they passed under the bridge, hoping she'd keep her promise to honor his privacy. The sound of the bagpipes continued to echo off the trees as they came to the first bend but began to be drowned out by the sounds of the river with each stroke of the paddle. Squirrels chattered and frogs barked as they floated lazily down the river.

"Are you okay?" Paul asked, staring at Rachel's back and realizing she'd said next to nothing since the funeral.

She nodded, but didn't speak.

The canoe that had been behind them pulled ahead into the swifter water and the middle-aged man and woman who captained the boat waved and smiled as they passed.

"Do you want to talk about it?"

Rachel didn't answer for a moment, and when she did, her answer surprised him. "How deep do you think this river is?" she asked softly.

"Probably only about four feet right here. Why do you ask?"

"Just wondering."

"If you look over the side, you can see patches of the bottom through the moss."

She didn't respond, holding onto her paddle, but not paddling.

"Are you okay, Babe?"

"Do you think we could pull over to the bank?"

"Sure, why? What's up?"

"I'd like to turn around and talk to you, but I'm afraid I'll tip the boat over, and I don't think I want to swim in this river."

Paul bit his lip, trying not to smile. "Sure, we can go to the bank, or I could just steady the canoe for you if you want to turn. Just don't stand up."

She wiggled from side to side on the seat, as if she was considering it, but stopped after a few seconds. "I think I'd feel better if we went to the shore."

"Sure," Paul said, dipping his paddle deep into the water on the right side of the canoe, maneuvering to the left bank where the spindly branches of an enormous weeping willow formed a beautiful green canopy over the river. Paul pulled the canoe securely against the bank, holding tight to the red willows that lined the swampy ground. "Whenever you're ready," he said.

"I'm sorry I'm such a pansy," Rachel responded as she slowly moved one foot and then the other over the side of the canoe and back around into the boat, pivoting on her bottom. "Thanks," she said, looking into Paul's eyes when her feet were firmly planted on the floor of the canoe.

Paul let go of the willows and pushed off again with his paddle, trying to act like he knew what he was doing, and grateful Rachel wasn't paying attention to their crooked path back into the current.

"Thanks for making me come to this," Rachel said after they'd regained cruising speed.

"*Making you come*?" Paul chided, raising one eyebrow.

"Yeah, well, you know what I mean. I'm sorry I had a bad attitude about it. It was good for me to be here, to hear these things, to hear how so many people changed from knowing Max—and reading your journal." She paused and then looked at Paul for a long moment until she knew she had his attention. "You've been wanting to talk to me about this stuff forever, haven't you?"

"Which stuff are you talking about?"

"The spiritual stuff, I guess—the stuff you learned by going to all those funerals. The stuff about God helping us change. I know you've been trying to help me see and feel those things for a long time, but I'm just realizing again how much I shut you down, not wanting to get sucked into … I'm sorry."

"It's okay.'

"No it's not," she responded quickly. "I felt sorry about it yesterday when you were telling us your story, but today, I see it even more, how much I've missed out on by not being able to hear you. I'm sorry that you've had something to share with me that I wasn't willing to hear. I've missed out on a lot of good stuff—stuff, I see now, that would have made my life better if I'd been capable of hearing it."

"Honey, it's …"

FIGURE OUT WHO YOU ARE.

DON'T BE ANGRY.

"Paul, this is hard for me to say, but I really need to say it. I've been working through this all morning. Can you put aside your need to make things better and just listen for a minute?"

Paul nodded. She'd never spoken to him like this before, and he wondered where she was going with it.

She ran her fingers through her hair, tucking it behind her ear, something she always did when she was thinking. It told Paul that whatever she was about to say had been waiting for a long, long time. There was a long silence as Paul watched her carefully, waiting expectantly.

"Something happened to me when I a teenager that I've been carrying with me for a long time," she finally said, breaking her silence. "I … I," she paused, biting her lip. "When my dad moved out and life changed for my family, part of me broke and I'm not sure if it's ever healed. I needed to be loved and understood, but when my dad stopped coming around, stopped spending time with me and Jared, I was hurt badly. I felt like it was my fault, like I'd somehow disappointed him. For a lot of years after that, I wondered if I was unlovable. Mom was busy trying to figure out how to take care of us, working at any job she could find, trying to work through attorneys and custody battles, and fighting with my father over money. It was a miserable time for all of us."

She wiped a tear from her cheek. "I used to play a game where I'd pretend I was invisible. It wasn't a very hard thing to do because no one paid any attention to me anyway. It made me feel better because when you're invisible, you don't have to be self-conscious. You don't have to worry about what people think of you, and you can pretend that you don't need love. Nobody cares if you spend all day crying inside your cave. But no matter how hard I tried, I wasn't invisible, not really. I was a lost teenager, filled with rage and frustrations and pain without any outlet or anyone to listen to me.

"I was a late bloomer, both emotionally and physically. I didn't start puberty until I was a freshman. It's easy to be invisible when you're the only girl in your class who doesn't need to wear a bra. I used to wonder if I was some kind of freak of nature, but when my body finally started changing, I felt fat and ugly and completely insecure. I had no one to talk to about anything and … and that's when I began starving myself. I called it a diet, but for most of my junior and senior years, I lived on soda crackers and Diet Pepsi. It's hard to even imagine that now, living on a couple hundred calories a day. Mom didn't seem to notice and Jared was grateful to eat my portions, too, which only made me feel more invisible. There were times when I felt like I was going to die, so I'd respond by binging. Sometimes I'd eat a whole pizza, and then I'd feel sick and fat, and make myself vomit. I weighed a hundred and five pounds when I graduated from high school, and I was sick and depressed and broken."

Paul shook his head, hardly believing his ears as he raced through his memory, wondering if she'd ever tried to tell him these things, wondering if he, like her own parents, had been unable to see and hear her. "I'm sorry," he spoke softly, not wanting to interrupt, but feeling the need to reach out to her across an unstable canoe with his words if not with his hands. But Rachel, if she heard, did not respond.

"When I went to college, I discovered, after I got away from the kids I went to high school with, that I could reinvent myself and become whatever I wanted to be. I'd always liked writing. It had been the only outlet I'd found that helped me express myself, and for the first time in my life, I felt like people were taking notice of me. I didn't need to pretend I was invisible anymore. I wanted and needed to be loved. I got a job at the school newspaper that gave me a chance to use my talents, and I slowly started coming out of my shell. One of the guys on the newspaper staff told me that his roommate enjoyed my stories and asked him to introduce me to him. I thought he was kidding at first, but he kept asking, and finally I agreed to meet him for coffee.

"I was eighteen years old, and that was the first time in my life that any boy had ever even looked at me. It was exciting. I was young and stupid and desperate for attention. His name was Brian, and he was from somewhere in England. He was a senior, majoring in psychology and

had plans of going to Harvard and eventually going to back to England to teach at Oxford. I was charmed by his accent and his ambition, but more than anything, it felt good to be interesting to someone else. His parents had all sorts of money and had sent him to the States to follow in his father's footsteps and get an American education. We spent a lot of time together over the next few months, and I began dreaming about marrying him and living in Oxford and raising children with beautiful accents in our English garden. He treated me well, and for the first time since I could remember, I felt loved."

Rachel paused, looking out at the water, and when she spoke again, there was emotion in her voice. "When he asked me to sleep with him, I was uncomfortable at first. I'd never had sex before, but I thought I loved him. And from everything I'd read and seen in the movies, it seemed like a natural step in the progression of our relationship. So one weekend, we drove up to The Dells to a swanky inn near the ski resort. It was romantic and comforting, and I believed he loved me.

"We went back to school and continued hanging out, but things were different. He was distant and cold, and I began feeling hurt and used. But a few weeks later, I started getting nervous that I hadn't had my period. I waited another couple of weeks, hoping and praying that I wasn't pregnant, but I finally took a pregnancy test and … and found out."

Paul watched and listened calmly, intensely, hanging on every word. He knew he'd been waiting for years for her to open up to him about her past, but this was a shock. She'd never mentioned this before—any of it. He knew Rachel had had boyfriends before she'd met him, and having had previous relationships of his own, he wasn't naive about the realties of physical and sexual attraction. When they began dating, they'd agreed early on to take things slowly, and when their relationship became more serious, Paul had suggested that maybe they should wait, putting off the consummation of their love for each other until after the wedding. Rachel had been quick to agree. It had been a difficult thing for both of them as their attraction to each other had been strong, but holding back had allowed them to build a strong friendship in ways none of their previous relationships had ever offered.

An intimate relationship was one thing, but a pregnancy was something else. He didn't know how to respond, so he didn't; waiting cautiously, wondering how whatever information she would share next had influenced who she became, how it had become a portion of her life that she'd buried, never talking about it. As his mind wandered in the silence, he was pricked with a pang of betrayal, but he pushed it aside, knowing these events happened before he met her, reminding himself that Rachel loved him regardless of the things she'd kept from him. He looked at her and was saddened to see her orange life jacket becoming streaked with tears. He wanted to reach for her, wanted to take her in his arms and hold her, but he held back, knowing if he did, he might never know the contents of this secret she'd hidden from him all these years. He watched her cry for nearly a minute before he spoke.

"Rachel, I'm still here," he said softly, reassuringly. "Tell me what happened."

She looked at him and stared for a moment before turning away again. "I can't do this," she mumbled.

"Rachel," he said again, softly. "I'm not going anywhere."

Slowly, she looked up, and the distance between them shortened as she leaned forward resting her elbows on her knees.

"Please," he said. "Tell me what happened."

"I freaked out," she said, not looking up. "I was barely nineteen years old, and I was in no way ready to have a child. I'm not sure exactly what happened—the next few weeks were kind of a blur for me. I was in shock, trying to make sense of the desperate realities I was facing. I spent a lot of time in bed, crying, dealing with morning sickness, and feeling sick about every other aspect of my life. I hoped I might feel better if I told Brian and at least have someone who could commiserate with me. But there was also part of me that hoped he'd marry me, thinking that the problems would go away if we could just get married, and he could take care of me … but I was naive … I was so naive."

Paul quietly set the paddle in the canoe and knelt down on floor, bracing himself on the gunnel as he leaned forward to reach for her hands.

"What happened?" he whispered softly.

She shook her head. "He was angry."

"At you?"

She nodded. "He accused me of being a gold-digger, of purposely getting pregnant to have some claim on his family's fortune. He called me a whore," she said, looking at the bottom of the boat as if into a portal that put her back in that time and place where the damage had been done.

After a moment, Paul squeezed her hand, bringing her back.

She looked at him, and they cried together as they floated downstream, each of them searching for understanding.

"What happened to the baby?" Paul finally mustered up the courage to ask.

"There was no baby," she sobbed. "He made sure of it. I tried to talk to him about other options, but he told me I was stupid and selfish and accused me of trying to ruin his life and his future. He pushed me into getting an abortion. He said it was the only way things would ever be better."

Paul shook his head, feeling the intensity of Rachel's anguish.

"He drove me to the clinic in Chicago and paid for the abortion. It was going to be easy and painless, he told me, and we'd both be able to continue on with our dreams without having to worry ...." She shook her head. "I was desperate. I knew I wasn't ready to be a mother—I was still a child myself. I was scared … and lost. I felt like I didn't have any other answers or possibilities."

She took a deep breath as tears continued in a stream down her cheeks, painting long shadows on her life jacket. "No one ever told me how I'd feel when it was over. Even the nurses and doctor told me I'd be able to get back to my life and live my dreams, but they never told me that I'd think about it every single day for the rest of my life, knowing I'd selfishly put an end to …" She stopped and looked away, unable to form words as she sobbed, but she pushed through, taking deep breaths, trying to gain control of her emotions.

"He dropped me off at my apartment like it was the end of a bad blind date, and he never called me again. He graduated a month later and moved to Boston and probably forgot all about me. It was easy for him, I'm sure, but I've carried this with me for eighteen years. Every time I see a baby, every time I look at a child, it reminds me of what I did. If I'd chosen to have the baby, he or she would be almost the same age I was when I made that choice. I don't pretend that I could have been a decent mother to that child, but so many times I've wondered what could have happened if that baby could have been adopted and raised by a family who wanted her, who could have provided a good life for her. I'm sure it would have been difficult to give her up, after carrying her for nine months, but I can't imagine that pain being any worse than the sorrow and pain I've felt for the last eighteen years. When I look at Eve, knowing the joy and love I've had with her in my life, in the back of my mind and heart, there is always the intense sorrow and guilt from that decision."

She took in a deep breath, and squeezed his hands. "When I was in that accident and Andrew died, I felt like God was punishing me for what I did," she said, sobbing again.

Paul swallowed hard. "Do you really think that's how God works?"

"I don't know—I mean, I don't want to. After Eve was born, and I had to have a hysterectomy, I wondered again if God was cursing me as a consequence for what I did."

Paul sat silent, stunned by these revelations and sad that Rachel had carried this burden of guilt, silently blaming herself for the problems and challenges they'd faced together.

"I'm sorry, Paul," she said, interrupting his thoughts. "I'm sorry I never told you these things before. I'm so sorry."

She wept bitterly as Paul held her hands, trying to be of comfort while sorting through these dark revelations, hoping to make sense of the things he'd just been told. As he searched his heart for words he could say to her, feeling the burden of this heartache she'd carried with her all these years, he was struck by the gift of understanding that it was not his place to judge her. As he considered the sorrow and guilt she'd carried with her for all these years, he felt a calm, peaceful spirit wash over him, filling his heart with an intense love for Rachel. He'd known since the very beginning that there was darkness in her past, but this was different from anything he'd imagined. He opened his mouth to speak, but nothing came, so he remained silent. He allowed the peace to course through his veins as he offered a silent prayer for her and for direction for himself. As soon as the thoughts of compassionate prayer passed through his mind, an overwhelming feeling of love washed over him, and he heard a voice in his heart speak.

"Love her," the voice spoke softly. "Love her," the gentle voice repeated again, melting away any hesitation he'd felt as a most intense feeling of love poured over him, causing his body to tingle from the crown of his head to the bottom of his feet.

"Love her," the voice said again, and Paul opened his mouth to speak the only words that came to him.

"Rachel, I love you."

She looked up, pressing her lips together. At first he wondered if he'd said the wrong thing as his words seemed to cause her to sob even more, but she squeezed his hands tightly, reassuringly, hopefully, as if she was desperately gripping a rope that had been tossed to her in a deep hole.

"I'm sorry you never felt like you could talk to me about this before. Why did you keep this from me?"

"Because I was afraid I'd lose you. I've never felt worthy of your love and patience, and I always worried that you'd wake up one day and realize you married the wrong person," she said through her tears

"Rachel, I love you," he repeated, unable to speak louder than a whisper, but it was enough. She leaned forward, kneeling on the floor of the canoe, wrapping her arms around him. They held onto each other as gracefully as they could with two life jackets adding awkward distance between them.

"Just a minute," Paul said. He unlatched his life jacket and pulled it over his head before struggling to stand up.

"Honey, aren't you going to tip us over?" Rachel asked, looking concerned.

Paul smiled and shook his head, reaching down to take her hand. "I think we're stuck on a sandbar." He unbuckled the strap on her life jacket and lifted it up over her head before taking her in his arms again. They just stood there, standing in a canoe in the middle of the river, holding onto each other and being nurtured by the silence. Time stood still as the miracle of love and forgiveness encircled them, filling them both with hope, understanding and compassion.

"We still fit, don't we?" he asked, breaking the long silence. As she squeezed him tighter, the spirit of peace they'd felt surged again in both their hearts, leaving them with the knowledge that God's grace was a balm big enough to cover all their sorrows. And in that peace they knew that their love for each other, made stronger through the love of God, would be strong enough to see them through.

-CHAPTER 36- FINDING THE SOMETHING

IF WE FIND OURSELVES WITH A DESIRE THAT NOTHING IN THIS WORLD CAN SATISFY, THE MOST PROBABLE EXPLANATION IS THAT WE WERE MADE FOR ANOTHER WORLD.
-C.S. LEWIS

"Are you guys okay?" somebody asked. Paul and Rachel turned their heads, bringing them back to the present.

"Thanks, yeah, we're fine," Paul said, waving to the two men in an orange canoe who were passing on his right.

"We've got a troop of scouts coming through just behind us here. Are you stuck?" the man sitting on the back seat asked, raising his hand to shield his eyes from the sun.

"No, no, we're just taking our time. Thanks though," Paul said, waving to them.

"All right, but unless you want to get wet, you might consider staying put until the boys pass. They've been having a water fight since we launched, and I'm not sure they'd discriminate if you got in their way."

"Thanks for the heads-up," Paul replied. "Maybe we'll just hang tight for a minute."

He gave Rachel another hug before letting her go. Then he sat back down on the seat and unlaced his shoes.

"What are you doing?" she asked.

"I don't think we'll be able to get off this sandbar without me getting out of the canoe."

"Do you need me to get out, too?

"No, I can handle it."

He'd just put his foot into the water when they heard the first war cry. Around the bend came a green canoe with four young scouts aboard, paddling desperately to avoid being overtaken by a red canoe captained by two teenaged boys who were armed with an arsenal of liquid assault rifles. The younger boys' frenzied strokes were no match for the older boys' experience and strength, and they quickly succumbed to their wet wrath. Paul and Rachel smiled at each other as they watched fifteen canoes float past them at varying speeds, their passengers soaking with varied amounts of water, but all of them looking like they were enjoying the day. When they were gone and their war cries faded, Paul rolled up his pants and stepped out of the boat and onto the soft yellow sand that had seized their vessel.

He walked to the bow of the canoe and tugged, slowly freeing the boat. He walked along side Rachel for ten yards until the water rose to his mid-calf and he felt it was deep enough to keep them from getting stuck again. He stepped back into the boat carefully, watching Rachel's white knuckles gripping tightly to the gunnel, trying to counter each tilt of the canoe. He paddled out into the deeper part of the river, and soon the current was carrying them again.

"Thank you," Rachel said, looking into his eyes.

"For what?"

"For listening … for loving me when I feel the least worthy of it."

Paul nodded, looking thoughtful. "Love is the answer to every question that really matters, isn't it? I don't believe God ever waits for us to be worthy—whatever that means—before He's ready to love us. I believe He's always hopeful that we'll come back when the choices we make separate us from Him. I feel like He waits for us, patiently, hoping we'll turn to Him for help and advice and direction. I thought I understood this, but as Eve gets older and is beginning to exercise her ability to make her own choices, I've found myself thinking how difficult it must be for God to watch us bumbling around without direction, doing stupid things, making mistakes and hurting ourselves and others. But maybe that's part of this whole big plan."

"What do you mean?"

Paul shrugged. "I don't have all the answers, but I feel like a big part of God's plan for us is learning what to do with the choices we have in front of us every day. I feel like He's waiting to give us inspiration and guidance. He waits patiently for us to ask, and when we ask, it seems that we always get more than we need, even if it's not exactly what we asked for. Sometimes the answer is 'no' when we want it to be 'yes.' Sometimes it's 'not now,' when we were hoping for yesterday. But if we wait on God and give Him a little more credit for the good things in our life, it seems like it can be a lot better than it is if we go at it alone."

Rachel nodded. "We don't have to, huh? Go it alone, I mean? That's what you've been trying to tell me, isn't it?"

Paul laughed softly at the change in her attitude. "Yes."

She sat silent for a moment. "I was just going to ask you why you didn't tell me all of this before, but I just answered my own question. I never let you. I'm so dumb." She shook her head. "I've wasted a lot of time, haven't I?"

"Rachel, if we spent our lives thinking about how much time we've wasted, we'd be wasting even more time. Let's just focus on doing something good with whatever time we have left."

"You're right. I'm just … there's something here, isn't there—your journal, the funeral, talking to Mom and Bud, and that lady at the museum yesterday? There's something here, isn't there?"

Paul smiled and nodded.

"I've felt this before, but never like I have in the last twenty-four hours. This is different, more intense, almost tangible."

Paul smiled again, grateful she'd felt it too.

"You know what I'm talking about, right?"

"Yes."

"Do you know what it is?"

"I think so. This is the magic I went looking for at Dr. Dinglebottom's funeral. I didn't know what it was back then, but I think that's the miracle of all of this. It makes me feel like God hasn't left us alone, and I've noticed that feeling comes again and again when I'm doing what I know I should be doing. It makes me want to keep going, knowing that everything is going to work out."

"That's why you taught Eve that true things have good feelings?"

"Exactly."

"And you learned that from going to funerals?"

"Yes and no. I was trying to reconnect or rediscover whatever it was I'd felt the night I almost died–and every other time I've had that dream. That's what I went looking for, but in order to have a funeral like Max's, you have to know something about life and what makes it worth living."

Rachel nodded thoughtfully. "Do you think you could teach me those things?" she asked humbly.

Paul nodded as tears returned to his eyes. "I've been waiting for you to ask me that for eleven years." He smiled. "I happen to have a book about a crazy kid named Wolf who went looking for the purpose of life and found it at a year's worth of funerals."

Rachel smiled. "I was just thinking, that if it's as good as everyone says it is, maybe more people would want to read it."

"You think so?"

"Yeah," she said nodding. "I think more people need to know that there's something out there, that there really is a meaning and purpose to life. More people need to feel this, Paul. They need to know that they're worthy of God's love, and He's waiting for us to invite Him in."

"Do you think people will read a book like that?"

Rachel shrugged. "I suppose it all depends."

"On what?"

"Well, are there any ponies in it?"

"No," Paul said, laughing, "but the story isn't over yet."

THROW OUT THE FEAR

TRUE THINGS HAVE GOOD FEELINGS

ALL THINGS ARE SPIRITUAL FIRST.

-CHAPTER 37- BACK TO THE BEGINNING

IT MAY BE HARD FOR AN EGG TO TURN INTO A BIRD: IT WOULD BE A JOLLY SIGHT HARDER FOR IT TO LEARN TO FLY WHILE REMAINING AN EGG. WE ARE LIKE EGGS AT PRESENT. AND YOU CANNOT GO ON INDEFINITELY BEING JUST AN ORDINARY, DECENT EGG. WE MUST BE HATCHED OR GO BAD. —C. S. LEWIS

As they rounded the bend, Lake Michigan came into view. The last stretch of the river lay before them, and Paul winced, recognizing that this conversation would soon be ending. The scouts that had passed them earlier were now scurrying about the banks of the river, moving the last of their canoes to the trailers and trucks in the parking lot. Rachel turned her head at the sound of the boys, and when she turned back, her face expressed the same disappointment Paul felt.

"I'm not ready to go back to the real world," she said, looking up at Paul.

Even though her words were filled with tones of disappointment, they were comforting to Paul. He knew what she meant; that she wanted to continue to talk and share and learn.

"Should we turn around?" he asked.

"Do you think we could?"

Paul shrugged then shook his head. "I don't think so. But maybe your Mom and Bud could hang out with Eve for a while, so we could keep talking."

Rachel's eyes brightened at the mention of the idea. "We don't have anywhere to be, do we?"

"No," Paul said, unable to keep himself from smiling at the idea. He maneuvered the canoe into the slower waters on the right side of the river, waiting for the noisy scouts to finish packing up their things. By the time they reached the beach, the scouts were pulling out of the parking lot, leaving only Bud's truck and trailer to be seen.

They coasted into the shallow waters, slowing with the drag of the sand against the bottom of the canoe. Paul stepped out into the water and pulled the boat ashore, offering his hand to Rachel. She stepped onto the muddy banks, but didn't let go of his hand, pulling him closer and embracing him.

"We were just beginning to worry that you guys might have fallen in," Bud said, coming up behind them.

Paul turned. "No, we've just been talking. Sorry to keep you waiting."

"No problem. Eve's just been telling us about your stop at the museum. That's quite a story."

Paul nodded.

"Say, Marilyn and I were just talking, and we were wondering how you might feel about us taking Eve for the afternoon and give you kids a chance to spend some time together. I'm not sure if it would be any fun for her, but we need to get some work done at the studio for tomorrow's market, and she could play in the clay if she wanted."

Rachel smiled. "You wouldn't mind?"

"Of course not. We actually already talked to Eve about it, and she seems pretty excited." Rachel looked at Paul then back to Bud. "That would be great."

While Paul and Bud moved the canoe to the trailer, Rachel retreated to the shade under the trees where Marilyn and Eve were sitting on a blanket, enjoying the afternoon. Arrangements were made to meet back at the park at 6:30 for a picnic unless Paul and Rachel got bored and wanted to see Bud's studio.

"What do you want to do?" Paul asked as they watched them pull out of the parking lot.

"I want to go to our bench, and I want you to finally tell me all the stuff I haven't let you tell me before."

Paul smiled.

"Will you buy me some lunch, though? I'm starving." She pointed to the shiny modified Airstream trailer that was parked on the far end of the parking lot, its awning advertising its edible offerings.

Paul reached for his back pocket then shook his head. "I must have left my wallet in my other pants. Do you have any money?"

"Yeah, I do," Rachel said, reaching into the side pocket of her skirt. She pulled out a twenty-dollar bill and a small, white envelope. "Oh, I forgot about this," she said, handing Paul the envelope.

"What's this?"

"I don't know. It fell out of your journal this morning when I was reading on the patio. I'm sorry; I meant to give it to you earlier, but I got distracted trying to get Eve's hair done."

Paul turned the envelope over, looking for anything that might offer a clue to what it was or where it had come from, but there was nothing. He looked at Rachel before tearing open the envelope to find a card, embossed with monogrammed letters, JMG.

-J G M-

He ran his fingers over the letters, "It's from Max."

Rachel nodded. "What does it say?"

Paul took a deep breath before looking up. He looked past the lunch wagon, past the lawn and the trees to the far end of the park where a solitary bench stood near the beach.

Rachel followed his line of site. "Let's get some lunch and go over there," she said, pulling him along. They purchased sandwiches and drinks, then walked through the grass towards the bench. As they approached it, Paul noticed something on the back side that he'd never noticed before.

"What's that?" he asked, pointing to the bright yellow lights that seemed to be glowing on the back side of the bench's backrest.

"I'm not sure," she responded.

They came closer, and Paul stooped to look at the three rectangular brass plates that were reflecting the sunlight.

Rachel set their lunch down on the bench and stooped down beside Paul.

"What is it?" she asked.

Paul looked at her and smiled, before turning back to read, shielding his eyes from the light that continued to reflect off their shiny surfaces. He ran his fingers over the surface of the first plate, reading it as he went:

He moved to the next one, but Rachel stopped him.

"Hey, isn't that Max's wife?"

Paul stopped and looked back, running his fingers over the name and date. "She died on Christmas," he said solemnly. "Can you imagine how painful that must have been?"

"Look," she responded, pointing to the next one.

Paul turned back and began to read.

"Oh, my gosh," he said, turning to Rachel. "This was their bench before it was ours. His family must have just put these up."

"There's one more," she responded, pointing to the last one.

Dedicated to the memory of a boy named Wolf, who sang the sweet songs of redeeming love.
All pain is temporary, all sorrow is fleeting, but love is eternal!

Rachel put her hand on Paul's shoulder, and he turned to her, smiling through his tears. He stood and pulled her close to him, and they looked out at the lake from this bench that had been the birthplace of so many memories for each of them. A feeling of peace and love enveloped them again, causing their tears to mingle as they fell. They held each other for a long time, neither of them wanting to let go.

"Aren't you dying to read that note?" Rachel finally spoke.

"As a matter of fact, I am." He reached into his pocket and withdrew the envelope, pulling out the card once again.

Rachel tugged at his elbow, and they moved to the other side of their bench, taking a seat very close to each other.

Paul smiled at Rachel and opened the card to find a note, written in cursive with a shaky hand and spilling onto a piece of blue paper that had been folded and placed inside. He cleared his throat and began to read aloud.

May 10, 2012

To my dear friend, Wolf,

For the last twelve years I have been looking for you, hoping to find you and thank you for your generous Christmas gift. When you gave it to me that night at the restaurant, you couldn't have known the impact your journal would have on my life. I hoped I could have reached you by now, but after searching for years and running out of ideas, I am writing this letter, hoping that somehow it will find you. Your journal and your sincere friendship came at a time when I needed them most. You couldn't have known it was the ten-year anniversary of the death of my wife, Millie. On the way to the restaurant that evening, I stopped at the bench where I'd scattered her ashes to remember her and to tell her I would be joining her soon.

You see, for years I'd been hoping to die a natural death, but I was tired of waiting, tired of living, tired of the pain and sorrow of loneliness. When you invited me to dinner that night, I was hesitant at first, not wanting to stick around that long, but I accepted your invitation, figuring it was the least I could do after all the time you'd spent with me.

Your gift, at the end of dinner, complicated a lot of things. It was very inconvenient. I considered throwing your journal away, but as I sat in my car at the marina, wondering what to do, I opened your journal and started to read. When I discovered who you were—that same ignorant kid who'd tried to kill himself—who I'd dragged to the hospital the year before—I started having second thoughts about my plans, and by the time I finished reading, late that night, I realized what a fool I'd been. Instead of driving into the lake that night as I'd planned, I drove home and went to bed, waking up to a new day and a new life.

Paul paused and wiped a tear off his cheek. He glanced at Rachel, who squeezed his arm, encouraging him to continue, her own cheeks wet with tears.

It has now been twelve years since that night, and my life has been blessed with the time I needed to change, to fix relationships I'd ruined, and make hundreds of new friends. After 92 years, I think I am beginning to understand the power of love-God's greatest gift to mankind. I don't know when the end will come for me, but I do know that I am much more ready to face it than I was the last time I saw you. For that, I will be eternally grateful for the kindness and hope and love you gave to a very undeserving, cranky, old man who was lost in the mess he'd made of his life.

I don't know where you are, or if you will ever read this, but I want to say thank you. Your gift has changed and blessed my life in ways too numerous to tell. I believe I will see you again someday, and when I do, I hope to thank you personally for giving me a second chance at life. Thanks to you, I have learned that all pain is temporary, all sorrow is fleeting, but love-love is eternal and will last forever.

Look to God, and live!

Sincerely, your friend,

Max

P.S.. If a young man ever offers you a Slurpee, please treat him better than I treated you.

Paul set the letter down on his lap. He put his arm around Rachel, looking out at the lake.

"What are you thinking?" she asked after a moment.

"I was thinking about what Bud said earlier today at breakfast, that there are no coincidences, only spiritual patterns we don't understand yet."

Rachel nodded. "I don't think I can deny that anymore. What else have I missed?"

Postlude

...TRUST THE PHYSICIAN AND DRINK HIS REMEDY IN SILENCE AND TRANQUILITY: FOR HIS HAND, THOUGH HEAVY AND HARD, IS GUIDED BY THE TENDER HAND OF THE UNSEEN, AND THE CUP HE BRINGS, THOUGH IT BURN YOUR LIPS, HAS BEEN FASHIONED OF THE CLAY WHICH THE Potter HAS MOISTENED WITH HIS OWN SACRED TEARS.

—Kahlil Gibran

Attending fifty-eight funerals for strangers would likely affect a hundred different people in at least a hundred different ways. I can only say how it affected me. This is my experience, but if you look a little deeper, I believe each of us will find a piece of ourselves within these pages. Hopefully, we can each find something that can inspire us to reach beyond who we are now, beyond where we came from, and through the prism of hope and love, begin to recognize all that we can become.

As I have shared some of the details of this book over the last two years with people who have asked about my latest project, I have experienced a huge range of reactions. Almost always, after the initial laughter—that anyone could be quirky enough to go to the funerals of strangers—I have been amazed and touched by the stories that follow. Almost without fail, people open their hearts and share stories of their loved ones with me. More often than I ever could have imagined, I have witnessed raw emotion as these stories have been shared. Many times I have found myself on sidewalks, at art festivals, in a church or another public setting where I have been moved to tears as friends and near-strangers have shared these personal stories with me. It is a wonderful thing to be able to laugh and cry at the funeral of strangers. It has been even more amazing to hear these stories, and to laugh and cry about loved ones who have long since passed away, and continue to live in the hearts of those who love them.

I have learned that we are far more connected as members of the human race than any of us know. We are all here sharing a mortal experience, trying to discover for ourselves the purpose of life, trying to make sense of our challenges and heartaches while holding tight to the good things life has to offer. Whether we care to admit it or not, part of this mortal experience includes the reality that someday, each of us will die.

It will likely not surprise you after reading this book to hear that I am a Christian, both by birth, and more recently by choice. I won't pretend that my views as a Christian have not informed and influenced my life in ways too numerous to count. I began writing this book with the hopes of being as objective as possible. But as a practicing Christian, I have recognized the futility of trying to be objective in matters of faith.

It has been informative and refreshing to walk into churches I've never been in before, to hear scripture and counsel and praise given from pastors and priests, bishops and chaplains, men and women, old and young, rich and poor. I have heard sermons in English, Spanish, Latin and Greek, as well as the universal language of music that invites communion with the spirit of love and truth in ways that nothing else can. I have heard great stories of faith and perseverance, as well as stories of suffering, tragedy, injustice and loss. I have learned that for most people, death comes too soon, but to others, it comes as the reward for a long and fruitful life.

I have felt the spirit of truth and love in nearly every funeral I have attended, leading me to believe that no one person, and no one religion can lay singular claim to the truth that is so readily evident (for those who have eyes to see) in the hearts of all mankind. I know my understanding may be different from yours, but as I have shared the things I have learned from this experience, I hope you have recognized that there is much more that unites us than divides us. In the end, the fact that we are all children of the same God makes us brothers and sisters in ways that no one religion can. I believe we all have things to share with each other—understanding, truth, wisdom, music, gifts of the spirit, light and knowledge, tolerance, love, charity, compassion, patience, and mercy; just to name a few. We are sharing this journey, and the more of God's love that we can share with each other, the better off our world will be.

As a Christian, I believe in the song of redeeming love. I believe God has a plan for each of us, one filled with joy and love and magic. I believe the vision of our personal plans can be opened to each of us as we ask God for direction, and listen in quiet places for His answer to come. My understanding of God and His plan for me has come in many ways, but usually one small piece at a time through gentle whispers and merciful nudges. I have sought understanding from the teachings of my parents, from the teachings of the scriptures, and other good books. I have been inspired by the teachings of wise men and women everywhere who have opened their mouths to share their songs and portions of truth with me. I have been impressed again and again that we were spiritual beings long before we were physical beings. And when our physical lives are over, our spirits will continue to live on through eternity.

As I have attended these funerals over these past two years, I have been impressed by the fact that we are all searching for understanding. Very often, but especially when death comes to the young, we find ourselves asking, "how, if there is a God, would He allow such sorrow to take place?" I don't know the answer to that question, but I believe in my heart that there is an answer to every question under the sun. I believe in a God who answers questions as well as prayers. If we will open our hearts, and ask with a sincere heart, exercising faith, with a desire to embrace truth, it will surely come. Remember that true things have good feelings.

I believe in the power of hope. Hope—in that which is true—is the beginning of faith. I believe faith is a verb; it requires action to become real and to grow. Like a muscle, it must be exercised if it is to gain any strength. If not, it will eventually atrophy and die. Faith is a journey, one that seems to have at least as many high mountain peaks as it does deep canyons. We all experience these highs and lows as we move forward along this journey. But the more we learn to embrace truth and to seek out every good gift and every true song, the less extreme those hills and valleys seem to become.

This experience has reminded me that there are very few constants in this world. To be honest, I can only think of one: God's love. Though we may not always be able to see it, or understand it, His love will never be far from us. Though we may not always be able to feel it, it is always there. Though we may not always choose to hear it, the song of redeeming love will continue to ring out. It calls out to us across the years and the great divides, inviting us to return to paradise.

As the Yiddish proverb says, "Man plans, God laughs." His timing is rarely our timing. His course for us is rarely the one we would naturally choose to travel. But God knows no distance, and I believe as we explore the will of God, recognizing His unchanging, unconditional love for us, life can and will be richer, fuller, and more meaningful.

I believe this world is made up of millions of interconnected spiritual patterns that we cannot understand or see without first casting off our natural tendencies to be cynical, sarcastic, crude, and unbelieving. I believe that with God, all things are possible. All pain is temporary, all sorrow is fleeting, but the love of God is eternal.

Let us look to God and live.

Ben Behunin

Author's Note

Few of us have not been affected in one way or another by the tragic occurrence of suicide. While speaking to a close friend about my intent to write this book, she expressed concern that I might be writing about a subject I knew little about and cautioned me about the sensitive nature surrounding this subject. Her brother had recently succumbed to depression and had taken his own life not long before our discussion took place.

My purpose in writing this book is neither to justify nor glorify the reality that suicide happens, but rather, to offer hope.

It will likely surprise many of my readers to hear of my own struggle with suicidal thoughts. Mine have largely been related to environmental and familial causes of hopelessness. And though I have never gone so far as to attempt the termination of my own life, there have been several times over the years when I have struggled to find reasons to continue to live.

I know depression is real. I also know that many who are challenged by it often need the help of professionals to manage and overcome those challenges. By discussing this now, it is in no way my desire to make light of or minimize the reality of those of us who suffer from different and often fluctuating levels of depression. All too often, many of those we love, choose a permanent end to what are usually temporary challenges.

It is a reality that life will one day end for each of us. But I hope that sharing the things I have learned about life and death will help you, no matter your station, to recognize the profound gift that is life. May you always know that life, despite its many challenges, is worth living, and living well.

Cheers to your journey. Ben Behunin

LEAD, KINDLY LIGHT,
AMID TH' ENCIRCLING GLOOM,
LEAD THOU ME ON!
THE NIGHT IS DARK,
AND I AM FAR FROM HOME;
LEAD THOU ME ON!
KEEP THOU MY FEET;
I DO NOT ASK TO SEE
THE DISTANT SCENE;
ONE STEP ENOUGH FOR ME.
"LEAD KINDLY LIGHT"
-JOHN NEWMAN

The Eulogy of Ben Behunin

Steve Speckman

Benjamin Aaron Behunin, (Ben) was born on October 23, 1973 in Provo, Utah to Stephen O. and Paulette Flint Behunin. He passed from this life into eternity on November 4, 2063 after being worn out from a life of hard work and not nearly enough sleep. He made his living as a potter and later a writer, his books include the "Niederbipp Trilogy", "Borrowing Fire" and twenty seven other books. But he always believed his most important work was that which he did with his wife, Lynnette: raising two wonderful children, Isaac and Eve, who were "the apples in his eye." He loved spending time with them, making up stories, wrestling, and coming up with silly nicknames that they will always remember like, "Snotmuffin," "Boogerhead," and "Dinglehopper," just to name a few.

Ben was a great father, spending time regularly with his children in the mountains, teaching them to yodel, polka dance, and play the harmonica—occasionally all at the same time (the high mountain air can inspire all sorts of things.) His children will remember him as an attentive father and grandfather who never grew up. He had a knack at telling silly jokes when they were eating their dinner, causing them to shoot broccoli out of their noses. He truly found joy in the smallest things in life, from walks with the family, to soft serve ice cream cones, to sitting down and reading books with the kids. He leaves behind one of the world's largest collections of worthless rocks he collected on his travels around the world.

Ben was an artist, a lover and a dreamer. Lynnette, who he always referred to as his first and always his favorite wife, (even though she was he only wife), was very patient with Ben, and together they enjoyed sixty-six years of marital bliss. Ben had nicknames for her too, including her favorite, "Sugarmuffin of Love," and several others that were edited from this text to protect the readers from sappy content. Together, they created a beautiful home, filled with the spirit of peace and faith, where people of all ages loved to come and visit—and if they stayed too long, Ben would always be the first to let them know.

Starting at the time he was 14, and throughout his life, Ben continued his work with clay. He told people it was because Lynnette locked him out of the house and he had to sleep in the studio. But really, it was the only thing he was good at and he figured it was more fun to make mudpies for a living than to be a dog catcher. He liked to think of himself as an entrepreneur, but in reality, it was mostly just regular manure. He was never rich, but he always had enough, and he liked to share with those around him.

In his later years, Ben became a professional badminton player. Touring the world, he showed off his patented techniques, especially his backhanded sideswipe that has come to be known around the world as the "Bad-hunin."

Despite his often quirky and irreverent comments and attitudes, Ben considered himself a Christian. He learned to sing the songs of redeeming love which he continued to sing throughout his life, helping others to open their hearts and minds to the love and grace of God.

Ben is survived by his children and their spouses, Isaac (Rosamunde) Behunin and Eve, (Peter) Snuffleupagus, thirty-six grandchildren, and four hundred and five great grandchildren. He is also survived by as many as seventeen imaginary pets, (he always said imaginary pets were better because they didn't eat as much, but just be careful where you step.)

Funeral services will be held on Thursday at the Old Geezer Victory Garden, where guests will be invited to throw a match on the funeral pyre. Bring your friends and a little gasoline, it ought to be a blast. In lieu of flowers, bring some marshmallows. Chocolate bars and graham crackers will be provided.

Personalized books can be ordered at
www.benbehunin.com
where you can also request to
receive updates about other publications.

Ben enjoys hearing from his readers. You can reach him at:

Abendmahl Press
P.O. Box 581083
Salt Lake City, Utah 84158-1083

Or by email to
benbehunin@comcast.net

More information on this book is available at
www.rememberingisaac.blogspot.com
and on Facebook
Ben's pottery is available at www.potterboy.com
and many fine galleries across the U.S.A.

If you would like to feature Borrowing Fire
in your book club, please contact Ben for a group discount.

For speaking engagements including book clubs and other activities
that include large payments of unmarked bills
please call (801)-883-0146

For design information, contact Bert Compton at bert@comptonds.com